What Is "College-Level" Writing?

Volume 2: Assignments, Readings, and Student Writing Samples

Edited by

PATRICK SULLIVAN
Manchester Community College

HOWARD TINBERG
Bristol Community College

SHERIDAN BLAU
Teachers College, Columbia University

National Council of Teachers of English
1111 W. Kenyon Road, Urbana, Illinois 61801–1096

Copy Editor: Peggy Currid
Production Editor: Carol Roehm
Interior Design: Jenny Jensen Greenleaf
Cover Design: Barbara Yale-Read

NCTE Stock Number: 56766

Library of Congress Cataloging-in-Publication Data

What is "college-level writing"? : Volume 2 : assignments, readings, and student writing samples / edited by Patrick Sullivan, Howard Tinberg, Sheridan Blau.
    p. cm.
  "A sequel to What Is "College-Level" Writing? (2006), the essays in this collection focus on matters that English teachers concern themselves with every day: assignments, readings, and real student writing."
  Includes bibliographical references and index.
  ISBN 978-0-8141-5676-6 (pbk)
 1. English language—Rhetoric. 2. Report writing. I. Sullivan, Patrick, 1956–   II. Tinberg, Howard B., 1953–   III. Blau, Sheridan D.
  PE1408.W5643 2010
  808.042071 '1--dc22
                                           2010031996

To Susan
 —Patrick

To Toni
 —Howard

To my students
 —Sheridan

To be of use

The people I love the best
jump into work head first
without dallying in the shallows
and swim off with sure strokes almost out of sight.
They seem to become natives of that element,
the black sleek heads of seals
bouncing like half submerged balls.

I love people who harness themselves, an ox to a heavy cart,
who pull like water buffalo, with massive patience,
who strain in the mud and the muck to move things forward,
who do what has to be done, again and again.

I want to be with people who submerge
in the task, who go into the fields to harvest
and work in a row and pass the bags along,
who stand in the line and haul in their places,
who are not parlor generals and field deserters
but move in a common rhythm
when the food must come in or the fire be put out.

The work of the world is common as mud.
Botched, it smears the hands, crumbles to dust.
But the thing worth doing well done
has a shape that satisfies, clean and evident.
Greek amphoras for wine or oil,
Hopi vases that held corn, are put in museums
but you know they were made to be used.
The pitcher cries for water to carry
and a person for work that is real.

MARGE PIERCY

CONTENTS

III College-Level Writing and the Basic Writing
     Classroom

IV Student Perspectives: Transitioning
    from High School to College

V Ideas, Observations, and Suggestions
   from Our Respondents

Permission Acknowledgments

INTRODUCTION

PATRICK SULLIVAN
Manchester Community College

HOWARD TINBERG
Bristol Community College

SHERIDAN BLAU
Teachers College, Columbia University

We cordially welcome you to our second collection of essays devoted to exploring "college-level writing."

Our goal for this new collection is to broaden and deepen the discussion we began in our first volume and to focus attention as much as possible on the *practical* and the *pragmatic* aspects of college-level writing. For that reason, the essays in this collection focus exclusively on matters that English teachers concern themselves with on a daily basis—assignments, readings, and student writing.

As was the case with our first volume, we do not seek here to produce a final, fixed, definitive answer to the question, "What is 'college-level' writing?" Our goal, instead, is to extend the conversation we began in our first book and to anchor this continuing conversation in real writing produced by actual high school and college students. In so doing, we hope to begin a process of defining "college-level writing" by example. In this regard, we see this volume serving as companion to the important outcomes statements issued recently by the Council of Writing Program Administrators and the Common Core State Standards Initiative regarding first-year composition and college readiness (see also *NCTE Beliefs*).

We certainly think this collection offers our profession a diverse and fascinating set of perspectives to consider as we pursue the important work of defining more clearly the kind of reading, writing, and thinking we want students to be doing in high school and college. It is also our hope that this collection will help promote dialogue among high school and college teachers nationwide. This is precisely the kind of conversation across institutional boundaries that has been identified as a national priority for educators in a number of recent reports, including *College Learning for the New Global Century* (Association), the Spellings Commission Report (United States), and Stanford University's Bridge Project report (Venezia, Kirst, and Antonio). This book can also be seen, then, as one response to calls to initiate substantive dialogue between high school and college English teachers. We believe this book will be of great value to English teachers at virtually all levels of instruction and to everyone interested in preparing students to be successful college-level readers, writers, and thinkers.

The idea for this collection developed from an authors' session held at the 2006 NCTE Annual Convention in Nashville to celebrate the publication of the first volume of *What Is "College-Level" Writing?* (NCTE). Four of the contributors—Merrill Davies, Jeanette Jordan, John Pekins, and Patrick Sullivan—spoke at this session, addressing a standing-room-only crowd full of enthusiastic and curious teachers. Most of those in attendance were high school teachers, and many were eager to talk about college-level writing. Some even expressed the hope of finally discovering what college-level writing actually was. Many had specific and pragmatic questions about first-year college writing, and a number of those at our session that morning suggested that it would be helpful to have actual assignments and samples of student writing to share and discuss.

It seemed like a rather obvious idea—to use artifacts from high school and college composition classrooms to help define what we mean by college-level writing. But a scholarship review turned up very little published work that included actual student writing.

This new collection of essays is designed to address this obvious need.

Because we found collaborations between high school and college teachers especially rare, one type of essay we feature in this collection focuses on dialogue across these institutional boundaries. In these essays, high school and college English teachers discuss college-level expectations and the best ways to prepare high school students to be effective college-level writers.

We also feature a group of contributors who set out to define college-level writing by using writing assignments and sample student work from their own classrooms. The goal here was to build a practical working definition of college-level writing from contributors who represent the widest possible variety of perspectives from secondary and postsecondary institutions. These essays include work from high school teachers, basic writing teachers, and first-year composition teachers.

We also include essays that address other important issues related to college-level writing, including assignment design, the use of the five-paragraph essay, the Advanced Placement test, state-mandated writing tests, and second language learning.

In addition, we invited a number of student contributors to write about their experiences transitioning from high school to college. We asked these contributors to illustrate their progression toward college-level proficiency by discussing landmark pieces of their own writing.

Finally, we invited Edward White and Kathleen Blake Yancey to serve as respondents for this collection. We asked them to identify important points of agreement among contributors and to offer us pragmatic advice for moving forward.

Contributors to our first collection often found a kind of "guessing game" at work among high school and college teachers. In the essays collected here, we seek to move beyond this guessing game toward real conversation. We respectfully invite you to join us.

One final note: A project of this scope could not have been completed without the generous support of colleagues, family, and friends. We would like to thank Kurt Austin, our editor at the National Council of Teachers of English (NCTE), and the anonymous field reviewers at NCTE, whose support and constructive criticism were invaluable to us as we worked on this project. We would also like to thank our production and publicity team at

NCTE, especially Carol Roehm, and our amazing freelance copy editor Peggy Currid. We would also like to offer a special note of thanks to the students who so generously allowed us to use their work. Their work made this volume possible, and we thank them for letting us use it. We would also like to thank our families for their support, patience, and many kindnesses.

We hope that you enjoy this book and find it useful. It has been an extraordinarily gratifying project to work on.

Works Cited

Association of American Colleges and Universities. *College Learning for the New Global Century*. Washington, DC: AAC&U, 2007. Print.

Common Core State Standards Initiative. "Common Standards." Common Core State Standards Initiative, 2010. Web. 2 June 2010.

Council of Writing Program Administrators. "WPA Outcomes Statement for First-Year Composition." WPA, Apr. 2000. Web. 8 May 2010.

Sullivan, Patrick, and Howard Tinberg, eds. *What Is "College-Level" Writing?* Urbana, IL: NCTE, 2006. Print.

United States Dept. of Education. *A Test of Leadership: Charting the Future of U.S. Higher Education*. [The Spellings Commission Report.] Washington, DC: U.S. Dept. of Education, 2006. Web. 24 Aug. 2009.

Venezia, Andrea, Michael W. Kirst, and Anthony L. Antonio. *Betraying the College Dream: How Disconnected K-12 and Postsecondary Education Systems Undermine Student Aspirations*. Final Policy Report from Stanford University's Bridge Project. 2003. Web. 21 June 2009.

Writing Study Group of the National Council of Teachers of English Executive Committee. *NCTE Beliefs about the Teaching of Writing*. NCTE, Nov. 2004. Web. 25 Apr. 2009.

Crossing Institutional Boundaries: High School and College

When a College Professor and a High School Teacher Read the Same Papers

TOM THOMPSON
The Citadel

ANDREA GALLAGHER
Wando High School

It is counterproductive to pretend that the first year of college is simply thirteenth grade, just another step up from twelfth grade. Although college has some features in common with high school, it has a whole new set of rules and expectations. Andrea Gallagher teaches in a large high school where the majority of students graduate and proceed to two- or four-year colleges and universities. Tom Thompson teaches in a small liberal arts college.

Though our schools are less than twenty miles apart, we find ourselves in entirely different worlds. The institutional differences are significant. High school students are minors: They are required by law to be in class and can be cited for truancy if they don't show up, but they have only limited ability to choose their classes or teachers. College students are adults: They choose whether to attend class (though nonattendance might affect their grade), and they have much more freedom to select their classes and even the time of day they want to attend classes; further, if they don't like the professor, they usually have the option of changing sections during the first week of the semester.

High school teachers are held responsible for the performance of their students; if too many students perform poorly on the statewide assessments, the teachers can lose their jobs and the state can even take over the school. In college, the responsibility rests with the student: Professors keep office hours, but it's up to the students to stop by for help if they need it. High school teachers might be compelled to provide frequent updates to parents on the progress and performance of their students; college professors are forbidden by law from revealing grades to parents unless the student provides a written release.

The Assignment

Our discussion focuses on an assignment in a dual-credit education course offered at Andrea's high school. This is not a writing class, or even an English class, but a class in which high school seniors are expected to produce "college-level" work because they earn college credit for the class. For several years, Tom has been the guest teacher for a unit focusing on a research-based paper assignment, giving students a chance to have "a real college professor" read and respond to their papers. The objective for this research-based assignment, according to state standards, is this: "Students will research and debate a variety of educational issues that affect our schools." To meet this objective, Tom designed the following assignment.

The goal of this assignment is to have you select a "hot topic" in education, research the issues and differing viewpoints that make it a hot topic, and report your findings to your classmates in a paper. In the process of reporting your findings, you will also draw a conclusion about the claims or perspectives YOU find most compelling. (That is, you will ultimately argue that a particular position or solution to a problem is the "best" one.)

Hence, the assignment has two major parts: **RESEARCH** and **WRITING**. In doing the research, you will need to *generate as much information about the topic as possible*; if it's a "hot topic," you should be able to find articles promoting a variety of ways—and usually some conflicting ways—to look at the issue, or a variety of solutions to solve the problem. (Note: If you can't find much, then the topic isn't really "hot.") You must find at least **five** sources to cite (i.e., quote, paraphrase, or refer to by name) in your paper; at least **three** must be print sources.

The second step is to present your research findings in writing. In your closing paragraph you will tell us which views/solutions you find most compelling, but the first step is to lay out the issues or problems and explain the various views or solutions. Only at the end of the paper should you explain why you think one particular approach/perspective/view/solution seems better or more likely to work than the others.

Because you are addressing classmates, your tone does not need to be excessively formal. It's OK to use "I," and it's OK to cite local examples to make a point, but you still need to use standard grammar and spelling, and you need to follow the conventions of research papers as set out in the *MLA Guide for Writers of Research Papers.*

Your paper should be 800 to 1,200 words (roughly three to five pages, 12-point type, double-spaced), and it should include a Works Cited page.

Three Student Papers

Tom selected three papers that he thought represented below average, average, and above average responses to the assignment.

Average Paper

The first paper, written by Liz, looks at the issue of mega schools.

Is Bigger Always Better?
The Advantages and Disadvantages of "Mega" Schools

Ken Reightler Jr. once said, "Education is the key to success," but is everyone receiving the education that he needs in order to be successful? It was once thought that it would be best to expand the curriculum in a school so the students could learn more, even though it meant the number of students enrolled at that school would increase. Since the 1940s the number of students enrolled in a school across the nation has grown. (Moore 8). So the question today is: are mega schools giving students the education they need in order to succeed? The controversy between mega schools and small schools focuses on financial cost, athletic teams, extra opportunities and diversity, as well as academic success; however, a study conducted in 2006 gives a solution to this controversy that no one has considered yet.

When deciding on what type of school to build financial cost becomes a topic. It is expensive for districts to build and operate schools. By building a mega school, districts are able to cut down finances. The cost for the contractor, land, building supplies, and hours for labor are just some of the factors that make building one mega school cheaper than building a few small schools (Moore 8). Faculties' salaries, equipment, supplies, and technology all add up as well and their expenses become rather large. By combining small schools into one mega school these expenses are able to be lowered. Not as much staff is needed and equipment, supplies, and technology can be shared. However, a mega school costs more to organize and ensure safety than a small school (Quindlen 68). Even though a principal may be extremely organized and display good leadership, there are still costs in running a mega school successfully. Technology, such as walkie-talkies, electrical devices, and extra internet and phone lines, is required to run a mega school efficiently and have it organized (Pommereau 10). When looking at the cost of a mega school, safety is a big expense also. Some schools may have to incorporate metal detectors, security guards, cameras, police officers, and extra assistant principals. These things cost a lot but are necessary for the safety of the students (Toppo 10D). The options for a mega school versus a small school regarding financial cost vary because it is cheaper to build and operate a mega school but at the same time it is more expensive to organize and ensure safety.

Athletic teams are important to a school. They give students an activity to do outside of school, help students find a belonging, give an opportunity for those who cannot afford college a chance for them to still go, and bring school spirit to the student body. Most mega schools have good athletic teams. This is because many good coaches are drawn towards a large school since there are more opportunities and a greater number of athletes which does not occur at a small school. Mega schools have a larger fund for its sports and athletic opportunities because there are more ticket sales, fund-raising, and other ways for the teams to earn money. Although, the main reason for athletic teams being successful is that they have a larger talent pool to select from. Coach Brad Batson from Wando High says, "The larger schools are better as a whole because of selection" (Batson). However for every highlight there is a malfunction. Mega schools can often eliminate a student from the team because he is not good enough for the school's sport team but in general he is a good athlete. Small schools give all athletes a chance to make the team (Quindlen 68). When deciding if a mega school is better than a small school, athletics should be a topic. Just like the other cost regarding school size, there are positives and negatives.

The more students at a school the more opportunities and diversity the school can have. This means that mega schools are able to have more extra curricular activities, opportunities, and more of a diverse student body than a small school. A mega school allows more time and sponsors so students can get more involved. At most large schools there are more clubs and activities for a student to join. There is something for everyone. A major play, band, marine biology club, foreign language activities, or a talent show can occur because there are a lot more students and teachers who are willing to put in time and effort. There are also many more opportunities available to students who attend mega schools. Culinary arts programs, drama, and other various electives such as accounting, engineering, and pharmacy are available to students. These opportunities allow the students to get involved as well as focus on a career choice (Pommereau 10). Almost all mega schools are diverse, whereas most small schools do not have as many minorities and the social economic status of the families is similar (Schneider 18). When a school is diverse it helps students fit in with their culture, religion, or personality. There is a group for every student (Pommereau 10).

However, there may be unaccommodating consequences in these areas at a mega school. When a school is so large opportunities and diversity can fail. Even though there may be more extra curricular activities at a mega school, they do not always work. At a small school student participation in extra curricular activities is higher (Batson). In addition, small schools may not be able to offer the extra opportunities like mega schools can offer, but they can help in other ways. Small schools are able to reach out to everyone and help students make decisions about their future. They have the opportunities and resources to help students decide if they are going to college, where they are going to apply, and what they are going to major in. A mega school has too many students to make these individual opportunities available (Schneider 28–31). Also, diversity can have a pessimistic outcome. It makes it even harder on a student if he cannot fit in anywhere.

Batson says, "It is easier to find a belonging at a small school." This is mainly because the small schools have more of a personal environment (Moore 8). The extra opportunities and diversity that a small school does not have are both two great things a mega school has to offer but if not handled correctly they can have consequences.

In the end, the academic program is the most important factor determining whether a mega school or small school is better. After all, school is mainly for academics. A mega school is able to offer many different courses and levels for its students. Advance Placement classes as well as honors, college-prep, and regular classes are available at mega schools because there are so many students at the school that fit in these categories (Pommereau 10). However, students at small schools are more likely to have higher composite test scores than those at mega schools (Schneider 16). This is mainly because at a small school the teacher to student ratio is smaller. A student at Wando High, Kaitlyn Rubino, who previously attended a small school of 300 students, says, "The ratio was around fifteen [students] to one [teacher] and you did have a stronger bond with teachers." A student-teacher bond is created at a small school. This encourages students to learn more and succeed in academics, as well as contribute to a lower drop out rate and a higher attendance rate (Quindlen 68).When viewing a school's academic success one can either look at the different levels of learning available to students and their grades in their classes, or one can look at composite test scores and the student to teacher ratio. Which ever one is chosen will determine if a mega school or small school is the best for students when it comes to academics.

To find a solution to this controversy, a study was conducted in 2006. It determined if small is really better in high school size. Statisticians found out this answer by looking at twelfth-grade students' math achievement, their postsecondary expectations, the number of college attendances, and the type and number of colleges the students applied to. After testing, the statisticians found no significant difference between the mega school and the small school. Instead, they discovered that educational success depends on what the student wants and is comfortable with. Some students learn the best and take the most from a mega school, whereas other students need a small school to perform their best and receive what they need. Therefore, the answer to the question, is small really better, is no. The size of the school does not affect educational success but rather the student's characteristics and comfort affect his educational success (Schneider 18–32).

In conclusion, financial cost, athletic teams, extra opportunities and diversity, and academic success are all factors that can be considered in determining whether a mega school or small school is the best for success. Each school, no matter what the size, offers positive and negative cost in all categories. However, it is not the school that determines educational success but the student. Each student has a school size where he can learn his best and has the most opportunities (Schneider 31–32). I do not believe mega schools are better in contrast to small schools. If both are run efficiently and meet the needs of the students everyone will get rewards from them. The district can alter the financial costs to make each school less expensive to build and operate. Athletic teams can be good at any school. It is up to the members of the team to become champions. I can see where extra opportunities in a mega school exceed those in a small school, but they are more successful at a small school. Diversity is not a big factor because it is up to the student to want to fit in and have a sense of belonging. I think academic success is the biggest factor in deciding whether a mega school or a small school is better. However, both schools have encouraging viewpoints. A mega school offers more levels and classes for its students so they can get the most out of their education (Pommereau 10). A small school has a smaller student to teacher ratio and a more personal environment which encourages academic success (Rubino). After my research, I am in agreement with the statisticians who say that the size of the school does not affect educational success. It is the drive in the student in the right environment that holds the key to success.

Works Cited

Batson, Brad. Typed Questioned Interview. 6 Sept. 2007.

Moore, Deb. "Growth or small growth? Editor's Notebook; public schools." *School Planning and Management* 1 July 2003: 8.

Pommereau, Isabelle de. "Nation's largest school says that bigger is better." *Christian Science Monitor* 90.28 (6 Jan. 1998): 10.

Quindlen, Anna. "The Problem of the Megaschool." *Newsweek* 26 Mar. 2001: 68.

Rubino, Kaitlyn. Typed Questioned Interview. 6 Sept. 2007.

Schneider, Barbara, Adam E. Wyse, and Venessa Keesler. "Is Small Really Better?" *The Brookings Institution.* (2006/2007): 15–47.

Toppo, Greg. "Schools see breakout success." *USA TODAY* 2 Oct. 2003, fin. Ed.:10D+.

TOM: For me, this paper meets the main criteria of the assignment. The opening paragraph provides a context ("the number of students enrolled in schools across the nation has grown"), poses a research question ("are mega schools giving students the education they need in order to succeed?"), and lists some important issues in the debate ("financial cost, athletic teams, extra opportunities [and] academic success"). Each subsequent paragraph addresses one of those issues, with an additional paragraph offering a possible solution. Liz cites five published sources and two interviews, and her in-text citations and Works Cited page follow MLA guidelines.

But how well does the paper do what it sets out to do? By asking whether mega schools are "giving students the education they need to succeed," Liz obligates herself to look at features of mega schools that affect student success, but that's not what she does. She simply lists four features that people debate—perhaps the first four that turned up in her research. With respect to cost, for example, she looks only at benefits to the school district, not benefits to student success. Likewise, the "athletics" paragraph suggests that athletics help students "find a belonging [and give] an opportunity for those who cannot afford college a chance for them to still go," but again, athletic scholarships say nothing about academic success. With respect to diversity, she says that when a school has more programs and clubs, "students can get more involved"; while student involvement might somehow relate to improved student performance, Liz fails to make such a case. Only the "academics" paragraph explicitly addresses student success: she cites a statistic that "students at small schools are more likely to have higher composite test scores than those at mega schools." That's a reasonable point, but rather than trying to dig up more sources to bolster this argument, she seems content to mention the point, then let it go. With so little development, the paper merits only a minimally passing grade.

ANDREA: For me, sticking to the assignment carries more weight. In my reading of the assignment, students are to identify the context of a problem and potential solutions for that problem—in other words, they should write a problem/solution paper. But the only "solution" Liz addresses is building small schools. Instead of writing a problem/solution paper, she writes a comparison/contrast of mega schools and small schools. From the beginning, there is no attempt to look at other solutions for the mega school issue; it becomes an either–or situation, either mega schools or small schools.

Liz uses her source information fairly well in outlining the advantages and disadvantages of the mega school and the small school, and she arrives at the conclusion that it is not the size of the school that determines student success. The assignment asks students to decide which solution is best, however, and Liz says that the size of the school is not the issue; there is no analysis of a solution here. In fact, she avoids taking a side. Her conclusion isn't based on her broad research and understanding of the issue; it is based on *only* the Brookings Institution study that concludes that the size of the school is not an issue. It is clear that Liz is either unaware of these contradictions or is choosing not to respond to them.

In terms of language usage and command, phrases such as *a lot* really lack the maturity expected at this level, but trying to sound too mature is equally distracting. The sentence, "However for every highlight there is a malfunction" shows that Liz is writing with a thesaurus at her side.

In short, Liz's paper is typical of what I often see in students' research: Consult the required number of sources, but keep looking until you find one that says what you want it to say. The thinking skills involved in developing an argument are often sacrificed in favor of a "hide and seek" sort of approach to research. For me, this paper can be considered "college-level writing," but just barely.

TOM AND ANDREA: Although Tom is willing to allow for greater latitude in how Liz addresses the prompt and Andrea holds her more strictly to the assignment, we agree that the paper meets minimum criteria and therefore merits a passing grade.

Below-Average Paper

The next paper, by Kaitlyn, shows an effort to address the assignment but clearly falls short. Her problems are typical of those we both see in other below-average papers.

Part-Time Coaches in High Schools

Many schools are faced with the ever-present predicament of not having enough teachers show interest in participating, as coaches, in their school's athletic programs. This lack of enthusiasm, unfortunately, leads to a limited amount of athletic opportunities for students to join because there simply are not enough teachers who are willing to coach the various sporting programs. One might say that this problem does not solely rest in the fact that there are still ample openings for athletic coaches in our schools, but that our teachers are not being equally considered for those positions.

How can we properly address this present day coaching problem? Well, one such solution to this problem may be to hire "lay coaches" (Bryant 1) for the various available positions. A lay coach is a part-time employee who is just an athletic coach and not a teacher; many other countries, such as Germany, Belgium, France, and Great Britain, have hired lay coaches, and it has been a very successful program (Knorr). This may sound like the perfect solution to our coaching quandary, but there are still some disadvantages to this solution. One such disadvantage to hiring lay coaches is that these individuals may exhibit a "lack of continuity to the overall program" (Bryant 3). Another disadvantage could include "poor communication with school employees and the lack of concern for equipment and non-educational emphasis" (Bryant 3). Lay coaches also have their own outside jobs, which would naturally take precedence over their coaching jobs, and therefore would bring additional stress to school administrators. Lay coaches can also get fired more easily than non-lay coaches, because unlike most teachers, the firing of a lay coach does not need a valid, documented explanation. Additional grounds for firing lay coaches include:

- the purchase of equipment without authorization from an administrator or athletic director;
- the misuse of school facility keys;
- the violation of state, school or district rules;

◆ defiance of authority; and

◆ inappropriate relationships with students (Bryant 4).

A major advantage of using lay coaches is that "athletic programs could be more flexible in filling coaching needs" (Bryant 1). Additional advantages in hiring lay coaches include:

◆ increased program offerings to athletes;

◆ they are easier to hire than full-time teachers who coach; and

◆ the needed prevention of coaches overseeing multiple sports (Bryant 2).

Prior to hiring a full-time teacher all applicants should be questioned as to whether or not they show the knowledge and interest in filling any available coaching positions in the school district. If so, the enthusiastic applicant should be hired over any other non-interested individual. Hiring teachers to coach their students also gives administrators the reassurance that all state, school, and district policies will be followed accordingly and that rules will not be violated (Hoch 2). Also, since the teachers are already at the school they would have better communication with students and the administrators and would, therefore, have fewer misunderstandings about funding or equipment questions. Full-time teachers also have work schedules that permit them to easily coach after school. Therefore, there are many advantages of having a teacher as an athletic coach.

There are also a few unattractive concerns that may arise when hiring teachers as coaches. There is an existing fear that some teachers, who coach, end up making coaching their main priority and therefore neglect their curriculum. One reason that teachers may focus more on coaching than their teaching responsibilities is because sporting teams get "more publicity and prestige for the school" (Chelladurial 2) and therefore emphasize the present "reward systems favoring coaching over teaching in terms of job security and salary" (Chelladurial 2). For example, if a coaching teacher leads one's team to a state championship the school would want to make sure that this coach remains with the school. In order to do so the academic institution may try to entice the teacher by offering one the possibility of instant tenure or a substantial salary increase.

Coaches are important, major role models to our youth. They provide a greater leadership role to our youth than general teachers because they interact with smaller groups of students, provide motivation to our athletes, and spend longer periods of time together with them (Chelladurial 2). Unfortunately, personality and gender differences can also distract a teacher's attention from academics to athletics. One personality theory that explains why coaching can become a higher priority than teaching is "managerial motivation" (Chelladurial 3). This theory explores the distinctive need for individuals to be able to quantify their results and deadlines. In other words, the theory of "managerial motivation" explores control based scenarios.

"Interpersonal orientation" (Chelladurial 4) is another personality difference that determines why coaching takes priority over teaching. Interpersonal orientation includes those individuals who are self-assertive, active participants. Whereas a person who prefers teaching would be much more expressive in their ideas through creative measures (Chelladurial 4). Therefore, personality differences reflect whether a teacher's first priority is given to coaching or teaching.

Gender differences also affect whether coaching or teaching remains the first priority of a teacher. Gender is one of the few things that make men and women different. Yet another difference concerning these genders comes through their teaching and coaching styles, and therefore their "coaching philosophy is going to be different" (Chelladurial 5). For instance, a woman might have the philosophy that as long as you try your hardest you are a winner, whereas a man might value the result over the actual effort. Another difference concerning gender teaching and coaching is one's "perception of the culture of the sport and organization, and their socialization into teaching and coaching is very different" (Chelladurial 5). Through various studies it has been revealed that more men than women prefer to coach. Most men embrace the responsibility of coaching because they are not afraid to be strict and yell at their athletes, whereas some women still remain hesitant. Also, men and women have very different perceptions of coaching and teaching. A female teaching coach may be consistently warm and comforting to all her students, whereas a man may be nice in his classroom, but strict when coaching his athletes. Therefore, many aspects contribute to the focus of coaching over teaching.

One must continue to analyze the ever present dilemma of teachers as coaches. This is a very serious problem considering all of the numerous coaching positions still left unfilled.

Hiring lay coaches instead of full-time teachers to coach our youth is a very plausible answer to this problem. If an applicant is not certified to teach at our schools, yet wants desperately to coach our students, they should be hired. On the other hand, if a teacher was hired predominantly on her willingness to coach and not based on her qualifications, then our students will lose out academically. Therefore, it is in the best interest of our states and their schools to hire lay coaches to fill the necessary coaching positions. One may only hope that through these challenging staffing decisions that the integrity of both our academic curriculum and sporting programs prosper in the end.

Works Cited

Bureau of Labor Statistics, U.S. Department of Labor. "Athletes, Coaches, Umpires, and Related Workers." *Occupational Outlook Handbook.* 2006. <http://www.bls.gov/oco/ocos251.htrn>

Bryant, Lance G. "Para-Professionals: The Answer to Staffing Problems." Coach and Athletic Director. Nov. 1997. Proquest. <http://proquest.umi.com/pqdweb?did_22167 985&sid=14&fmt=3&clientld=3402&rqt=309&vname =pqd>

Chelladurial, Packianathan, Donna J. Kuga, and Camille P. O'Bryant. "Individual, differences perceived task characteristics, and preferences for teaching and coaching." *Research Quarterly for Exercise and Sport* 70.2 (June 1999): 179 (1).

General Reference Center. Gale. Daniel Library, The Citadel. 5 Sept. 2007. <http://fing.galegroup.com/itx/start. do?prodid=grcm>

Hoch, David. "The Importance of the Chain of Command. *Coach and Athletic Director.* Feb. 2005. Proquest. <http://proquest.umi.com/pqdweb?did=795116641&sid =4&fmt=4&clientld=3402&rqt=3 09&vname=pqd.>

Knorr, John. "The Need to Rethink Coaching Certification." *Coach and Athletic Director.* Jan. 1996.

TOM: The opening sentence shows a basic misunderstanding of the issue: "Many schools are faced with the ever-present predicament of not having enough teachers show interest in participating, as coaches, in their school's athletic programs." This sentence seems to set up a problem–solution paper with teacher apathy as the problem and part-time coaches as an answer, but the real problem in Kaitlyn's district—and the reason I offered this as a suggested topic—was that the school board had suddenly outlawed the long-standing practice of hiring part-time coaches, so some schools had lost almost their entire coaching staffs and needed to find replacements for the part-timers. I expected to see references to local news stories and interviews with local teachers or coaches, but the paper mostly just summarizes two articles, one of which focuses on general differences between coaches and classroom teachers rather than the value of part-time coaches; Kaitlyn never even mentions that the issue affects her own school.

The final sentence of the opening paragraph further muddies the issue: "One might say that this problem does not solely rest in the fact that there are still ample openings for athletic coaches in our schools, but that our teachers are not being equally considered for those positions." What's the problem: that teachers aren't interested in coaching, or that teachers who want to coach aren't given fair consideration? This lack of an appropriate focus, combined with other common problems such as too much reliance on one or two sources, overblown prose, and weak control of mechanics, keep this paper in the below-average category.

The first body paragraphs summarize an article about advantages and disadvantages of using "lay coaches" in high school athletic programs. Most of the rest of the paper summarizes another article, this one looking at differences between teaching and coaching and what happens when coaches also have classroom duties. Some of the points are appropriate to the discussion—for example, the observation that financial incentives could lead teacher/coaches to devote more time and energy to coaching duties than to the classroom—but the paper fails to connect this idea to any other relevant ideas, and it never moves beyond mere summary. Being able to summarize appropriate sources is an important skill, but for a position paper, the writer needs to *use* those summaries in the service of some kind of claims.

ANDREA: Organization is a major issue. After simply defining what a "lay coach" is, Kaitlyn says, "This may sound like the perfect solution to our coaching quandary, but there are still some disadvantages to this solution." Yet at this point in the paper, Kaitlyn has not discussed *any* benefits of lay coaches; she doesn't do that until the second set of bullet points. And the reader will see the continuity only by ignoring the first set of bullet points, which gives a list of reasons why lay coaches can be fired. It's hard to tell whether this is supposed to be an advantage of lay coaches or a disadvantage; perhaps Kaitlyn isn't sure which she wants it to be.

An even bigger issue for me, however, is that Kaitlyn seems not to understand what she's writing. For example, she quotes an article saying that lay coaches may show "a lack of continuity to the overall program," but she doesn't give any indication that she knows what this continuity is or why it would be important. Like the section later about "managerial motivation," Kaitlyn's quotes seem to be chosen for how impressive they sound, not how well they support what she wants to say. The real problem may therefore be not with *writing* (although there are certainly language command issues evident), but with *reading*—specifically, with her inability to understand and synthesize the information she has found.

TOM AND ANDREA: Whether the problem arises from Kaitlyn's reading or writing skills is difficult to determine, but we agree that this level of work will not allow her to be successful at the college level or even the high school level.

Above-Average Paper

Few students in this class have produced papers over the years that Tom would rate as above average. The D grades typically outnumber the C grades, and it's unusual to have more than a couple of A or B papers in a class of fifteen students. But these are high school seniors—sometimes first-semester high school seniors—trying to write like high school graduates. Curiously, Laurie Ann's paper, which Tom selected as above average, generated the most disagreement about what should "count" as college-level writing.

The Effectiveness of the Multiage Teaching Program

Multiage teaching has been around for a very long time, much longer than the graded classroom. The early Jews developed schools for boys from ages six to thirteen and taught them in the synagogues. In ancient Greece, young boys, ages seven to eighteen were brought together to receive physical and mental training. In medieval trade guilds, students studied with their teachers until they were ready to be on their own. Some would finish their apprenticeship soon; others might take a longer time. Each was considered as good as the artisan who had taught him. In the monasteries of the 1500s, "a sixteen year old and a six year old were likely to be seated side by side in the same class." Our earliest American schools were multiage. They included all the children of the village, from ages 6 to 16. Even the rural schoolrooms of 25 to 50 years ago contained children of a wide variety of ages with just one teacher. It was not until the early 20th century that the idea became to hold students into compartments until their social group is ready to advance as a unit began (Longstreet & Shane 1).

The teacher of a multiage class has an advantage in that he or she may look at the curriculum for two consecutive grade levels and know that he or she has two years where she is on that continuum of learning to the end or even beyond. The second year is where this program really begins to pay off because the teacher knows exactly where each student stands in progress and what the students have learned. The class can operate as a collective unit, or family, rather than having to adapt again.

Multiage educational practices are grounded in the philosophy that every child can learn and has the right to do so at their own pace, that learning is a continuum rather than a series of steps, that diversity is not only a reality but is something to be embraced, and that a classroom is a family of learners (Meisels, Steele, & Quinn-Leering 3).

Multiage classrooms believe that children learn best from interactions with other children who are also at different stages of learning, including cognitive, emotional, social, and physical. Teachers have determined that these types of "mixed" age classrooms reflect a more honest portrait of family life and community life, and a better chance of greater cultural diversity as well; all ideals that differ widely from the traditional practice of classroom selection of children by age and/or ability alone.

Kathleen Cotton states that the multiage teaching program is based on the following assumptions and truths about teaching and learning: Student diversity is a given. Diversity in the classroom is viewed by the teachers as a strength and is central in making the learning community effective. A multiage classroom operates more like a family operates to solve its everyday problems. The classroom is based on the belief in a teaching model that is interactive in nature, with everyone learning from each other. The multiage curriculum also operates on the belief that learning does not necessarily occur in a neat, orderly sequence, but rather that learning is dynamic, complex, and developmental. The multiage teaching program is based on the belief that how to learn is as valuable as what is learned. It is not assumed that covering curriculum is learning. Finally, the curriculum is based on the belief that the teacher will facilitate a variety of teaching and learning experiences that will be developmentally appropriate for students in the class, and that children will learn from these experiences (Cotton 17).

When instructing children at this early an age, it is very critical for the teachers and students to build relationships (Love, Logue, & Trudeau 2). Children construct knowledge about the world and learn skills through social interactions. They learn to make meaning out of their dialogues and adjustment with adults and older children. In particular schools, due to such differences in the teachers and children—cultural, racial, and linguistic—it is common for the teacher to keep the children for more than one year in order to solidify relationships and give children and parents comfort. This also would lend greater continuity to the effort to develop every child's social, ethical, and emotional potential, as well as his or her intellectual and physical capacities (Love, Logue, & Trudeau 2).

Based on research on the way in which children learn, the multiage teacher uses a process method of teaching. In this method, the teacher facilitates each child's learning success based on the child's individual developmental stages of learning (Stone, *Playing* 15). For instance, the child learns to write by writing, to read by reading, to develop social skills by being in a social environment with children of differing ages and ability levels. Peer collaboration and cooperation are important aspects of the multiage curriculum. As the teacher helps the child become a better reader, writer, and problemsolver, so does the older child facilitate the learning for the younger child (Stone, *Playing* 16).

The traditional school system infers same age equals same ability. Most parents and teachers know this is not the case, particularly in relation to the years 1–3. The multiage classroom allows learning to be more responsive to the developmental needs of young children. This rate is different for each child and is often characterized by spurts and plateaus (Bredekamp 35). Activities and learning experiences in the multiage classroom are planned to accommodate the varied needs of the children. The fact that a child can be part of this class for more than one year supports these developmental needs and allows children time in a supportive environment (Bredekamp 35).

In her book entitled *Creating the Multiage Classroom*, Sandra Stone emphasizes that those who advocate a multiage classroom do it for four reasons. These four reasons include an underlying premise that all in the classroom are special; each child has strengths and weaknesses, and the teacher and the students work as a collaborate unit. A second advantage is that learning is planted as a lifelong goal and that learning is never completed. A third advantage is that the teacher is able to become familiar with each student over a long period of time. Teachers, students, and parents develop close relationships similar to a family structure which further allows for positive social development, better decision making, less anxiety at the beginning of the school year, and less learning time lost to setting up classroom rules and explaining school year expectations. A fourth benefit of a multiage class is that the teachers are facilitating in a cooperative, collaborative manner, using an assortment of approaches to help students successfully master concepts and skills, which ensures students' continual progress at their own developmental rates, positive feelings of self-worth, and an eagerness to continue the process of learning (Stone, *Creating* 45).

Educators, parents, administrators, and students list countless advantages of multiage classrooms. These advantages can be grouped into several categories: advantages to students because of the mixed-age environment, advantages to students because of the multiple-year experience, and advantages to teachers (Thompson 5). One of the prominent advantages to the students due to the mixed environment is the modeling that takes place. Thompson defines modeling as "The natural process by which younger students pick up behaviors they observe in older students" (Thompson 5). Younger students will imitate academic and social behaviors demonstrated by the older students. Modeling and tutoring benefit both the older and the younger students and occur more naturally in multiage classrooms because of the age span. Continuity has also been shown to be one of the biggest advantages of multiage education (Stone, *Strategies* 12).

Through my analysis of the strengths and weaknesses of the multiage class, I believe that as a whole the multiage class seems to be very effective. I have experienced single graded classes as well as multiage classes, and from just observing there is little difference. Through further observations, the children in the multiage class seem to be more cooperative and helpful toward each other and the teachers. The first graders help the kindergarteners learn the rules that their teacher requires. There is less time spent on instruction and more time spent on learning. Instead of the teacher having to spend time on teaching the children how to operate in the classroom, the students are more focused on the actual lessons and more quality learning is completed. There are many advantages of multiage teaching as I mentioned earlier and through observations of the children, this becomes very apparent. This method is used in many schools in South Carolina and more specifically in Charleston County. Jennie Moore and Goodwin Elementary advocate this program. Many schools have implemented this into their curriculum. Many teachers actually request that his or her child be put in this type of environment because they feel that the student will be able to learn more if the teacher already has a background with the student and knows what type of learner he or she is. I think that one main reason for multiage classrooms not being as common as the single graded classroom is because parents are taken back by the fact that their child will be integrated with students older than theirs and may feel like they will be compared to those who are a year ahead of them. I feel that the multiage classroom has been proven effective in schools and should be implemented more due to the positive outcomes of the students and teachers.

Works Cited

Bredekamp, S. (Ed). *Developmentally appropriate practice in early childhood programs serving children from birth through age 8* (Exp. ed). Washington, DC: National Association for the Education of Young Children 1990.

Cotton, Kathleen. *Nongraded Primary Education.* School Improvement Research Series. NWREL. 1995.

Longstreet, W. S. & Shane, H. G. *Curriculum for a new millennium.* Massachusetts: Allyn & Bacon 1993.

Love, J.M., Logue, M.E., Trudeau, J.V., & Thayer, K. *Transitions to Kindergarten in American Schools: Final Report of the National Transition Study.* Washington, DC: U.S. Department of Education 1992.

Meisels, S.J., Steele, D.M., & Quinn-Leering, K. Testing, tracking, and retaining young children: an analysis of research and social policy. In B. Spodek (Ed.), *Handbook of Researched on the Education of Young Children* (pp. 279–292). New York: Macmillan Publishing Co 1993.

Stone, Sandra J. *Creating the Multiage Classroom.* Glenview, IL: Good Year Books, 1996.

———. *Playing: A Kid's Curriculum.* Glenview, IL: Good Year Books, 1993.

———. "Strategies for Teaching Children in Multiage Classrooms." *Childhood Education.* 102–105. 1994/1995.

Thompson, Ellen. "Ten Questions You Must Ask About Your Classroom." Workshop. Sixth Annual National Conference on Multiage and Looping Practices: Best Teaching Practices . . . Meeting Student Needs over Time. The Society for Developmental Education. Cincinnati. 19 Jul 1998.

TOM: For me, this paper rates better than average because it shows a command of material from a variety of sources and it builds a persuasive case for its position. Laurie Ann's sources all fit her topic, and her paper offers much broader coverage of the issue than either of the other papers. Also in contrast to the other papers, rather than simply summarizing a few sources, it uses those sources as evidence to support a position. Finally, Laurie Ann writes with an authority not apparent in the other essays, possibly because she has personal knowledge of this topic: As she notes in her closing paragraph, many schools in her district use multiage classrooms in additional to traditional ones, and she has personal experience with both formats. Choosing a topic with which she is familiar certainly makes for a different situation than choosing a topic about which she knows nothing, but topic selection is part of the writing process.

ANDREA: Although this paper unarguably demonstrates the best command of language and content, I still see significant problems with how completely this paper addresses the assignment criteria: There is no assessment of why this is a hot-button issue, no analysis of the weaknesses or disadvantages of this type of educational setting, and certainly no discussion of alternatives or solutions—all aspects of the issue that the original assignment seemed to be looking for. Laurie Ann expects the reader to acknowledge that she has already identified the problem and that the multi-age approach is the solution. What should have been a synthesis leading to an evaluation has instead become a thorough, well-written report on one facet of education. It meets the page requirement, exceeds the source requirement, and follows MLA format. But while it is in fact researched and well-written, it does not meet my expectations for a position paper. If we determine this to be the best paper, aren't we overlooking its weaknesses in addressing the assignment?

TOM AND ANDREA: Tom, for whom state standards are not a part of the professional landscape and who is therefore used to much more latitude when evaluating papers, is less concerned with strict attention to each component of the assignment and does, in fact, focus more on the clear, well-constructed and appropriately supported case that Laurie Ann builds. A major goal of this assignment is to introduce students to "college-level writing," and—at least for Tom, in this particular setting—using a wide variety of sources, demonstrating an understanding of those sources, using those sources to build a solid case, and speaking with an authority based on a clear understanding of the material are all features of college-level writing, especially in contrast to writing that summarizes a few seemingly random sources for no clear reason.

Andrea uses more task-specific rubrics in her work at the high school level, and she is inclined to think with a task-specific checklist for this assignment as well, even though one wasn't included with the assignment. Laurie Ann's paper, though well-written, doesn't allow her to check off the assignment criteria regarding the actual argument that was supposed to be constructed.

And therein lies a difference in how we read. Andrea, who is required to teach to the state standards, and who has therefore internalized those standards, reads with a mental checklist, regardless of (or in addition to) the rubric in play; Tom, operating without such guidelines, (unless he imposes his own), is left to read from whatever perspective (or for whatever features) he finds most appropriate or compelling. These differences, we believe, are related to the different worlds we inhabit.

Different Worlds, Different Readings

High school teachers and college professors—note the different titles—inhabit different worlds. In addition to the institutional differences described earlier, we also face significant instructional differences. High school teachers, who teach a full complement of classes every day, typically have more than twenty-two contact hours each week; college professors, who usually teach four courses per semester, typically have twelve contact hours per week. In terms of student contact hours, a college professor with four classes of twenty-five students each has about 4,500 student contact hours per semester; a high school teacher with an average of twenty-five students per class faces more than ten thousand student contact hours per semester. Most high school teachers have their own classrooms, which they can individualize to complement the classes they teach; most college professors have an office (and a departmental secretary), and they might have a different classroom for every class. High school teachers are expected to attend a certain number of inservice programs each year; college professors are expected to publish. Perhaps the most salient feature, at least in terms of our discussion, is the high school emphasis on standardization: standardized curricula, standardized tests, standardized rubrics. In "The Truth about High School English," Milka Mosley notes, "Just like the students, high school English teachers have to conform to and cover the curriculum approved by our school boards because everything we do is closely monitored by standardized testing" (60). The goal is to be sure that a student in a given course masters a standard set of skills and knowledge, regardless of the teacher or the school at which the class is offered. This emphasis, combined with high student numbers and a demand for accountability, leads to a need to simplify. The five-paragraph theme, with its clear, easy-to-grade format (which also makes grades easy to justify when challenged), continues to be a staple assignment, even in junior and senior classes. The complexity of an organically structured essay is time consuming to teach and often not subject to reliable measurement, so external factors steer teachers away from such essays. Simple forms are quicker to teach and easier to measure.

Rubrics can help standardize instruction and assessment. Andrea sees many rubrics in high school, since teachers who teach the same material are more likely to use a common rubric. Tom sees rubrics only occasionally in college, and professors who use rubrics tend to do so mainly for convenience, to speed up the grading process. Although (or because) they promote standardization, rubrics can lead to boring, overly structured papers. That is, teaching to a rubric can dictate too closely each step of the process, so that writing becomes a cookbook activity: "First, state the problem and explain why it matters; second, identify at least three possible solutions; third, identify positive and negative aspects of the first solution, the second solution, and so on; then say which solution is the best."

In college, professors chafe at the idea of standardization. When Tom tried to get members of his department to create some kind of description of what students should be able to do upon successful completion of the composition sequence, the general response was that "we don't need to do that; we all know what good writing looks like." Although some departments publish a generic rubric (at least for first-year comp courses) describing A work, B work, and so on, the more common situation seems to be that individual professors have considerable say over the standards in their own classrooms. This situation looks like a double standard: College professors hold high school teachers accountable for producing graduates with a standard set of skills, but they feel no responsibility to a similar system of accountability.

College professors can expect students to work with a degree of independence that high school teachers cannot expect or require. To be sure, teachers in both college and high school want to help their students pursue increasingly sophisticated levels of reading and writing. Based on admission standards, however, college professors can expect a certain degree of sophistication as a starting point, and they can expect their students to work with a fairly high degree of independence. High school teachers, however, enjoy no such luxury: They must accept whatever students show up, take them at whatever level they can function, and use whatever methods—however remedial—necessary to help students progress. To provide adequate and individualized instruction, the high school teacher probably has to create more handouts, as well as more worksheets, quizzes, and tests. The high school teacher might even be expected to post one or more grades every week for every student, or even daily grades, so parents can monitor the progress of their students. Such frequent grading is unheard of in college. Students generally receive grades less frequently in college, and they don't always appear to know how they're doing in a particular course. If they're not doing well, it's their responsibility to seek out the extra help (from student services, the writing center, or maybe a tutor) to improve.

To make the jump to college even more challenging, students who learned to do well in their high school English classes—who internalized the descriptors of high performance levels on the standard rubrics—suddenly find themselves facing unknown (and often unpublished) criteria; they don't know what an A paper looks like, and they might have a professor who won't (or can't) provide a clear description the way their high school teachers did. These students, who learned to play the high school game by following the high school rules, will find themselves playing a completely different game in college, where the rules may change from professor to professor. The first year of college isn't just another grade level—it's a whole new culture.

High School Writing and College Writing

In this volume and its predecessor, authors trying to define "college-level" writing have had to admit the elusiveness of such a definition; still, our task is to add what we can to the effort, based on our perspective and our discussions.

At least part of the difficulty with creating a definition arises from the lack of standardization in college classes. It's not hard to find a rubric that defines appropriate writing for students at any grade level in public schools, but many (if not most) colleges lack such a document. The SAT rubric offers one definition for successful writing, and the Advanced Placement test for English language and composition offers another. Colleges that use scores on these tests to substitute for first-year composition courses acknowledge passing scores as indicators of college-level performance. Beyond these documents, however, we have little common ground for describing our objective. What "counts" as adequate for one college might be substandard at another college; in fact, writing that earns a passing grade with one professor might earn a failing grade with another professor at the same college.

Mixed with the elusive definition of college-level writing is a further complicating distinction: There is clearly a difference between competent writing and sophisticated writing. A competent paper will respond directly to the assignment and show command of the subject, either through synthesis of adequate research materials or as a result of authentic experience. A competent paper will have an introduction, conclusion, and some logical (if perhaps predictable) flow of ideas in the middle. A competent paper will be free of errors in conventions (grammar, mechanics, and usage) that require the reader to reread in order to construct meaning.

And while a competent paper doesn't *require* rereading, a sophisticated paper *invites* it: that is, a sophisticated paper is one that the reader *wants* to reread. Word choice and sentence variety are used to bring out the voice of the writer, ideas are expressed with insight, and the organization subtly moves the reader from one idea to the next.

The same basic qualities appear to be present and required at each level (high school and college, competent and sophisticated), but then our difficulty shifts to how to measure the importance of those characteristics in each piece of writing we assign and assess. Following the trend toward holistic scoring, the weighting of individual components is unnecessary; the overall impression is what matters most.

One way we can help high school students prepare is by trading in our task-specific rubrics for skill-specific rubrics, since the "skills" associated with good writing are transferable to a variety of tasks and genres (Popham 98). For their part, it would be help-ful if college professors also used skill-specific rubrics so their stu-dents will know what's expected or how those professors define good writing. As things stand now, high school students can at least find published standards (for their school, their district, or their state) for acceptable work; college students may or may not be able to point to any such standards. In college, students must figure out for themselves what counts as acceptable perfor-mance—more evidence that the distance between high school and college is not just another step up some academic staircase but instead is a chasm.

Works Cited

Mosley, Milka Mustenikova. "The Truth about High School English." *What Is "College-Level" Writing?* Ed. Patrick Sullivan and How-ard Tinberg. Urbana, IL: NCTE, 2006. 58–68. Print.

Popham, W. James. *Test Better, Teach Better: The Instructional Role of Assessment*. Alexandria, VA: ASCD, 2003. Print.

Academic Writing as Participation: Writing Your Way In

SHERIDAN BLAU

Teachers College, Columbia University

Most college and university professors conceive of their undergraduate courses—including introductory courses in various fields—as sites for initiating students into a discourse (that is, into the technical terms, procedures, problems, and research practices) that define the field of study they are teaching (Thaiss and Zawacki). The model for academic papers for many professors in such courses (including many undergraduate English classes), therefore, tends to be some version of the scholarly paper that professionals produce in the scholarly journals written for other specialists in the same field. That model can be a problem, however, for a number of reasons, the first of which is that students frequently are required to write such papers before they have ever read one (and even before they are sufficiently conversant with the issues in a field to read one), rendering their act of writing an artificial kind of composing, guided by formula and outlines and formal requirements designed to ensure that student papers will at least appear to observe the formal conventions of published work in a particular discourse community.

A more serious problem created by the professional model is the fact that articles written in professional journals are by definition and cultural practice the discourse of experts who know a field intimately, can speak with authority about the background and history of the problem or question they are addressing, and usually know many of the readers who will be reading their work—know them personally from conferences, from hearing their presentations, or from reading their articles. In other words, academic authors are typically deeply embedded in an academic culture as participating members of an academic community, and their writing emerges from and reflects their status as members and contributors to the making of knowledge in their community.

The Developmental Perspective and the Problem of Transition

Student writers, on the other hand, and most especially first-year or other lower-division students in college courses, are hardly even neophyte members of such disciplinary communities, are often not conversant with the language of any scholarly community, and are generally unable to speak with any authority about the subjects or problems they are first encountering and whose histories are entirely unknown to them. The idea that they might contribute to knowledge in such a community is not even entertained as a present or future possibility (Penrose and Geisler). Nor do they know anything about their readers (which is to say their professor or teaching assistant) except that their "expert" readers are likely to judge their minimal knowledge, their inexpert language, and the form of their discourse against an entirely unattainable standard. Moreover, most students, particularly in lower-division courses, don't expect or aspire to ever become members of the disciplinary communities into which they are being introduced and cannot imagine themselves as genuine participants in such a community at any level of expertise. And since most students do not aspire to participate eventually as insiders in the academic disciplines of their introductory courses, the formal writing assignments that ask for parodic versions of academic discourse are more alienating than inviting, leading students to experience themselves as even more rather than less outside the academic community of the university to which their introductory courses are ostensibly inducting them. This is particularly discouraging and threatening to the developing academic identities (Ball and Ellis) of students who are most at risk of dropping out of the university early in their academic careers—students from underrepresented socioeconomic and ethnic groups including economically disadvantaged students who are the first in their families to attend college.

The problem then may be seen as a developmental one. How can faculty members who want to initiate students into the discourse community of their subject and prepare students for writing academic papers in their subject help their students to take initial steps into the discourse practices of a particular disciplinary community without alienating those students, when many of the students do not aspire to join that particular academic community and may not imagine themselves ever becoming members of any academic community? This may also be seen as a problem of transition, often between high school and college writing, but just as characteristically, perhaps, between first-year college composition courses and the specialized writing of upper-division courses. In that sense, it may also be seen as the problem of transition from community college writing to university writing.

Meeting the Instructional Challenge: A Workshop on Academic Writing

To meet the developmental and instructional challenge of helping students develop competence as participants in an academic culture and in an academic discourse, I describe in this chapter a workshop that I believe takes developmentally appropriate steps for inducting students into a legitimate academic community where they can inhabit roles and take on responsibilities and a discourse (Green and Dixon) that will prepare them for the demands of college writing in any course, discipline, or field of study they happen to enter. The informing premise of this project, in other words, is that students will best learn to produce academic discourse the way they learn to produce any other specialized discourse: through their cultural experience as members of a discourse community, where they master the discourse to the degree that they (sometimes very gradually) become active contributing participants in the community (Lave and Wenger).

Since I happen to be an English teacher, my workshop is framed for an English class and is a version of my practice in teaching academic writing to undergraduates in my university literature courses, including a course called Introduction to Literary Study designed

for first- and second-year students, and various advanced literature courses, including one in Milton. But I believe that the principles and procedures I demonstrate here can apply with equal
relevance to introductory or advanced courses in any academic
field and are especially adaptable for instruction in first-year
composition courses in college or college preparatory English
classes in high schools. My evidence for the adaptability of this
workshop for first-year college English classes and high school
English classes derives from the testimony of the teachers who
have reported to me on their success in replicating what I demonstrated to them at conferences and professional development
workshops, and I can now add to that testimony the preliminary
results of some recent experiments I have conducted in community college and high school English classes in New York City,
where I worked in classes that exemplify the diversity, the linguistic and cultural challenges, the economic disadvantages, and
the aspirations of typical students in most of the public schools
of New York City and other large cities in the United States.

To introduce readers of this chapter to my approach to teaching academic writing, I use a version of the presentational method
I regularly employ in workshops that I conduct for inservice and
preservice secondary and college teachers of English, where (with
fidelity to the professional development model of the National
Writing Project) my aim is to provide teachers with a hands-on
experience of a particular teaching strategy that I have used successfully over time in my own teaching practice, along with a
rationale for my practice, which is to say, an account of the theory
or principles that inform my practice. And since my actual teaching practice at every level is built around workshops I construct
for my students, my method of exposition in this chapter, as in
my professional development workshops for teachers, is to provide
a dramatic re-creation of a classroom workshop I typically conduct in my own classes with my own students.[1] In this case, it is
the workshop I conducted for several years with my undergraduate students in the first week of almost any literature course, where
my aim was to initiate them into the writing practice that would
become the most crucial and generative activity of our class—an
activity that also addresses what I have described as the developmental problem of enabling students to become participants in

the academic discourse that defines whatever discipline or field of study they are being taught in whatever course they are enrolled in.

Hence, I now ask readers of this chapter to imagine themselves in a conference center or university classroom, where they are among professional colleagues, and asked to participate in a workshop to introduce a particular genre of academic writing for use in a first-year college English class, an introductory college literature course, or perhaps a college prep English class in high school. In other words, I ask readers of this chapter to participate in a drama within a drama, the framing drama being that of the professional development workshop for teachers within which I try to provide a hands-on or dramatic experience of the workshop I conduct for my undergraduate students. But since in this chapter I am, in fact, engaged in a superordinate discourse for teachers (as I am in my professional development workshops), I step outside the drama of the student workshop from time to time to make theoretical and pedagogical observations and explanations about why I am doing what I am doing. In this chapter I call such asides *side notes* (pedagogical or theoretical or both). At the end of the interactive portion of the workshop, I take advantage of the fact that this workshop is a virtual one, experienced only through a reading, and I complete the workshop with some additional details about how I implement it in my classroom and with some additional reflections on the informing principles and research base for my practice—much as I would in a room full of teachers—but at considerably greater length than I would allow myself in an oral presentation.

A couple of additional notes before we begin: on representation, on format, and on factuality, or verisimilitude. First, the dialogue presented here is not a transcript of any particular workshop but a dramatic reconstruction of a typical workshop drawn from my own notes and memory and confirmed by the memories and notes of colleague and student participants. Second, while I use pseudonyms for the names of the participants who read their own writing during the workshop, I do not otherwise invent names for the teachers and students (at various levels of education) whose voices are dramatically presented here, except to identify separate voices as those of the workshop leader or teacher (T) and various participants or students (S1, S2, and so on). Sometimes, in the middle of the drama, I give what amount to stage directions, or instructional directions for teachers. I enclose these comments in brackets without further comment. Finally, when I present samples of the writing produced in my workshop, I sacrifice verisimilitude for the sake of elucidation and show samples collected from very different groups of participants, ranging from graduate students and teachers to first-year community college students to high school students, as if they are all in one classroom together. But I continue to frame my discourse as if I am talking to teachers or student teachers.

Inside the Inaugural Workshop

Step 1: Setting Up the Experiment

T: I want to begin this workshop with an experiment in writing about literature, so I'm going to give you a very short piece of literature to read and then ask you to write a commentary on it. Please enter the heads of your students for a moment and imagine you are students in a classroom where I have just announced what we are going to do. What would you now say? What would students ask or want to know?

S1: What's a commentary?

T: Good question. Perhaps I should have defined it immediately, since it is an unknown genre, and that's largely why I identified it by such a name. A commentary in this classroom is a contribution to a discussion about a literary work or literary issue or question arising from a discussion about literature. Any other questions?

S2: How long does it have to be?

T: Ah! Well, since I'm only going to give you seven minutes to write your commentary today, it can't be very long. But I'll tell you now that we are going to write commentaries almost every week in this class, and you'll post them on our classroom online forum, and I'm also going to ask you to write responses to each other's commentaries online. So while you'll be able to take all the time you need to write your commentaries before you post them online, if they are very long, nobody is going to read them and respond to them. And your commentary won't be much of a contribution to a discussion if nobody reads it. But, to be more helpful, let me say that I anticipate that most commentaries will about one page in length, though they might sometimes be closer to half a page or as long as two.

S2: Single space or double?

T: I guess we'll see. Why not a space and a half?

S3: Does it have to have a thesis?

T: I don't know. Let's see what happens.

S4: Can we use *I*?

T: Why not? How else are you going to talk about what *you* think? You want to say, "In this writer's opinion . . . ? I guess you can do that if you like it. But it might sound weird. Remember that a commentary is part of a conversation in which you are a participant.

S5: What about grammar?

T: What about it?

S5: And spelling. Do we have to use complete sentences and put the commas in and spell out words correctly?

S6: Does it have to be perfect?

T: Well, I imagine that you would at least want to be sure that your readers will understand what you say and that you wouldn't want to embarrass yourself with childish errors. And surely you can all use your spellcheckers before you post your contributions. But you can't do that here today in the short time you'll have for writing.

S6: So is it going to be graded?

T: Not today. But over time, no and yes. I won't grade any individual commentary, but at the end of the term I'll grade your performance as a contributor to our online discussion of literature, which means evaluating the entire collection of your commentaries and responses. And all through the course I'll also be responding myself from time to time to individual commentaries.

S7: Do we have to talk about whether we like the literature and analyze it and stuff?

T: I don't know. Let's see what happens.

S6: Can we say we don't like it?

T: I don't know. Let's see what happens.

S6: Why don't you know? You're giving the assignment.

T: Because we have never written commentaries in this class before, and I'm not sure what will happen when we start writing them. Have any of you ever seen rules for writing commentaries? No? Then maybe there are no rules that anybody can hand down to us and we'll have to see what a commentary looks like in our class, based on what we do with it, with our only agreement in advance being that it is a contribution to a discussion about literature.

Theoretical and Pedagogical Side Note

The idea of this exercise, as I will later explain in more detail, is to recapitulate the emergence of a new genre within a discourse community, much as the written genres of academic and professional communities emerged from the activity systems that generated and shaped them (Russell). Hence, a teacher should give as little direction as possible, beyond specifying the ostensible function of the new genre within the class. Some features of the genre may be deduced in advance from that function (the need for contributions to be short, for example), but it is crucial that most of the features of the genre be allowed to emerge through use and be recognized as the creation of the community through the contributions of its members.

Step 2: Instructions for Reading and Writing

T: So let's get started. If you all have the handout with the poem "Nineteen" on it, I'd like you to read that poem attentively (after I read it aloud) and write a commentary on it—remembering that a commentary is a contribution to a discussion of a literary work. If you find yourself stuck and unable to get started with your commentary, try beginning with the phrase *I wonder . . .* and then, after you have written for a while and find yourself running out of gas, see if you can get some extra mileage by writing, *which makes me think . . .* , and go on from there. You may not need such starter phrases, but if you feel stuck, don't hesitate to use them.[2]

So now let me read the poem out loud, before you read it again for yourselves one more time (or possibly more). Then when I see you are all ready, I'm going to tell you to start writing, and I'll time you, giving you seven minutes to write.

Nineteen

On the first day of Philosophy 148, a small girl walked in,
freckled, solemn, cute, whom I liked right off.

Next time, our eyes met and she smiled a little.
I was already in love.

I always tried to arrive before she did so I could watch her
coming through the doorway, each time loving her more.

She began to look at me, too, hoping for a word, I suppose,
but when our eyes met mine would drop.

Once I heard her ask someone for a pencil.
I passed mine back without turning or speaking.

Spring came and we saw each other on the campus
open-throated, wordless, everywhere.

On the last day of exam week I was reading at the far end
of the Philosophy Library. Not a soul there but the librarian.
Dust in the sunbeams. End of college.

The door opened. It was my girl. I looked down.

In all that empty library she came to my side,
to the very next chair. Sweet springtime love.
Lovely last chance first love.

I could have taken her by the hand and walked the whole 60 blocks
to the piers right onto a steamer to France or somewhere,
but I said nothing and after a while got up
and walked out into middle age.

GEORGE BOGIN[3]

T: Now read the poem again (once or twice) by yourself and when you have done that I'll begin timing the writing.

[After three or four additional minutes]

T: Okay. Now I'm going to ask you to write your commentary. But you're only going to have seven minutes to do it. That's enough time to get some thoughts down on paper but not enough for serious editing or extensive revision. So for this exercise you're going to have to do what some people call *quick-writing*. Write fast to get down your ideas before you lose them, and don't worry much at this point about cleaning up your paper for an audience. Nobody will look at it but you. And remember, if you feel stuck and don't know how to get started, try starting with the phrase *I wonder . . .* and then after a while try using *which makes me think . . . .* So let's get going: I'm going to write with you. When we finish our writing, I'll have more instructions for you.

Pedagogical Side Note

I think it is very important that teachers write along with their students for this exercises as a way to include themselves in this community of writers, so they can serve as models for practices they wish to encourage. It also enables the teacher to determine whether students might need an extra minute of two to complete the assigned task.

Step 3: Processing the Writing

T: Okay. I see we've actually taken a little more than seven minutes. So now please get ready to stop . . . and bring your piece to a close . . . and now really stop . . . and that's it. What I'd like you to do now is share your commentaries with two other writers, listening to what your partners wrote. Read your commentaries aloud to each other. Don't summarize it or tell about it. Read what you wrote on the paper and make sure your partners do the same thing.

Pedagogical Side Note

It is important that students be required to read their writing aloud rather than tell about what they wrote. For one thing it usually takes less time. But, more important, the experience of "publishing" (literally, making public) their writing in their own voice allows them to appreciate the power of their prose to contribute to a shared project and also to notice where their prose might not communicate accurately.

T: You will then be free to talk about the poem briefly in your small group, but your focal task is to notice what might be said to be the features of a commentary, so you can answer the questions I couldn't answer before about what a commentary does or looks like. Imagine a student entering our class for the first time tomorrow and being told to write a commentary at home for the next class. And he turns to you and asks, "What's a commentary?" Aside from saying it's a contribution to a discussion about a text, what could you tell him? Your job in your groups is to discover from listening to the commentaries in your group how to answer that question and the questions that might follow it, like what do you talk about in a commentary and how formal does it have to be, and so on.

Be sure to have a member of your group take notes, recording the features noticed in your group, so they might be reported to the larger group. Also, please remember that what you will be finding are rules about what a commentary may or might include, not what it must include. You have only limited evidence, so be careful not to conclude that what you found must be present in every commentary or that what you didn't find can't be allowed in a commentary. Let's begin by merely trying to discover what we see in this class as a range of possibilities for what a commentary might be. I should add that if we had enough time today, I'd ask you to write responses to each other's commentaries and process those, too, extrapolating the features of a response, since you will all be writing even more responses than commentaries. But for the sake of time, we'll deal with responses another day.

[15 minutes in groups for reading pieces and discussing features of commentaries]

T: How about if before we hear reports on your findings about the features of a commentary, we hear some commentaries that your group and you found particularly interesting or illuminating or that did something unexpected that you think we'd want to hear. Then as we hear those commentaries, we may be able to add to the list we constructed with our small group of the features of a commentary. So please feel free to volunteer yourself or volunteer some member of your group to read. Your whole group seems to be pointing to you, Lisa.

LISA: Okay, I'll read it.

Student Commentary #1
(Master of Arts student, student teacher)

> I wonder how this poem might be different or make the reader feel differently if the subject had overcome his fear. If, instead of walking away from his yearlong crush, he did whisk her away to France or the courtyard or just to the end of the stacks. Would it seem too cliché, like a tired romance comedy? Would I have wanted to read it again and again? Probably not. Which makes me think that the image of our protagonist, failing yet again, resonates deeply with most readers. Bogin's image of a college boy "walking out into middle age" is not only depressing, but universal . . . it's the dream deferred all over again and Bogin answers the question . . . does it pop? Does it dry up like a raisin in the sun, or does it just get up and walk off into old age? Is it the dream that shrivels or the man? Bogin's protagonist has a dream and she is alive and well on the page. Captured in all her beauty and awkwardness. But it is the man who passed her (his dream) out of fear who ends up "shriveled" and deferred . . . straight into the loveless springless time of middle age.

T: Wow! Let's applaud for that, as we will for all the pieces we hear. So, what are some features of this piece that might be mentioned in describing a commentary?

S7: It can use lines from another poem to talk about this poem. That's very cool!

T: Right. Do you all recognize the lines or at least some language and images from the Langston Hughes poem on the dream deferred? What's the proper title of the Hughes poem? I can't remember.

SEVERAL STUDENTS: "Dream Deferred!"

T: Oh! Of course. So we can say that a commentary might allude to and even draw language from another literary work in order to describe or illuminate the text under discussion. That's terrific. What other features of a commentary might we derive from Lisa's piece?

S8: She identifies the theme of the poem as the explanation of why the poem is interesting to her and other readers.

T: Yes, and that observation is very interesting to me, because it's not that she identifies a theme because she thought she was supposed to, but she identifies a theme in the course of wondering what makes the poem so interesting to her and, she presumes, to other readers. In fact, it's really her thinking about the theme that brings her to the Hughes poem and accounts for why in the end she drew on the language of the Hughes poem. It's the idea of deferring one's dreams and not acting on them. And this isn't any crude thematizing either, because I'm just now realizing that she isn't suggesting that the theme of this poem is the same as that of the Hughes poem. She is actually contrasting the two poems in their themes. In our poem, the speaker is the agent of the drying up of the dream, not merely the victim of it. But that isn't something Lisa thought about and then decided to write about. It's one of the things I love about quick-writing, when a writer is engaged in real thinking. Is it the case, Lisa, that it was the process of writing your thoughts that brought you to the discovery of the idea about the connection or contrast with the Hughes poem? You didn't think of it until your writing brought you to it?

LISA: Yes, that's true. When I wrote that he walked out into middle age, I thought about how he didn't try to make his dream come true but put it off, and that made me think about deferring a dream and the images of the Hughes poem.

T: She is talking about the power of writing to lead us into deeper and more interesting thoughts than we may have thought we were capable of. Okay. Let's hear another. I know it's hard to follow that one, but let's have some brave soul volunteer to read—or again you can volunteer a neighbor. Ah, I see Derrick is volunteering for our benefit. Thank you, Derrick.

DERRICK: Okay. I'll take a chance. Here's mine.

Student Commentary #2
(community college, beginning first-year student)

> This guy is an idiot. I can understand admiring from afar and trying to act cool by just passing the pencil back without eye contact. For him to play it cool even in the library when it's the last chance to see her. Maybe I watch too many Japanese cartoons, but I would have asked her out although probably in a nervous manner. Of course I'm a little confused about the last line where he says he "walked out into middle age." Does that mean he ended up alone or lonely at middle age?

ALL: [*Applause*]

T: That's gives us a lot to work with. What can we add now to our description of a commentary?

S9: It can evaluate the poem or the speaker in it.

T: That's right. It treats the narrated events as if they are real and comments on the character in the poem much as he would comment on a character in real life who behaved in the same way. Yet we know that we are reading a poem, a work of art, something made. Maybe it's all fiction? Is it naïve to treat narrated events in fiction as if they really happened?

S10: I wouldn't give away my money if I read a story about the world ending. But I wouldn't be interested in a story or its characters if they didn't seem real.

T: Sure. A usual requirement of fiction is verisimilitude—the feel of truthfulness or reality. A common criticism of a play or film or novel or even a poem is that one doesn't find the characters or situation believable, even if the setting is in an alternative universe. It may be fantasy, but it has to have the kind of plausibility that allows one to enter its world imaginatively and "suspend disbelief." So what else can we say about the features of Derrick's commentary?

S11: He puts himself in the same situation and tells what he would do.

T: Right. That's a way of entering the world of the poem, which is a sign of a good reader.

S11: He also asks questions. Not just the kind of wondering we heard in Lisa's, but questions trying to figure out the meaning of lines.

T: That's right, and the value of doing that is evident here in the way Derrick asks his question and then, in thinking about it, offers a tentative answer that seems to me highly plausible. Is the character in middle age and still alone and lonely? Why might we think so?

S6: Because he's looking back at when he was nineteen and seems remorseful about his failure to act on his feelings—a failure that led him into middle age. So he must be looking back from a place where he is now unhappy.

T: I see most of you are nodding in agreement. So asking questions is a productive move in commentaries, and I would add that it is probably the most reliable avenue we can take to advancing our understanding of what we read. But let's hear another commentary. I see some people pointing at you, Miguel.

MIGUEL: Okay. I'll read.

Student Commentary #3 (high school senior)

The whole poem, but especially the last phrase, "I got up and walked into middle age," made me very melancholic. I can't help but think of the fact that most people (at least the ones I know) by the time they've reached middle age have had at least one "simple yet seems to be so significant" event in their lives that they regret, or would have changed the course of. And who can really blame them? It is to my opinion, after all, human nature. So I have selfishly taken it upon myself to wonder: "WHAT ABOUT ME?!" Will it be the same for me, am I going to hang on one simple event of my life and never really be able to fully move on with it? It would make anyone that's growing up paranoid. But good thing I'm not too much of a pessimist. I rather live life by the moment (which is probably what the still very young nineteen-year-old author should have done) and hope to live a full-on-never-"shouldhavedonesoinsteadofso" life.

ALL: [*Applause*]

T: Thank you, Miguel. Anything here we may want to add to the features of a commentary.

S3: You can make up words.

T: Is that what he did? Well, sort of; he strung familiar words together in an unsegmented fashion. And it has a witty effect. So I guess we can say you can do that in a commentary—especially if it has a witty effect. Anything else?

S7: You can use the poem to talk about your own life. Sort of like Derrick did.

T: Yes. But he starts out by wondering how he might be like or unlike the speaker in the poem. Often a poem or story is important to us for the degree that it illuminates our own lives, either by resemblance or by contrast or as a cautionary tale, which is partly how Miguel reads this poem.

S12 et al.: Read yours. Our group picks you. You read it to us. Read it to everybody.

T: Okay, but I'll just read the beginning and end of it.

> I used to think this was a charming and sad poem about missed opportunity and lost happiness resulting from the shyness and inexperience of two young people—a poem about how youth is wasted on the young. But several subsequent readings of this poem and several additional opportunities to write about it have enabled me to recognize it for what it is: a cheap, sentimental cliché of a poem, indulging in a fundamentally adolescent fantasy about true love and happiness and destiny—a fantasy that is as dangerous as it is stupid. That's the beginning.
>
> Here is the end: If the young man in George Bogin's poem had worked up his nerve and declared himself to his unnamed beloved, he might have found that he had hooked up with a cold-hearted, gold-digging twit with whom his life would have been unbearably lonely, painfully boring, and financially ruinous. And surely that is a more likely outcome of a grab at love with a beautiful stranger than the outcome imagined

by the permanently regretful speaker in Bogin's poem. That speaker didn't walk out of college straight into middle age. He never grew beyond adolescence.

T: Well. What feature of a commentary might my piece add?

S13: A commentary may attack a text. [*General laughter*]

T: Sure. What's so funny about that? Lots of literature deserves to be attacked, and even classic works can be controversial and subject to serious critical censure.

S3: It has a thesis.

T: That's true. It advances a thesis and then backs it up with examples and reasons. And I need to acknowledge that I am generally opposed to and have conducted research and published arguments to discredit the widespread opinion that academic writing must or ought to make an argument and be driven by a thesis (Blau). Yet given the chance to write a commentary on a poem, I produced a thesis-driven argument. So why did I do it?

S6: You like to argue with everybody, including yourself.

T: That may be true. But in this case the answer is that my experience of the poem over time and of the discussions of it that have transpired whenever I have used it have led me to an opinion of the poem that puts me in opposition to what I know to be the prevailing sentiment about the poem among the readers I am likely to encounter. Hence, I now read the poem with an expectation about what most readers will say and, needing to produce a commentary on the poem, find myself drawn most immediately to the contribution I assume I can make to the discussion by opposing what I know will be the prevailing viewpoint and what was formerly my own viewpoint. In other words, my piece advances a thesis, not because I felt obliged to write from a thesis, but because my relationship to the poem and its readers over time puts me in a position that happens to be adversarial.

S6: That's what I said. You like to argue.

T: Okay. But what this particular context also suggests is that argumentative, thesis-driven writing arises in the academic community (as elsewhere) from social and intellectual contexts that place some writers in opposition to a prior discourse, and not from any arbitrary requirement for thesis-driven writing as an essential feature of academic discourse (see Graff and Birkenstein). Indeed, most writers—at any level of academic and literary accomplishment—who comment on the Bogin poem for the first time do not advance a thesis or make an argument in their commentaries. How many of you advanced a thesis? Nobody? Well, what about Derrick? He began by calling the speaker an idiot. So maybe he has a thesis, though I'm not sure it's what drives his commentary. In any event, very few of you wrote in support of any thesis (even though you may have been taught over and over to do so or may teach your own students to do it), mainly because it was your first encounter with the poem and you used your writing more productively to explore problems, raise questions, make observations about youth and love, express sympathy or regret for the poetic speaker, and try to understand the motives of the speaker and his unclaimed girlfriend. I have never conducted this workshop with any group of students or teachers at any level where I have seen more than one or two thesis-driven commentaries, beyond my own. But, of course, it would be counterproductive and intellectually indefensible either to require or to forbid them.

Can we now hear from the groups about the features they identified for a commentary, especially ones we haven't already noticed in the pieces we have heard?

S14: We'll go. We said that a commentary expresses feelings and thoughts in the first person, uses an informal language, but that it doesn't use emoticons or the shorthand spelling of text messaging.

T: Okay. Does your list imply that a commentary has to observe the features you named?

S14: Well, I'm not sure I can speak for our group, but I think we were thinking that it usually does these things, and I don't think text-messaging language should be allowed in any kind of academic writing.

T: I'm inclined to agree, though I've never had to face the problem in this first exercise, except for a couple of instances of the abbreviated *u* for *you* that I noticed in the commentaries I recently collected in a high school class. And I confess that I've found myself doing that in my own draft writing lately. I do want to argue, however, for reasons I'll elaborate on more fully a little later, that at this stage our experiment entails seeing what people do with commentaries, not what they should or must do, and that we ought to be intellectually consistent in our inquiry, noting what we observe and not concluding that what we happen to observe in three samples can be interpreted as a general rule of inclusion or exclusion. It is at this stage, rather, a rule of allowances or affordances or common practices. We can say that a commentary allows a writer to talk about personal feelings and other works of literature and so on. And maybe we can say that the observed practice is to use relatively informal (but not very casual) written language—a style that the linguist, Martin Joos would call *conversational* or *consultative*, rather than *intimate* on one end or *formal* or *frozen* on the other, and that is generally consistent with the conventions of edited American English. We'll talk later, I hope, about how to deal with nonconforming practice.

But that can't be all. What other features did you notice in the commentaries you heard in your groups that we haven't yet mentioned?

S6: We had an example that talked about some technical features of the poem and about its structure, so we added that kind of discussion to the possibilities for a commentary.

S11: In our group, somebody wrote their commentary in the form of a poem. So we said your commentary can be a poem. Or maybe a story in response to a story.

T: But so far all you have actually seen is a poem, which I hope its author will share with all of us a little later.

S15: In our group, we got a couple of stories or personal narratives. We liked them, too.

T: I'm not surprised. I suspect that some of the most interesting pieces and the ones that most illuminate or complicate the psychological or prudential issues are often pieces that employ personal narratives as examples. That's important to mention. Any more?

S16: Well, it seems like none of our commentaries are just brief assertions. All of us seem to elaborate our ideas and explain our point of view. Maybe this is related to the text-messaging issue.

T: That's right. The commentaries we've heard aren't bare statements or empty clichés, invoking commonplace ideas presumed to be already understood. Rather they involve the development of ideas for readers who will be willing to pay attention. And maybe that's another feature. They seem to be written for readers who are interested in what the commentator has to say. Or is that my imagination? I wonder how I could verify that feeling or show that it is based on some observable textual facts?

S15: In our group, we were certainly interested.

T: But did you write your piece with that expectation in mind, and can that expectation be recognized in any discernible features of your piece of writing?

S15: I think there is some evidence of it in the personal stories people tell, in their willingness to reveal themselves, and even in their willingness to ask questions.

T: That may be so, and it's certainly what I have found in later stages of the discursive enterprise into which this workshop is an initiating exercise. And here I want to remind you and remind myself that the genre-creating project I have been initiating in this workshop applies as much to the genre of the response as the commentary, but I have never figured out how to include responses in an initial workshop that has to be completed within the span of something like an academic period or even a somewhat longer professional workshop session. In my courses, if I treat responses at all in a workshop, I have to do it somewhat later, after we start to see some. In any event, it is probably the case that the responses, and the responses to responses that characterize many exchanges on the class online forum, also contribute to the construction of a community where supportive personal engagement and self-disclosure can both flourish.

Beyond the First Workshop: The Classroom as an Academic Community

The workshop we have just completed is ostensibly designed to introduce students to the genre of the commentary (and eventually the response) that will occupy a central place in my literature class, but, more crucially, it serves as the foundational experience for building the kind of classroom culture that will foster the development of students as contributing members of a legitimate academic community, an academic community not unlike those to which college and university faculty members belong in their identity as microbiologists, or psychologists, or historians, or composition specialists, or literary scholars. But while students, particularly in their early undergraduate years and surely in high school, are unwilling and unready to identify themselves as even neophyte members of disciplinary communities, which, for them, occupy a remotely distant if not alien universe, classrooms themselves can still be organized as authentic yet accessible versions of such communities. That is to say, classrooms can be organized—largely through shared writing—into academic communities where students can experience a developmentally appropriate induction into the practices and world of disciplinary discourse, where students experience themselves as contributors to that discourse, as they quite literally produce and share knowledge with other members of the academic community whose work they have read and whose positions and ideas they are familiar with from conversation and "publication." The online body of commentaries and replies, moreover, serves the same function in such a classroom community as scholarly journals and books serve in advanced professional communities. Assigned class readings and online postings of passages from the published writing of distinguished scholars (along with the teacher's contributions) can also bring the discourse of the classroom community into closer contact with the more advanced work and intellectual traditions of the parent discipline.

Note, too, that, for the most part (beyond the initial definition of a commentary), it is students who, through their own shared and visible writing—their practice—become responsible for determining the conventions that emerge to define the genres of writing (the "commentary" and "response" and possibly other genres as well) that characterize the main body of publications sponsored by and accepted in this academic community. Significantly, that process of allowing the conventions that define a genre to emerge from the practice of members of a discourse community recapitulates the birth and emergence of the genres of academic discourse in most established academic and professional disciplines (Bazerman; Miller), where the genres of the scholarly article, the review of research, the legal brief, the probation report (Converse) and so on continue to develop and undergo changes in response to the ongoing practice of those members who contribute to discourse in the field and the exigencies of the activity systems (Russell) served by the genres that have emerged in that field.

Thus, student ownership of the genres of writing in their classroom community and their familiarity with classmates whose work they read and respond to confer on students the kind of authority and relationship to knowledge, to knowledge producers, and to knowledge production that contributors to professional and scholarly journals typically possess. Such genuine authority and real relationships render the student writing more like professional academic writing than any superficial observance of any externally imposed conventions of form or organization would ever achieve. In other words, what students are learning (not learning *about* but learning *how* to do) is how to produce knowledge through their contributions to an academic discourse in a genuine academic community. They are legitimately engaged in the real thing, not going through motions in a dutiful but less meaningful parody of it.

The teacher in such a classroom is also positioned to have a particularly potent influence on the character of the online discourse and the quality of student publications. Aside from setting the requirement of participation in the first place, the teacher, as member of the community, also shares a responsibility to publish commentaries and to respond to the commentaries of other members of the class, and thereby insert his or her voice, knowledge, and example into the online discourse as an authoritative resource and potential model for students. The teacher's interventions need to be respectful and supportive, however, much as they would be (or perhaps much more than they would be) in any academic community where he or she might function as a senior member. In cases where the teacher needs to discipline or admonish a student or where the teacher's response to a student's work might be embarrassing for the student, the response can be delivered privately through email or in person. It is also the case that the teacher serves in a role that is much like that of a journal editor. And in that role the teacher has the capacity to set some rules and impose some norms that may not develop organically over the course of a term or academic year. Hence, a teacher-editor might eventually proscribe (or allow the community to accept) the spelling and shorthand conventions of instant messaging or require the observance of some conventions of courtesy or acknowledgement (citing the work of other students from whom one borrows language or ideas, for example) widely practiced in the broader academic community. I would be inclined to advise patience on such matters, however, and some trust in the power of genuine scholarly activity to recapitulate in the consciousness of student scholars the same sense of proprietary interest and indebtedness, for example, that may have produced the conventions of citation and attribution that are now common in academic publications.

In my own experience of requiring commentaries and replies, typically amounting to one each week, excluding weeks when larger papers are due (more about these later) and allowing students to excuse themselves from participation in any two or three additional weeks each term, I believe I exert the most powerful influence through the way I make use of the written commentaries in class. In almost every class meeting, I select at least a couple to read aloud (and sometimes distribute them as a handout or show them on an overhead, though I should—but don't, unless a student does it for me—retrieve them online and project them on a screen) and use them to initiate discussion of what seem to me important critical issues that they raise. In the course of using these commentaries as critical resources for advancing our discussion of particular texts or issues, I honor their originality or insight or interesting perspective, and I sometimes comment on the language, style, or form of the piece as a model of (or sometimes an obstacle to) rhetorical effectiveness. In this way I honor student work for its contribution to knowledge in our classroom community at the same time that I point out strategies for thinking or writing that seem to me exemplary and that sometimes stretch our notions about what is rhetorically or substantively possible within the genres that we have been employing in limited ways in our class. I try to provide some of the same sort of instruction, more subtly, I presume, in the commentaries I publish myself on our online forum. And let me add here that I instituted a version of this program of instruction some two or three years before I began to use any online forum in my class. I asked students to bring three copies of their papers to class and share them in groups of four and write responses to at least one. I could still manage to create an academic community in my classroom, without using online resources. But once I began to use an online forum for the publication and sharing of student work, the pedagogical advantages of my approach became increasingly obvious and multiplied exponentially.

Here I should also mention, as promised, that I do require my students to write what might be considered more formal papers twice during an academic term. These are probably much like the papers assigned to students in most other literature courses, except in a couple of their special features. First, students choose their own topics, and, for the midterm paper, I urge them to address problems that have troubled them in their reading or troubled the class in class discussions or online commentaries and replies. For the final paper, I invite students to examine a problem or topic they have already explored to some degree in their commentaries and replies and to try to write their paper mainly by combining and revising commentaries and responses they have already written for our course. Finally, for both papers I require students to consult the writing of their classmates (available on our online forum) on the problem they are investigating in their paper and to cite the work of their classmates in their references.

Producing College-Level Writing: The Confirmation of Experience and Theory

While I cannot claim that the practice I have demonstrated and described in this essay is guaranteed to succeed in engaging student interest and fostering more attentive reading and more powerful writing in every class, my own students (with a few exceptions)[4] have found their experience in writing commentaries and replies online, within the classroom context I have described, a positive one, and sometimes an extraordinarily valuable or even transforming one. And a number of teachers and former students who have contacted me after attending my recent workshops have reported experimenting with my approach to academic writing in their secondary or college classes and getting similar though somewhat more mixed results.

Although my principal interest in this workshop has been in the way it positions students to engage in the production of knowledge and thereby experience what it means to participate in a genuine academic discourse, I want to point out that the particular genre I have chosen as the experimental focus of my genre-creating program serves especially well as an instrument for producing an academic discourse that can also make a strong claim to the status of college-level discourse. Notice that the practice presented in my workshop is built on the principle of requiring students to participate in an academic discourse by placing them in a social environment where the culture of the classroom and the exigencies of social and academic life in the classroom occasion participation in a form of writing that is academic, because it addresses literary texts (in the commentaries) and commentaries on literary texts (in the responses) and is by its nature interpretive, reflective, and metacognitive. That is to say, it represents thinking about texts, thinking about thinking, and thinking about the problems that texts pose and that are raised by readers of texts. Such discourse, by definition (Dewey) represents reflective thought or "critical thinking," which is virtually the defining characteristic of college-level discourse (Smith 229).

Finally, though I am obliged to observe space limitations in this chapter that won't allow me to elaborate on the elegant and powerful theories of discourse and learning that inform and support the practices I have enacted in my workshop and class-room, I do want to assert emphatically that the practice I have been proposing and variations on it are worthy of our continu-ing experimentation and some persistence on our part, as we try to improve and perfect our practice in the face of any problems that might arise, because the method—though still needing refine-ment—is so richly supported by a number of converging strands of highly persuasive research and theory. It seems to me, in fact, that everything we have learned from contemporary research and theory on language acquisition (Bruner) on discourse competence (Freedman and Medway), on the development of writing abili-ties (Rogers; Sommers and Saltz; Sternglass), on situated learning (Lave and Wenger); and on the conditions that foster academic achievement (Hillocks) argue for a workshop such as I have dem-onstrated and a classroom community such as that workshop is designed to inaugurate.

Notes

1. For an account of the theory and pedagogical history of this genre of teaching, see *The Literature Workshop: Teaching Texts and Their Readers* (Blau).

2. This particular starter prompt I owe to my colleague Ruth Vinz. It has been very helpful in this exercise for a number of student writers and for teachers, too.

3. George Bogin (1920–1988) is now best known for the annual poetry prize awarded in his memory by the Poetry Society of America. During his career as a poet, he published widely in such leading journals as *Ploughshares, The American Poetry Review,* and *The Nation.* A volume of his selected poems, *In a Surf of Strangers,* was published shortly after his death.

4. Twice I have encountered a student in my class who never would take the risk of posting written work online or even submitting a draft of a commentary or reply in private to me. Visits for these two students to our campus writing center and repeated office conferences with me did not suffice to rescue them, though I believe that my own growing under-standing of the nature of alienation and peripheral participation over the

past couple of years would now give me new resources for easing them into some kind of participation that would make further development possible within the scope of my course.

Works Cited

Ball, Arnetha F., and Pamela Ellis. "Identity and the Writing of Culturally and Linguistically Diverse Students." *Handbook of Research on Writing: History, Society, School, Individual, Text.* Ed. Charles Bazerman. New York: Erlbaum, 2008. 499–513. Print.

Bazerman, Charles. "System of Genres and the Enactment of Social Intentions." *Genre and the New Rhetoric.* Eds. A. Freedman and P. Medway. London: Taylor and Francis, 1994. 79–101. Print.

Blau, Sheridan. *The Literature Workshop: Teaching Texts and Their Readers.* Portsmouth, NH: Heinemann, 2003 pp. 1–20. Print.

Bogin, George. "Nineteen." *In a Surf of Strangers.* Gainesville: UP of Florida, 1981. Print.

Bruner, Jerome. *Child's Talk: Learning to Use Language.* New York: Norton, 1983. Print.

Converse, Caren. "Unpoetic Justice: The Pre-Sentence Investigation Report and the Criminal Justice System." Diss. in progress. U of California, Santa Barbara, 2010. Print.

Dewey, John. *How We Think.* 1910. Buffalo, NY: Prometheus, 1991. Print.

Freedman, Aviva, and Peter Medway. *Genre and the New Rhetoric.* New York: Taylor and Francis, 1994. Print.

Graff, Gerald, and Cathy Birkenstein. *They Say/I Say: The Moves That Matter in Academic Writing.* New York: Norton, 2006. Print.

Green, Judith, and Carol Dixon, "Talking Knowledge into Being: Discursive and Social Practices in Classrooms." *Linguistics in Education* 5.3 (1993): 231–39. Print.

Hillocks, George, Jr. *Teaching Writing as Reflective Practice.* New York: Teachers College Press, 1995. Print.

Joos, Martin. *The Five Clocks: A Linguistic Excursion into the Five Styles of English Usage.* 1961. New York: Harcourt, 1967. Print.

Lave, Jean, and Etienne Wenger. *Situated Learning: Legitimate Peripheral Participation*. Cambridge, UK: Cambridge UP, 1991. Print.

Miller, Carolyn R. "Genre as Social Action." *Quarterly Journal of Speech* 70.2 (1984): 151–67. Print.

Penrose, Ann M., and Cheryl Geisler. "Reading and Writing without Authority." *College Composition and Communication* 45.4 (1994): 505–20. Print.

Rogers, Paul. "The Contributions of North American Longitudinal Studies of Writing in Higher Education to Our Understanding of Writing Development." *Traditions of Writing Research*. Ed. Charles Bazerman, Robert Krut, Karen Lunsford, Susan McLeod, Suzie Null, Paul Rogers, and Amanda Stansell. New York: Routledge, 2010. 365–77. Print.

Russell, David R. "Rethinking Genre in School and Society: An Activity Theory Analysis." *Written Communication* 14.4 (1997): 504–54. Print.

Smith, Cheryl Hogue. "'Botched Performances': Rising to the Challenge of Teaching Our Underprepared Students." *What Is "College-Level" Writing? Volume 2: Assignments, Readings, and Student Writing Samples*. Ed. Patrick Sullivan, Howard Tinberg, and Sheridan Blau. Urbana, IL: NCTE. 2010. 209–232. Print.

Sommers, Nancy, and Laura Saltz. "The Novice as Expert: Writing the Freshman Year." *College Composition and Communication* 56.1 (2004): 124–49. Print.

Sternglass, Marilyn S. *Time to Know Them: A Longitudinal Study of Writing and Learning at the College Level*. Mahwah, NJ: Erlbaum, 1997. Print.

Thaiss, Chris, and Terry Myers Zawacki. *Engaged Writers and Dynamic Disciplines: Research on the Academic Writing Life*. Portsmouth, NH: Boynton/Cook, 2006. Print.

Advanced Placement English and College Composition: "Can't We All Get Along?"

DAVID A. JOLLIFFE
University of Arkansas

When I consider the question motivating this collection—what is "college-level" writing?—in light of my eighteen years as a reader, table leader, question leader, and chief reader for the Advanced Placement English language and composition examination, I am tempted, tongue in cheek, to emulate our beloved forty-second president and propose that the answer "depends on what your definition of *is* is."

Seriously, though—tongue out of cheek—when we ask what "college-level" writing is, are we asking what the *writing* is in terms of process, product, purpose, genre, audience, and so on? Or are we asking what a college writing *course* is, in terms of what its content is, who teaches it, what its level of rigor is, and so on? In either case, neither an Advanced Placement English[1] course, which a student might complete in preparation for taking one of two Advanced Placement English examinations, nor the writing done in the course and on the examination is college writing. The course is a high school course, taught by high school teachers. The students who take it are in high school; therefore, their writing cannot be college-level writing.

But if we are asking what college-level *writing* is, we are in less certain territory. Is the writing that students do in an Advanced Placement course college-level writing? Is the writing that students produce on the timed, impromptu Advanced Placement examination a decent predictor of their ability to succeed in college courses that require substantial critical reading and argumentative writing? At the risk of provoking an argument, and remaining completely mindful of the many critiques that can be leveled at the writing produced on the Advanced Placement English language and composition examination,[2] including the one by Edward White in this volume, I want to assay that, in many ways, an Advanced Placement English language and composition *course* might be superior to a typical first-year college course in terms of its preparation of students to succeed as readers and writers in the remainder of their college years and in their lives as responsible citizens of a democracy. I propose to get to this assaying by means of a good, old-fashioned comparison and contrast list. That is, I propose to point out what I see are both the benefits and the drawbacks of taking a good Advanced Placement English language and composition course, and I aim to show how each of the benefits and drawbacks stacks up against a traditional first-year college composition course. Before I get to this list, however, I need to offer a bit of background information, both programmatic and personal, about the Advanced Placement English language and composition program. At the end of this essay, I'll try to offer some advice reminiscent of Rodney King: Since neither AP English nor college composition is going away, can't we all get along?

Advanced Placement English— The Programmatic Perspective

Advanced Placement is an educational program owned and marketed by the College Board, a not-for-profit organization based in New York City. The College Board promotes AP as a chance for students to do "college-level" work in high school and as an "opportunity to earn credit or advanced standing at most of the nation's colleges and universities" (http://www.collegeboard.com/student/testing/ap/about.html). In May of every year, the College Board offers more than thirty examinations in different content areas. It contracts with the Educational Testing Service, based in Princeton, New Jersey, to develop and score the examinations. A high school student may take any Advanced Placement examination that he or she wants to take. A student does not have to take a course called *Advanced Placement* in order to take an examination, but many high schools offer a wide range of AP courses in all content areas, and the College Board openly encourages the development of Advanced Placement curricula.

Two Advanced Placement English examinations are offered: one in English literature and composition, which was among the first AP examinations offered, beginning in 1955; and one in English language and composition, which has been offered since 1980. Most of the students who take the English literature and composition exam are seniors, and most who take English language and composition are juniors. The format of both exams is similar: Students first have one hour to answer about fifty-five multiple-choice questions, based on four or five reading passages. On the English literature exam, the passages are brief pieces of fiction, poetry, and drama, and most of the questions call for close readings of the texts. On the English language exam, the passages come from nonfiction prose—there is no fiction, poetry, or drama at all—and most of the questions call for students to analyze the rhetorical effectiveness, either of the entire text or sections of it.

After the one-hour, multiple-choice exam, students have two hours on the English literature test and two hours and fifteen minutes on the English language test to write three essays in response to prompts. On the English literature test, one prompt calls for a close-reading analysis of a poem, one calls for a close-reading analysis of a piece of prose fiction, and one—the "open" question—calls for students to write an essay about some thematic issue or motif found either in one of the twenty or so novels or plays listed under the prompt or in a "literary work of comparable merit." On the English language test, the first prompt calls for students to read six, seven, or eight brief sources (at least one of which is a visual—a picture, cartoon, graph, or chart) on an issue and then write an argumentative essay that synthesizes at least three of the sources in their composition. (Students get the aforementioned extra fifteen minutes on the English language exam to read and annotate the sources.) The second prompt requires students to write a rhetorical analysis of a piece of nonfiction prose. The third prompt calls for students to write an argumentative essay based on a brief prompt that may contain an excerpt from a piece of nonfiction prose. (The order of the second and third prompts is reversed on some examinations.)

The students' answers to the multiple-choice questions are, of course, machine scored. To rate the students' essays, the Educational Testing Service (ETS) recruits a large cadre of high school and college instructors to come to a single location (most recently Louisville for both the English literature and English language exams) for an entire week in June. These readers work for seven straight days from 8:00 a.m. to 5:00 p.m., rating each essay on a 1-to-9 scale, using a scoring guide that has been devised by the chief reader, a university faculty member who oversees the entire scoring process, and taught, using a range of benchmarked training papers, to the question leaders (one per prompt), table leaders (around forty per prompt), and readers (between 350 and 400 per prompt), who periodically pause during the week and recalibrate their scoring standards. More than 360,000 students take each of the English examinations, and, since each student writes in response to three prompts, well over two million student essays are read and rated during the week of scoring.

At the end of the scoring session, ETS uses a formula that weights the students' performance on the essays at 55 percent and their performance on the multiple-choice test at 45 percent to generate a raw score for each student. Then, making careful comparisons between the difficulty of tests from year to year and the apparently relative strengths of the students from year to year, ETS, in consultation with the chief reader, establishes cut scores that separate students into five categories: 5 is "extremely well qualified" to receive college credit or Advanced Placement, 4 is "well qualified," 3 is "qualified," 2 is "possibly qualified," and 1 is "no recommendation."

These scores are then reported to the student, his or her high school, and any college or university designated at the time of testing. Individual colleges and universities must decide whether they are going to award exemptions or credits for courses on the basis of students' Advanced Placement scores. A great many institutions will waive students from one or two required first-year writing courses if they earn a 4 or a 5 on one of the Advanced Placement English examinations. Some institutions will accept a score of 3 as well. More and more colleges and universities are accepting only high scores on the Advanced Placement English language and composition examination in lieu of required composition courses since relatively few first-year writing programs emphasize writing about literature.

Advanced Placement English—The Personal Perspective

I must admit that I knew almost nothing about the Advanced Placement English program until I became director of English composition at the University of Illinois at Chicago (UIC) in 1987. The high school where I taught from 1976 through 1981 did not offer AP courses, nor did the high school I attended in my small hometown in West Virginia back before the Punic Wars.

Like many of the early graduates of doctoral programs in rhetoric and composition in the 1980s, I felt prepared to develop a rigorous and challenging first-year writing program, and I did so at UIC. I was proud of the courses in the program, and I felt strongly that every student who graduated from the university should have to take them. Thus, when a student sashayed into my office one day and told me that, based on an examination he had taken when he was a junior in high school, he was waiving the courses that I had so proudly and meticulously developed, well, I got my nose a little out of joint. I wondered, "What the devil is this AP program?"—only I imagine I probably substituted another word for *devil*.

Rather than being immediately dismissive of AP English, I decided to gain some insider knowledge. I applied to become a reader for the English language and composition exam, and, in the summer of 1992, I traveled to a hotel at exit 8 on the New Jersey Turnpike and spent a week reading student essays that analyzed the rhetorical effectiveness of Nancy Mairs's "On Being a Cripple." I returned to the AP English language and composition reading every June for almost all of the next eighteen years. I moved up in the hierarchy, becoming a table leader, then a question leader, and then, in 2003, chief reader—a position I held through 2007. I was appointed to the test development committee, a group comprising three college or university instructors and three high school teachers, in 1999, served on it as a voting member until I became chief reader, and then served ex officio until the chief readership expired.

I discovered three things during my tenure with the AP English language program, and I list them here in ascending order of importance: First, I discovered an examination that has all the flaws of any examination administered to several hundred thousand students—an exam that relies on multiple-choice questions with answers that are sometimes ambiguous and also requires students to write impromptu essays. Second, I found a wonderful group of teachers from high schools and colleges alike, many of whom return every summer to the reading. (Some people jokingly refer to the reading as "summer camp for nerds.") Participating in the reading is difficult work, but attending it allows folks not only to bond with old friends and new but also to participate in an extremely valuable professional development experience. At the reading, one sits at a table of eight, generally with four college or university instructors and four high school teachers.

While the reading itself happens in silence, the conversation during the breaks and after the reading day ends is valuable beyond measure: Here are groups of excellent, dedicated teachers who spend seven straight days reading the same set of student work. The questions abound: "How would you score a paper if it does X?" "How would you work with a student whose writing does the things we saw in the sample paper we all looked at together?" "How do you teach writing?" "How do you teach reading?" "What works for you?" Certainly, high school and college instructors have the opportunity to attend the same conferences and hear the same papers being read at them, as is the habit at professional conferences. At the AP English language reading, on the other hand, these teachers actually talk with one another, work with one another. In my thirty-four years of teaching at the high school and university levels, I have found no more valuable professional development experience for teachers who are concerned about high school to college articulation.

Third, with the AP English language and composition program, I found a complex set of activities—the exam itself, the curricula that emerge from the exam, the professional development activities that the College Board sponsors to support both new and experienced teachers of AP English language—that have the potential to make high school English (1) focused on rhetorical theory and practice, in academic and "real-world" settings, rather than simply on appreciation and analysis of canonical literature; and (2) harder.

When I was a high school student in the 1960s and a teacher in the '70s, English was about reading fiction, poetry, and drama and writing analyses of and themes about these pieces. I suspect the course I took in the '60s and taught in the '70s is still being taught in thousands of classrooms across the United States. That course is way too easy. It lacks analytic rigor. It lacks any connection to the ways language is actually used to shape meaning, to achieve different purposes, to effect change in real rhetorical situations. Ideally, an Advanced Placement English language and composition course can teach students how to operate as effective consumers and producers in these situations.

Advanced Placement English Language versus Traditional First-Year College Composition

Picture, if you will, a hypothetical high school junior. If this person is fortunate enough to attend a high school that offers an Advanced Placement English language and composition course, and if she can afford to pay to take the examination or if someone will pay the tab for her, here is a probable scenario: She will take the course. She will take the examination. If she gets a 4 or 5 (or a 3, depending on where she intends to go to college), her postsecondary institution[3] will exempt her from one or two of its required first-year composition courses or perhaps even offer course credit as well as the exemption. At some colleges and universities, she may have to take another required, upper-division writing or writing-intensive course, and, ideally, she will have to read critically and write copiously and effectively in both general education and major courses. At many institutions, however, she will have satisfied the general education writing requirement. She will officially be "done" with studying reading and writing.

Should our hypothetical student follow this plan of action? As an ardent supporter of college composition programs—I have been the director of composition at two large universities and have sat on the executive committees of both the Conference on College Composition and Communication and the Council of

Writing Program Administrators—I am going to argue that she should, even though I am quite troubled by the fact that doing well on the AP English language and composition exam might mean that this student had no impetus actually to study rhetoric and composition at the postsecondary level. I will return to this issue in the final section of this chapter.

In the following comparison of the benefits and drawbacks of following the AP scenario, I am going to focus solely on the ideal AP English language and composition course and the examination. As much as I value students' abilities to engage in close readings of fiction, poetry, and drama and to write themes about literature, as they do on the AP English literature and composition test, I do not believe that demonstrating proficiency in these abilities should exempt a student from first-year composition. College composition ought to be about learning to read critically and write effectively about different subject matters from an array of academic and public forums. Writing about literature is a small subset of the range of academic and public writing.

So what would our hypothetical student learn in the ideal AP English language and composition course? With plenty of instruction, discussion, guided practice, and independent practice, she would learn the principles of rhetorical theory that would allow her to critically read texts of all kinds—essays, articles, websites, advertisements, short stories, novels, poems, and plays—as rhetorical artifacts, as the instantiation of a rhetor's efforts, in a particular rhetorical situation, to achieve meaning, accomplish a purpose, or create an effect with a reader or group of readers. With the same depth of instruction, discussion, guided practice, and independent practice, she would learn about the principles of rhetoric and argumentation that underlie the production of texts of all kinds in academic and civic contexts. In other words, as Ronald Lunsford, John Kiser, and Deborah Coxwell-Teague advocate in their chapter in this volume (77–97), our hypothetical student would learn how to inscribe in her own compositions the same principles of rhetorical effectiveness that she studied under the rubric of "rhetorical analysis." With the same level of care and effort, she would learn how to conduct academically respectable research, how to evaluate material discovered in the research process, and how to synthesize research in her own argumentative writing. As she wrote pieces that analyzed, argued, and synthesized research, she would learn about and develop processes that would move her along the developmental path toward becoming an excellent writer—ideally, a path that she started traversing several years before coming to the AP course and that she will continue to travel after the course ends.

At the end of the course—that is, after a full year's instruction in rhetorical theory, rhetorical analysis, critical reading, and argumentative writing in its richest definition—she would take the examination. If she scores high, all well and good. Ideally, she will attend a college or university that places her in an advanced writing course, not simply waive her from required basic ones. But even if she does not score high enough on the exam to earn college credit or exemption, our hypothetical student is so much better prepared for reading and writing in college and in the polis than students who haven't taken the AP English language course—and, I want to offer, she is better prepared for reading and writing in these two realms than many students who take college composition.

What would be the benefits of living out this hypothetical scenario in Advanced Placement English language and composition, rather than simply taking required first-year composition? Let me list them:

◆ In the best AP English language and composition course, she would get a thorough exposure to the principles of rhetorical theory and analysis and to the idea that all the texts and documents that swirl about her—in school and beyond—are rhetorical artifacts designed to shape meaning, purpose, and effect. In the best AP course, rhetoric is the content. I'm not certain what the content of the typical college composition course is. In some cases, I imagine, it is an elementary version of cultural studies/cultural critique, in which students are exposed to essays about controversial issues from the popular press—work, the environment, gender and sexuality—and taught to use those texts as springboards to their own reactions and arguments.

◆ In the best AP English language and composition course, our hypothetical student would pay lots of attention to careful, close, analytical reading—to seeing how the organization, structure, diction, syntax, imagery, and figurative language of a text, textual or visual, shape its *logos* and influence its appeals to the author or creator's credibility and to the audience's emotions and stages of life. In a typical college composition course, I fear, not nearly enough attention is paid to such close, analytic reading. (For a similar view, see David's Bartholomae's "The Argument of Reading" and my "Who is Teaching Composition Students to Read?")

♦ Despite its flaws—a reliance on multiple-choice questions and on students' impromptu essays—the Advanced Placement English language and composition examination provides a set of inherent end-of-course, student-outcomes-oriented learning goals that can give shape and order to instruction over the year-long course. If the AP instructor has any familiarity with the concept of backward mapping,[4] he or she knows that an effective instructor inscribes end-of-course learning goals in the curriculum and pedagogy and teaches toward them from day one of the course. Unless its instructors have become familiar with the Council of Writing Program Administrators' "Outcomes Statement for First-Year Composition" (http://www.wpacouncil.org/positions/outcomes.html), most typical first-year college composition courses that I have observed are not structured, either explicitly or tacitly, to define and work toward accomplishing learning goals that are student-outcomes oriented.

♦ The best AP English language and composition courses are taught by instructors who receive specific training in rhetorical theory and analysis and who take their professional development seriously. While the College Board has no specific requirements for teaching an AP course, its national office, regional offices, and affiliated state offices do provide a wide range of one-day, two-day, and weeklong institutes for AP teachers, taught by college and high school faculty members with AP experience who are certified as consultants by the College Board. Moreover, many states and school districts require AP teachers to have either initial training or periodic retraining or both.[5] In short, an excellent AP English language and composition teacher has lots of avenues to experience and excellence. On the other hand, a typical college composition instructor, especially at a large university, whose professional interests or aspirations lie somewhere other than rhetoric and composition studies, or a teaching assistant who is just learning his or her craft, may have had relatively few opportunities to develop expertise in teaching critical reading and effective writing.

♦ In the best AP English language and composition courses, the level of both instructional rigor and student performance expectations is high. I'm not sure I can say that is the case categorically in a typical first-year college composition course.

The Imperfections of AP English Language and Composition

I don't want to suggest that the AP English language and composition program is perfect. In fact, it must confront imperfections presented by its personnel, its de facto curricula, and the examination itself:

- About the issue of "staffing"—of both teachers and students: Like most high school English teachers, relatively few AP English language and composition instructors have had any concentrated coursework in rhetorical theory and analysis as part of their professional preparation, and not all of them have taken advantage of the College Board's one-day, two-day, and weeklong sessions on rhetoric. Many of them are fine teachers of literature, reading, grammar, and composition, but the principles and terminology of rhetoric are often foreign to them. And if many AP English language and composition teachers are in the dark about rhetoric, how much more so are the students taking the course? Predominantly juniors,[6] most these students have been the beneficiaries of eleven years of English/language arts instruction that has emphasized close reading of poetry, fiction, and drama. They have often had scant experience analyzing a text created by a writer for readers in a specific rhetorical situation, and they have had little exposure to nonfiction prose or texts that rely on words, visuals, and graphics working together.

- The de facto curriculum that many AP English language and composition instructors must teach can also create a roadblock to success. Because the course is usually offered to students in the junior year, and because many school districts require that an American literature curriculum, focusing on poetry, fiction, and drama, be taught in the eleventh grade, many teachers have to try to map a curriculum focusing on rhetorical theory and analysis onto a traditional "great-square-inches-of-American-literature" syllabus. One can, of course, learn to teach imaginative literature from a rhetorical perspective, and one can supplement one's teaching of American literature with nonfiction texts appropriate for teaching rhetorical analysis, but not all AP English language and composition instructors have had much experience or training in doing so.

- The examination itself represents a can of worms. Because it is given to such a large population, it must measure all the abilities it tests using multiple-choice questions and impromptu essays. Multiple-choice answers are often, by design, ambiguous, and test-takers frequently have to select the answer that's "most correct." Moreover, one hopes that the writing-as-process movement, now approaching its fifth decade in composition studies, has convinced all and sundry that no writer ever does his or her best work impromptu, with no chance for the writing to "percolate," to benefit from formative feedback, and to be revised. Finally, because the College Board promotes the test as one way to earn credit for college composition, the examination is complicit with the kind of thinking, also fostered by colleges' and universities' own language portraying composition requirements as something students want "to get out of the way," that one's abilities as a critical reader and careful, effective writer can be put in place at age sixteen, seventeen, or eighteen and need no continuing development or improvement over the years.

Despite These Imperfections . . .

These problems notwithstanding, the reason I have supported and worked for the AP English language and composition program for nearly two decades is this: It does provide a structure and a rationale for high school English instruction that emphasizes the close analysis of the rhetorical effectiveness of texts, the production of rhetorically effective argumentative essays, and the incorporation of texts in source-based synthesis essays. I find such a curriculum a vast improvement over one that overemphasizes canonical literary history, repeated practice in New Critical close reading, and isolated, drill-based instruction in grammar.

Moreover, I am willing to assert that the impromptu writing produced by students who score solidly in the upper half of the 9-point scoring guide—that is, compositions that score 6 and higher—offers a decent indication that, if the students continue in college to learn new ways to read and write effectively, they will be able to succeed (and perhaps excel) in the rhetorical environments that their college courses and their civic lives present to them.

Here, for example, is a student's composition produced under exam conditions (forty minutes of impromptu writing) by an Advanced Placement student at Fayetteville High School responding to a prompt from the 2008 AP English language and composition examination.[7] Here was the prompt:

For years corporations have sponsored high school sports. Their ads are found on the outfield fence at baseball parks or on the walls of the gymnasium, the football field, or even the locker room. Corporate logos are even found on players' uniforms. But some schools have moved beyond corporate sponsorship of sports to allow "corporate partners" to place their names and ads on all kinds of school facilities—libraries, music rooms, cafeterias. Some schools accept money to require students to watch Channel One, a news program that includes advertising. And schools often negotiate contracts with soft drink or clothing companies.

Some people argue that corporate partnerships are a necessity for cash-strapped schools. Others argue that schools should provide an environment free from ads and corporate influence. Using appropriate evidence, write an essay in which you evaluate the pros and cons of corporate sponsorship for schools and indicate why you find one position more persuasive than the other.

The student produced this essay:

With low government funding and a less stimulated economy, many schools are looking for different routes of earning financial support. Partnerships with corporations—a long time coming financial backer of schools—may take a turn in a new, more official direction. Do these advertisements have a positive or negative affect on the student body? Despite any potential drawbacks, schools should seek corporate sponsorships to improve school facilities and positively influence the general opinion of the student body.

Because schools are often underfunded by the government, forming financial partnerships may be necessary to meet the needs of a school's student body. For example, if building a new and improved art room requires the display of the sponsor's name, students would benefit more from the new art room than they would be affected by the subtle advertisement. The same scenario works for buying new textbooks, renovating the exterior of the school, and expanding the parking facilities. While students may be influenced by the nature of the sponsorship, they will benefit more from the boost in their education brought about by financial support. Assuming the advertisement *does* affect the students, partnerships may be crafted in a way that makes this influence mutually beneficial.

Partnerships may have an influence on student opinion. Such an influence may distract from student's education, increase or shift their spending habits, or create a school bias regarding an organization. While some may lobby for an educational environment free of this corporate influence, such advertisements would be minimal in comparison to the advertisements students see every day. Furthermore, students may be more inclined to support an organization or business that supports their school. Thus, by supporting said business, they are indirectly supporting their own education. However, to decrease any potential distractions or unfair bias, any partnerships with businesses should be carefully made. Businesses should be financially stable, socially sturdy, and comply to the general vision of the school.

Schools should form partnerships with businesses that they believe their students should support (as decided by steering committee, board of directors, etc.). For example, if a school decides its students should eat more healthily, the school may form a partnership with an organization like Appleseeds, which intends to foster healthier eating habits in youth. If a school wants to encourage a more athletic, physically active student body, it should seek a partnership with a sporting company. Such efforts ensure a win-win situation; schools receive needed funding while encouraging students in a desired direction. Despite these good intentions, a partner organization may change directions over time. For example, when Michael Phelps was photographed smoking marijuana, many of his sponsorships cut back their funding. Said sponsors did not support his actions, nor did they want their customers to support his actions. Schools should avoid such public disputes by troubleshooting potential partners. This may be done with an interview, background check, or other means of investigation regarding a business's intentions. With a sturdier partnership, there is a smaller likelihood of scandal, thus detracting attention from the partnership. When fewer students notice a partnership, it has less of an impact on the general student body and their spending habits. Such preventative measures may not be necessary if both parties of a partnership benefit from the relationship.

While some may argue that public education should be free of financial matters and advertisements, students may benefit more from such endeavors than they would without them.

Certainly this is not a perfect essay. It has the occasional clumsy sentence—the second one in the first paragraph, for example, with its noble try but inelegant execution of a parenthetical—and its diction sometimes slips, as in "comply to" rather than "comply with." But if I were to receive such a composition from a student during the first week of my first-year composition course at any of the six colleges or universities at which I have taught, I would wonder whether this student might profitably spend his or her time and tuition money in a course in which both the instructor and the classmates would push him or her into deeper explorations of reading, rhetoric, and composition than the mainstream first-year course typically sponsors. The writer seems to understand that an argumentative essay must engage and interact with readers. Notice the prevailing stance: This is a writer who reasons with her reader, who assumes that people may be taking issue with her claims and may need to be convinced logically, rather than preached at. The writer shows skill with exemplification: The fourth paragraph, for instance, is dominated by examples that demonstrate how corporate partnerships can be win–win situations.

Some readers might notice that this composition has five paragraphs and criticize it as just another stultifying, formulaic five-paragraph theme. It's not. As I have repeatedly taught my own writing classes, and as Cathy Birkenstein and Gerald Graff make clear in their coauthored *Chronicle of Higher Education* column, a student's composition is not stultifying and formulaic simply because it has five paragraphs. The bad five-paragraph theme is one in which the "arguments . . . are disengaged and decontextualized, severed from any social mission or context" (A40; see also Graff's *Clueless in Academe*). Such is certainly not the case with this sample composition, which engages with readers, anticipates and addresses their possible objections, fleshes out its evidence with appropriate detail, and amplifies and intensifies its argumentative reasoning.

Does this composition represent college-level writing? I'm not sure I know how to answer that question. Does the writing ability manifest in this composition suggest a writer who is ready for more advanced college courses requiring him or her to learn how to read critically and write effectively? I believe it does.

Toward Learning to Get Along

In a nutshell: I maintain that good students benefit greatly from taking a good AP English language and composition course. In my eighteen years working with the AP English language and composition program, I have both understood and become used to the vitriol that the mere mention of AP English stirs up in my colleagues in the college composition community. Certainly, all their assertions had some truth to them: The AP English program can be seen as a kind of outsourcing of college composition; college composition as an academic rite of passage does help students effect a successful transition from high school to college; an examination that students take as juniors in high school might not be able to certify that they are as prepared for college reading and writing as they would be at the end of a solidly demanding first-year composition course.

I meet these objections with two conclusions drawn from the world of *Realpolitik*—a supportable assertion about the AP English language and composition course and two suggestions for the college composition community. First, the *Realpolitik* reality: AP English is not going to go away. It has solid support among school administrators, teachers, students and their parents, and university administrators who want to attract the best and brightest to their institutions. College composition is not going to go away. Despite the periodic resurgence of the "new abolitionists,"[8] one or two required first-year writing courses seem an irreplaceable staple of most college and university general education programs. Next, the assertion: Despite the aforementioned flaws, the AP English language and composition program generally provides high school students with a very good course—much better, in my experience, than the mainstream, traditional high school course. I continue to hope that, someday, high school teachers, curriculum designers, and administrators will perceive that the focus on rhetorical theory and analysis and the emphasis on rigor inherent in AP English language and composition is appropriate for all levels of high school students, not simply those privileged enough to take AP courses.

So, the two suggestions: First, college composition professionals can work with the AP English program to help improve the test. Beginning in the early 1990s, representatives of the test development committee began to attend the summer workshop of the Council of Writing Program Administrators (WPA) and have been doing so since then. A series of frank, open conversations at the WPA meeting in Park City, Utah, for example, led to initial efforts to focus the multiple-choice questions on the AP English language and composition exam more on rhetorical analysis and less on new-critical close reading, to add multiple-choice questions that assessed whether students could understand the content of bibliographic citations, and to add a new type of essay question to the exam—one calling for students to synthesize secondary sources in their own arguments. If any college composition administrators or instructors, acknowledging that the AP English program is not going to go away, have other suggestions for improving the examinations, I'm certain that the College Board and the Educational Testing Service would be delighted to hear them.

Finally, a great many benefits would accrue if the folks involved in AP English language and composition and college composition decided they could get along. My experiences in directing the reading and in leading professional development institutes suggest that AP English language teachers are extremely eager to learn about rhetorical theory and analysis. The best and brightest teachers of college composition are in the position to help them learn about this material. If more students had better training in rhetoric in high school, I think they would become more successful college students. If college composition administrators are not keen on the fact that students who do well on the AP English examinations are exempted or waived from required composition courses, then the administrators need to get involved in campus discussions about the policy for accepting AP courses for credit. Rather than simply complaining about the AP students' placing *out* of college composition, why not work to get a more advanced writing course in place for the students to place *into*? Why not try to take advantage of having students enrolled at the college and university who have had at least some solid instruction in rhetoric? Why not try to recruit these students into peer-tutoring programs in writing centers? Why not get them get them involved in writing-enriched service-learning programs. In short, why not take advantage of better-than-average students showing up at the door?

Notes

1. For a high school to offer a course that is specifically labeled *Advanced Placement*, the school must submit a syllabus to a College Board review panel, which audits the syllabus and either approves its being offered under the Advanced Placement label or informs the school that it may not refer to the course as Advanced Placement.

2. See, for example, David Foster's "The Theory of AP English: A Critique" and Joseph Jones's "Recomposing the AP English Exam."

3. While I know of no comprehensive listing of which colleges and universities do and do not award waivers or credits for AP, the issue remains contentious. For a recent overview of the controversy at Tufts, Williams, and other highly selective universities, see "Professors and Students Split on AP Credits."

4. Backward mapping is a curriculum-planning technique promoted by Grant Wiggins and Jay McTighe in their book, *Understanding by Design*.

5. For a summary of some states' required professional development programs for AP teachers, see "A Review of State Policies Supporting Advanced Placement, International Baccalaureate, and Dual Credit Programs."

6. That the AP English language and composition course and exam are mostly given to juniors is an historical accident. The AP English literature and composition course and exam had been in place at the senior year for a quarter of a century when the English language and composition exam was introduced, in 1980. Rather than have two AP courses in the same year, most high schools opted to make English language a junior course. There is a good bit of debate in AP circles about whether the English literature course should actually be the junior-year offering and the English language course be given to seniors.

7. The prompt and sample paper are reprinted from the College Board's *AP English Language and Composition Workshop Handbook, 2008–2009.*

8. The history of the debate about whether college composition as a whole or the universal requirement of college composition should be abolished is reviewed in the introduction to Joseph Petraglia's collection, *Reconceiving Writing, Rethinking Writing Instruction.*

Works Cited

AP English Language and Composition Workshop Handbook, 2008-2009. New York: College Board, 2008. Print.

Bartholomae, David. "The Argument of Reading." *Argument Revisited; Argument Redefined: Negotiating Meaning in the Composition Classroom.* Ed. Barbara Emmel, Paula Resch, and Deborah Tenney. Thousand Oaks, CA: Sage, 1996. 199–211. Print.

Birkenstein, Cathy, and Gerald Graff. "In Teaching Composition, 'Formulaic' Is Not a 4-Letter Word." *Chronicle of Higher Education* 4 Apr. 2008. A40. Print.

Foster, David. "The Theory of AP English: A Critique." *Advanced Placement English: Theory, Politics, and Pedagogy.* Ed. Gary A. Olson, Elizabeth Metzger, and Evelyn Ashton-Jones. Portsmouth, NH: Heinemann, 1989. 3–24. Print.

Graff, Gerald. *Clueless in Academe: How Schooling Obscures the Life of the Mind.* New Haven: Yale UP, 2003. Print.

Jolliffe, David A. "Who is Teaching Composition Students to Read and How Are They Doing It?" *Composition Studies* 31.1 (2003): 127–42. Print.

Jones, Joseph. "Recomposing the AP English Exam." *English Journal* 91.1 (2001): 51–56. Print.

Lerner, Jennifer Brown, and Betsy Brand. "Review of State Policies Supporting Advanced Placement, International Baccalaureate, and Dual Credit Programs." Center of Excellence in Leadership of Learning, U of Indianapolis, Oct. 2008. Web. 12 Feb. 2009.

Lunsford, Ronald, John Kiser, and Deborah Coxwell-Teague. "Advanced Placement English and College Composition: A Comparison of Writing at the High School and First-Year College Levels." *What Is "College-Level" Writing? Volume 2: Assignments, Readings, and Student Writing Samples*. Ed. Patrick Sullivan, Howard Tinberg, and Sheridan Blau. Urbana, IL: NCTE. 2010. 77–97. Print.

Petraglia, Joseph, ed. *Reconceiving Writing, Rethinking Writing Instruction*. Mahwah, NJ: Erlbaum, 1995. Print.

"Professors and Students Split on AP Credits." *Inside Higher Ed* 10 Feb. 2009: n. pag. Web. 12 Feb. 2009.

Wiggins, Grant, and Jay McTighe. *Understanding by Design*. Upper Saddle River, NJ: Prentice-Hall, 2005. Print.

Advanced Placement English and College Composition: A Comparison of Writing at the High School and First-Year College Levels

RONALD F. LUNSFORD
University of North Carolina at Charlotte

JOHN KISER
Charlotte-Mecklenburg Schools

DEBORAH COXWELL-TEAGUE
Florida State University

Should students be granted college composition credit for scores received on Advanced Placement English examinations? The three of us are friends, colleagues, and veteran teachers, and this is a question that has long intrigued us. Two of us are very much involved in the training of Advanced Placement teachers, and the third is a writing program administrator with strong reservations about granting college credit for AP test scores. We are pleased to have the opportunity to address this question in the context of the other essays included in this collection.

Before doing so, we would like to pause here to introduce ourselves. Ronald F. Lunsford is a former writing program administrator and English department chair who now teaches undergraduate and graduate courses and serves as director of graduate studies in English at the University of North Carolina at Charlotte. John Kiser is a former high school teacher and director of the English curriculum for the Charlotte-Mecklenburg Schools. He currently serves as a consultant for the Advanced

Placement program. Deborah Coxwell-Teague is a former high school teacher who now serves as writing program administrator at Florida State University.

We began this conversation by gathering a small number of writing samples from students in Advanced Placement high school classes and first-year composition (FYC) courses in college. Ron Lunsford collected essays from the first-year writing program at UNC Charlotte. John Kiser collected essays from teachers of AP language and composition courses in the Charlotte-Mecklenburg school system. Deborah Coxwell-Teague collected sample essays from the FYC program at Florida State University, along with sample essays from AP English teachers at a north Florida high school. In all, eighteen essays were collected.

We present and discuss three of those essays. They were chosen because they seemed representative of the types of essays students were currently writing in AP and FYC classes. The essays are presented in their entirety, along with the assignments provided by the teachers. Following each essay is a brief conversation among the three of us about the essay. As we have talked informally about this student work, we have had numerous lively interchanges, and we would love to have transcriptions of those conversations to offer you. Since we do not, we decided to offer something of the flavor of those conversations in the limited venue this chapter affords. After each of the student essays, one of us initiates the conversation with a few comments about the paper. The other two respond, and then the person who began the conversation offers a final comment. But that comment should not be considered the final word about any of these papers.

Essay #1

The following essay was written by a student in a North Carolina AP eleventh-grade English class. When John asked AP teachers in the Charlotte-Mecklenburg area to share with us examples of the kinds of writing that their students composed, we were given essays such as the one that follows that were taken through several drafts with both peer response and teacher feedback to drafts in progress.

Assignment: American Definition Essay

What does it mean to be an American in the twenty-first century? What does it mean for you?

Student Essay

James A. Baldwin, an American novelist, once said, "I love America more than any other country in this world, and, exactly for this reason, I insist on the right to criticize her perpetually." Baldwin acts toward America the way a watchful parent acts toward a small child. He criticizes, as any concerned and involved parent would, not out of malice or spite, but rather to nurture the country he loves so deeply and to help it mature. This ability to criticize and to voice opinion, whether positive or negative, is one of the options unique to Americans. We, like Baldwin, can say whatever we like about America and our government without fear of repercussions. We are children with a very unusual privilege: we can voice any number of negative, dissenting views about our parent country without ever being punished.

Americans have a unique and complex relationship with our country. As a result of our unusual rights and privileges, we can act as both critical parents and discerning children. These rights originate from America's unconventional origin and composition, from the founding fathers in the eighteenth century to the millions of immigrants here today.

In the first part of the eighteenth century, America was still comprised of small colonies, which were subservient to England. The colonists eventually grew tired of British control and interference, however, and they decided to revolt against their country of origin. In 1776, Thomas Jefferson, one of America's founding fathers, drafted the Declaration of Independence, establishing that America was separate and independent from Britain. He wrote, "We hold these truths to be self-evident, that all men are created equal, that they are endowed by their Creator with certain unalienable Rights, that among these are Life, Liberty and the pursuit of Happiness.—That to secure these rights, Governments are instituted among Men, deriving their just powers from the consent of the governed." The document served first as a list of complaints toward Britain, the country Americans had left. Since very early in the nation's history, Americans have criticized their government. We are opinionated, bold, and not afraid to express ourselves. In this case, however, when Americans expressed their displeasure with England, their criticism was unwelcome. England waged war on Americans to punish them for their disobedience. At this point, Americans did not have the unique privilege of to criticize an authority figure that we have now.

The Declaration serves to define Americans as separate from people of other nationalities. In America it is "self-evident" to us that "all men are created equal." And we believe that every person has "certain unalienable rights." This document sets the foundation for what Americans as a people stand for. We believe in equality and natural, essential rights for all people.

In 1781, the United States Constitution built upon these defining principles and set them into law. When the founding fathers drafted the Constitution, they became parents, granting Americans, their children, special privileges in the form of unalienable rights and liberties. The Bill of Rights, the first ten amendments to the Constitution, guarantees Americans the right to speak, worship, and protest as we wish. The founding fathers gave Americans the right to criticize, unlike England, which punished Americans for opposing British rule. Perhaps more importantly, when the founding fathers gave Americans so many freedoms, they also granted their children the right to be different without consequences.

As Americans we celebrate these differences. America is sometimes referred to as the "Melting Pot" because of the many ethnicities, religions, and customs present in the country. We pride ourselves on our diverse and textured composition, just as children pride themselves on being different and distinct from their peers. The children of America have always been different. Since the time of the founders, Americans have comprised a large diverse family. In part, this is because the American family began this way. In colonial America, people emigratred from all different places; therefore, compared to other nations, America is not a traditional country at all. Gordon Wood wrote in *Revolutionary Characters: What Made the Founders Different* that though the identities of other nations, such as France or Germany, have been lost in the mists of time, America was deliberately formed and became a nation in 1776. Instead of belonging to a common race or a common religion, as did the French or the Germans, Americans were brought together by geography and a common pioneering spirit.

Americans don't share a common religion or a common ethnicity; we are unified instead by a common belief that everyone is created equal. Americans celebrate their differences, but we also celebrate this one very important similarity. In the Declaration of independence, Jefferson defined Americans as believing that "all men are created equal." Today, this belief brings America's diverse family together in a common philosophy and brings forth a common love for our country. As Mr. Baldwin said, Americans love their country more than any other country in the world.

Our relationship with America is a complicated one, however. We love our country more than any other, but we "insist on the right to criticize her perpetually." As Americans, we have those special privileges and opportunities to voice our bold opinions and criticisms. But though critical, we are also dutiful. If someone from another country criticizes America, we defend our country. We may criticize because both the Declaration of Independence and the Constitution allow us to do so, but no other nationality is allowed that privilege. When someone criticizes America, we become the defensive parent once again, protecting our child from whatever evils may attack it.

We are the perceptive, discerning children and the protective caring parents of a huge and multilayered country, unified by our belief in equality and our celebration of cultural and ethnic differences. We love America and being American because we can be different yet at the same time blend into a vast melting pot.

JOHN: Although this essay is largely vacuous, this student in this AP English language and composition class does show, I think, potential for writing at the college level. The essay, after all, does contain some elements of good writing—it's not poorly written, it's not full of grammatical or mechanical errors, and the level of diction and syntax is good. Typical of beginning AP students (and high school students in general), the writer does not clearly establish an audience—something that is generally neglected in the teaching of high school writing, and students typically just write for the teacher. While the author uses *we*, it's not clear who *we* are. The paper seems to indicate it is fellow Americans, but if that's so, they would already know everything in the paper. I think the major failure here is the writer fails to adequately respond to the assignment because the paper lacks focus. Instead of defining an

American in the twenty-first century, she or he deals largely with historical events and digresses on the "melting pot," although she or he implies being an American means freedom to criticize one's country. Part of the paper's failure may be based on the nature of the assignment, which needs to be more specific, about audience especially.

RON: I agree with you, John, on two important points: (1) this essay lacks substance, and (2) despite this lack of substance, this writer is ready for a college writing course. This is very much the kind of writing I expect to find at the beginning of a first-year writing course; if all goes well, it won't be what he or she is writing at the end of that course. I also agree, John, that a major factor accounting for this type of writing is the student's lack of audience awareness. You are right, I think, that the student imagines his or her teacher as the audience for this paper. However, herein lies a complication. I suspect there are many teachers who will give this paper a high mark. As long as the student and teacher agree that the purpose of this paper is to render clichés and platitudes in a school exercise designed to show that the student has mastered the basics of grammar and essay structure, then the essay will be deemed a success. In fact, the audience doesn't even have to be limited to the teacher. If the student imagines a formal speaking situation in which he or she might give an epideictic speech—one in which a person, place, or thing is held up for "praise or blame," then this panegyric on America might be seen as quite successful. Since the focus in my writing classrooms is critical thinking, I will be asking students to imagine audiences that will question. Such readers would want to know why this writer believes the America formed as a result of the American Revolution would handle rebellion differently than Britain handled the American revolt. They might ask the writer to explain America's reaction to the attempt by Southern states to secede from the Union. In writing for such critical readers, the student will learn to look at the words he or she puts on the page as the first move in a conversation rather than an exercise in speech making.

DEBORAH: While I agree with your comments, Ron and John, I'd like to point out a couple of additional aspects of this essay that bothered me. First, the sweeping generalizations made by the student writer are annoying. The student states: "We are opinionated, bold, and not afraid to express ourselves. . . . We pride ourselves on our diverse and textured composition, just as children pride themselves on being different and distinct from their peers. . . . [We are] unified by our belief in equality and our celebration of cultural and ethnic differences." These statements accurately describe many Americans but certainly not all. There are those among us who are shy and hesitant to speak their minds. There are many who do not appreciate the diversity among our population. There are more than a few individuals who do not want to be different—individuals who want to blend in. The student should have acknowledged that while many Americans have the characteristics he or she emphasizes in the essay, many don't.

Another aspect of the essay that bothered me even more than the generalizations was the lack of attention to providing source material. The student begins the essay with a quote from James A. Baldwin but provides no information regarding the publication in which the source appeared. Two pages later, the student refers to a publication by Gordon Wood and goes on to paraphrase an assertion made by Wood, yet the student provides no parenthetical documentation. This is troubling. The student should know better, and, furthermore, as the student was drafting the essay, both peers and the instructor should have stressed the necessity of providing the appropriate source material.

Essay #2

The following essay was written in a Florida twelfth-grade AP English class. When we asked AP teachers at a highly ranked north Florida high school for examples of the kinds of writing students compose for their classes, we were given only examples of timed writing such as the essay that follows. (When we contacted the teachers again and asked for examples of other types of writing that were not timed, we received no response.) Although this was a timed practice essay in an AP class, students did read and respond to one another's papers.

Assignment: AP English Literature and Composition Practice Essay
Time: 40 minutes

Read the following poem carefully, paying particular attention to the physical intensity of the language. Then write a well-organized essay in which you explain how the poet conveys not just a literal description of picking blackberries but a deeper understanding of the whole experience. You may wish to include analysis of such elements as diction, imagery, metaphor, rhyme, rhythm, and form.

Blackberry-Picking

Late August, given heavy rain and sun
For a full week, the blackberries would ripen.
At first, just one, a glossy purple clot
Among others, red, green, hard as a knot.
You ate that first one and its flesh was sweet
Like thickened wine: summer's blood was in it
Leaving stains upon the tongue and lust for
Picking. Then red ones inked up and that hunger
Sent us out with milk cans, pea tins, jam pots
Where briars scratched and wet grass bleached our boots.
Round hayfields, cornfields and potato drills
We trekked and picked until the cans were full,
Until the inkling bottom had been covered
With green ones, and on top big dark blobs burned
Like a plate of eyes. Our hands were peppered
With thorn pricks, our palms sticky as Bluebeard's.

We hoarded the fresh berries in the byre.
But when the bath was filled we found a fur.
Rat-grey fungus, glutting on our cache.
The juice was stinking too. Once off the bush
The fruit fermented, the sweet flesh would turn sour.
I always felt like crying. It wasn't fair
That all the lovely canfuls smelt of rot.
Each year I hoped they'd keep, knew they would not.

Student Essay

Blackberry-picking is a time-honored tradition passed through generations in many families. In his poem, "Blackberry-Picking," Seamus Heaney captures the childhood wonder and enthusiasm of this simple, treasured experience through the use of imagery and personification. Though the poem has a surface meaning of going blackberry-picking, Heaney has used this universal event to convey a deeper meaning that nothing can last forever and all good things must come to an end.

From the start, Heaney bombards the reader with imagery, describing the weather, colors, sizes, shapes, and tastes of blackberry season. The reader is immersed in adjectives and details to force the reader into that late August day and become a part of the poem, rather than an outside observer. After the first stanza, there is a dramatic shift in imagery. The details are no longer satisfying. The "sweet flesh" idealized in the fifth line has "turn[ed] sour" and there is a "rat-grey fungus." This drastic shift in imagery darkens the tone of the poem and parallels death and an end to a good thing.

Heaney's imagery buries the reader in his world, but his personification brings the poem to life. Blackberries have flesh, and summer blood which "leave[s] stains upon the tongue." Hunger sends you out to the fields for picking. In short, elements of summer blackberry-picking become something to transform Heaney's memories and show his closeness and devotion to these late August days. After the shift, the personification dies. No more do briars scratch or lust stir a yearning for picking. Instead, Heaney turns to stinking juice and "fruit fermented." The "lovely canfuls smelt of rot," all these alluding to death in an unusual way—through stench.

Heaney's poem is a story of coming to terms with reality, particularly that of death. Though the beginning is lighthearted and carefree, the end is bleak. Heaney regrets this harsh reality, as he particularly shows in his final line, "Each year I hoped they'd keep, knew they would not." This shows the contrast between hope and reality and trying to keep hope despite the cruelty of inevitable death.

DEBORAH: I have such mixed feelings after reading this essay. The student is a very good writer—of that there is no doubt in my mind.

If this student could compose this essay in 40 minutes, I am certain he or she would do well in writing in college courses. However, what bothers me is the idea that the student will receive credit for a college composition course by making a decent score on timed essays such as this one. What he or she does in this type of writing is so completely different from what we do in FYC courses in the Florida State program. For this student, there's no time for invention, no peer review and teacher feedback as he or she writes, no drafting going on. So much of what we focus on in FYC is apparently ignored in the sort of timed writing that resulted in this essay.

RON: I agree with you, Deborah, that this is, in many ways, a very good essay—especially in comparison with other essays that were written in response to this prompt. One of the peer evaluators of this essay was right to underline this phrase "all these alluding to death in an unusual way—through stench" and write in the margin "Yay! You got it!" There is a very real sense in which the student does get it. But for all the reasons you mention above, this type of rhetorical essay is problematic. Instruction in the skill of producing essays such as this cannot take the place of the kind of process instruction the student would receive in the first course of our composition sequence at UNC Charlotte.

JOHN: I agree with you, Deborah, that this writer has potential; however, to receive college credit, I believe there would have to be more in-depth discussion of imagery (too general) and personification than found here. What she or he says is good, but it's not good enough. Since you have never taught AP, you might keep in mind that essays of this nature are only one type of writing done in any AP English course. When Ron and I train AP teachers, we stress that the types of writing should be a variety, and the foundation of writing in the course should be the writing process in which students would do the kind of writing done at UNC Charlotte and FSU. The College Board makes this very clear in the course descriptions for both AP English language and English literature.

I agree with your assertion, Ron, that the essay is rhetorically problematic, but would point out, as stated above, that this essay does not (or should not) be the bulk of the writing done in AP English. After all, there is life after AP, and students must be prepared to meet the challenge of writing other college papers, assuming they earn college credit through AP, and that cannot be unless there is adequate emphasis on the writing process with attention to audience and tone.

DEBORAH: Your comment, John, that "essays of this nature are only one type of writing done in any AP English course" is an interesting one. I realize that timed writing such as this is *supposed* to be only one type of writing taught in AP, but all evidence suggests that in the AP program from which this essay was received, this is the only kind of writing students are doing, and that greatly concerns me.

Another point I'd like to make before we move on to the next essay is that in states such as the one where I teach, students receive credit for the first of two required composition courses at our university (and at universities throughout our state) by making a mediocre score of 3 (on a scale of 1 to 5) on the AP literature or language exam. John, you say that you " . . . believe there would have to be more in-depth discussion of imagery (too general) and personification than found here" for the student to receive college credit for this essay, but I feel certain this student would receive at the least a score of 3 for this essay—and that would count for college credit.

Essay #3

The next essay was written by a first-semester, first-year college student in her composition class at Florida State University.

Assignment: Literacy Narrative

For your first essay this semester, I'd like to learn about your history as a reader and writer of academic texts. I'd like you to think about the factors, people, and situations in your life that played a major role in making you the student you are today. Think about the schools you attended, the people who taught

---

you, and the situations you found yourself in that shaped you as a reader and writer. Reflect upon both positive and negative influences, how you reacted to those influences, and how they played a role in shaping you as a student.

There's no one way to approach or structure this essay or any of the other essays you write in this class. What you say in this paper and how you say it will depend on the ideas you want to communicate to your readers—the other students in this class and me.

My Most Spectacular Failure

When I was in the fourth grade, socializing was paramount. Recess was my favorite part of the day because I could congregate with my friends, reminisce about the previous day's happenings, and play to my heart's content. Day after day I anticipated the moment when my classmates and I would stomp out of the classrooms and make our way to what seemed like a haven from the rigors of fourth grade. Nevertheless, I completed my homework assignments and class work, in a less enthusiastic manner, but on time. My sole purpose was to stay focused long enough to get the work done, but not to learn the concepts being taught. Tests as well were completed in much the same manner, lightheartedly. Needless to say, education was not my priority and I had no drive for success, achievement, or focus. But there was nothing wrong with my lack of drive in my eyes because that philosophy made my life simplistic and carefree.

That academic year I failed the Florida Comprehension Assessment Test (FCAT). I was crushed. Students who failed could not move onto the fifth grade. The next year I had to watch my former classmates go on, without me, and eventually watch as they graduated from elementary school, leaving me behind. This pivotal experience was forever imprinted in my memory and haunted me throughout my secondary education. I had failed myself, my family, and everyone who had ever believed in me and my abilities as a scholar. With this "failure" I began to realize the importance of an education and how it could help me reach my future goals, not yet known to me. So I resolved to change. That next year, homework became something I did to learn, not merely to get by.

I paid attention to what all my teachers said and did. I asked questions each and every time I didn't understand something. Learning became a desired and obtainable venture. With that newly formed outlook I believed success was possible. What was once stressful became a challenge which I was determined to overcome. When I took the FCAT again, with a new-found determination, I felt more confident. But as time went by, I wondered if I would find myself in the fourth grade yet again. However, when I reported to school the next year, I was delighted to find that I was placed in the fifth grade. I had passed! This was a great accomplishment for me because I had recently immigrated to America just a year prior.

Raised in Port-au-Prince, Haiti, with a strong value on education, my parents were preparing me to achieve something they could not. So they made a tough decision. I was about five years of age when my dad left for the United States, leaving the family behind. The plan was that my dad would work and send money back to Haiti to fund his daughters' education. After seeing what the United States could offer our family, he decided to turn his mission into bringing the whole family to the United States. So three years later I entered the United States, knowing neither English nor the country and its culture. Although we were positive about this endeavor, nothing came easy for either my family or me. With just high school diplomas and some vocational training, my parents worked to provide for four girls with high ambitions.

Having been born in another country meant that I was already a step behind the rest. Although I knew how to speak and write both French and Creole almost fluently, I had just moved to the United States, which meant I had to learn the English language and its style of writing just as fluently or even better. Facing the FCAT reminded me that I still had a long way to go. Also it allowed me to see what I was still struggling with, which happened to be both syntax and reading comprehension. My struggle was also evident, later on, in my Scholastic Aptitude Test (SAT) and American College Testing (ACT) scores. What made me exceptional is that I refused to let the fact that English is not my first language be an excuse for low performance. So in high school I challenged myself with Advanced Placement (AP) literature and composition and Honors English courses, which facilitated my continual improvement in reading and English syntax.

For two of my high school years I was fortunate enough to be guided to success by Mrs. Pinckney, who was both my English II and AP literature and composition teacher. The most profound aspect of both courses was that most people in the class had her as their English teacher for three years in high school. She knew all our strengths and weaknesses as well as our potential and our goals. Once senior year came around, senioritis left no one untouched. Those who had the drive and were willing to excel before lost their tenacity. Other who had never grasped the drive to succeed reconfirmed their attitudes. Although Mrs. Pinckney realized that the class did not believe in their abilities and was not willing to do the work it would take to pass both the course and the AP exam, she was determined. Her convictions were unwavering. She would not tolerate blatant laziness.

That year she presented her senior class with what we thought would be an insurmountable assignment. Our school district had a program they referred to as the laureate program. Only students with unquestionable drive braved to enter the grueling requirements to complete the program and gain the prestigious laureate diploma. Even though this was an optional program she decided to present us with the challenge. The class was in every way capable; we all met the criteria to start the program and, therefore, had no reason not to pursue the recognition it entailed. Many were not willing to challenge themselves and cracked, dropping the course as soon as possible. Others, like me, took on the challenge, with great reservations. The assignment included a 5,000-word research paper on a topic of our choice; because I had a strong desire to expand my knowledge of the medical field, I choose the topic "The Effects of Long-Term Antibiotic Usage on the Immune System." Upon completing the paper we had to prepare a PowerPoint presentation of our topics and present them to a group of teachers, faculty members, and a portion of the student body. After the presentation we would be asked challenging questions regarding our topic and research. This was an arduous task; however, upon completing this project, very successfully, I was convinced that there was now nothing that I could not do if I dedicated myself. I not only overcame my crippling fear of public speaking but also a fear of putting my work out there to be judged by others.

My purpose in life is to help others thrive and prosper. Steered in the right direction by my experiences and mentored by a dedicated and motivational teacher, I have seen the impact that one can make on another's life. My goals are now known to me. I am attending a major university and pursuing a passion of mine, which happens to be the arduous field of medicine. With that aspiration in mind I will major in biology, while minoring in chemistry, on a pre-medicine track in hopes of later attending my university's school of medicine. I aspire to become a general surgeon. Once well into my practice field I would like to join Médecins Sans Frontières (Doctors without Borders) or another similar goal-oriented organization and travel the world providing medical aid to people in need.

Does this all seem impossible? I mean, less than nine years ago I did not know where I was headed or wanted to go educationally. However, the experiences I have gained and the confidence I have obtained have forever changed me as a scholar. I do not think my goals are impossible because sometimes life teaches us our most important lessons, not by our successes but by our failures. Many aspects of life change over time. While some aspects of life move down the hierarchy of life pyramid, others move up. My search for knowledge has increased in importance over socializing, which was at one time essential. One life-changing event led me to contemplate this switch in priorities. Through failing the FCAT, my perception of schooling has now been greatly altered. Currently, I value education as a search for knowledge, which has and can lead to continued successes. Only when I was held back did I realize the serious side of school, along with the importance of an education. In the nine years since my most spectacular "failure," I have continued to improve my listening, reading, writing and study skills. Maintaining a very stringent work ethic, I am now diligent and meticulous at all I undertake. As a result, I graduated third in my class, successfully completed eight AP courses in addition to completing the grueling laureate presentation, although I did not receive the diploma. I am grateful for my novel characteristics, which have helped me set my priorities straight. I value knowledge, the thrill of overcoming challenges, and the payoff of diligence. Knowledge . . . I crave it.

DEBORAH: We begin many of our FYC classes at Florida State by having students write an essay such as this one—a literacy narrative. We do this for a couple of reasons. First, we like to help make students comfortable with writing and help them discover the writing processes that work best for them by having them begin by writing about what they know—themselves and their experiences. We also assign this sort of essay because this type of writing helps us learn a little about our students' backgrounds so that we can better meet their needs.

And Ron, that leads me to a question for you. I know that you believe that students should write argumentative essays in FYC classes. This essay does not present an argument. It's a personal experience essay that helps the teacher and the other students in the class learn more about the author's literacy experiences. Do you think this type of writing has a place in the FYC classroom? Is the type of writing going on in this essay less valuable than writing argumentative essays?

RON: I'll begin with an attempt at answering your question, Deborah, and then move on to a few more general comments about this essay. While I do believe argumentative writing is important, it is certainly not the only kind of writing we should value; I ask my students to write reflective, informative, and argumentative essays. From your comments above, Deborah, I would guess that this teacher sees this not as a reflective essay but rather as a chance to learn something of the student's personal history and her ability to craft an essay.

I would not make such an assignment. But I might well ask for a reflective essay. And if I did, I would not be happy with this response; I would want to push the student to clarify whom she is writing for and why. In hopes of helping the student do so, I would begin by asking why she didn't talk about any specific reading or writing situations she has encountered. When she tells us at the end of her paper that she craves knowledge, I would ask her to talk about some particular act of reading or writing that has whetted her appetite for this knowledge.

Clearly, the student sees her failure on the fourth-grade test as a turning point in her academic career. But, as she narrates the story, it is not clear that she has come to terms with why this event was so important to her. Given the value that her parents put on education, a value that pushed them to make great sacrifices to get their children in American schools, how does she account for the nonchalant attitude she was taking to her studies before failing this test—was it simply a matter of not knowing how important education was—for her or her parents? That leads to a follow-up question that gets at the heart of my dis-ease with this essay: namely, what one of my mentors, William E. Coles Jr., used to refer to as "magic dust." She fails the fourth-grade test and then a fairy spreads magic dust and suddenly she understands how wonderfully important education is. How did that understanding come about? To make this more than a "I once was blind but now I see" narrative, we would need to know something of her thought processes during this transformative time.

JOHN: I'm prone to agree with you, Ron, that the assignment sounds like a diagnostic essay, but I surmise the student perceives it to be a reflective essay in light of the content. I don't think I agree with you about the student's need to explore her understanding of how the change came about. I find it hard to believe that a fourth grader would have the maturity to wrestle with the need to make a change. The fear of failure for a second time is enough to motivate any child, even a fourth grader. After all, she's a child, and she loves doing what children love to do. (Note she dutifully does her work but without enthusiasm.) While your point about the "magic dust" is well taken, I don't think it seriously mars the paper.

Deborah, students in AP English language and composition are expected to write reflective and informative essays as well as argumentation. In many cases, AP students will be asked to write a reflective piece as their first piece of formal writing in the course.

DEBORAH: I think you make a good point, Ron, when you say that you would like to see the writer discuss " . . . specific reading or writing situations she has encountered" and " . . . talk about some particular act of reading or writing that has whetted her appetite for this knowledge." Those added details would make her paper stronger.

However, like John, I disagree with you when you state that the writer should have explored her understanding of why she changed. She tells us that she was a carefree, lighthearted fourth grader—that recess was her favorite part of the day—and then she failed the FCAT, which resulted in her failing the fourth grade. Failing a grade is a huge deal. That failure made her realize that she had to get serious about studying and applying herself in school. That explanation was all I needed. Unlike you, I didn't feel the need for the writer to share "something of her thought processes" that led to her change in attitude after she failed the FCAT in fourth grade. But then again, we're readers, and readers react differently to a text, even when we're teachers of composition who are trained to respond to student writing.

Concluding Remarks and Recommendations

As we reflect on these conversations, it is clear that we differ in our responses to the student texts, and these differences reflect subtle differences in the theoretical underpinnings of our writing instruction. They probably also reflect key differences in who we are as people. Viva la différence! If we want to hear our students' individual voices in their writing, then we can offer them no less that our authentic voices as teachers. But along with these differences, we find a good many areas of agreement in these responses.

We agree that the Advanced Placement program is a valid program. By that we mean that we all agree that students who take AP courses and perform very well on the AP test should receive credit when they arrive at college. As the reader might expect from our discussions above, there are several caveats that come with this agreement. First, in saying that students should receive credit for a college writing course, we are assuming (1) a first-year program that comprises two writing courses—so that students will still have the benefit of at least one college writing course and (2) a student who has taken the AP language and composition course (we'll address literature and composition next) and made an excellent score on the AP Language and Composition exam—as experienced readers of this exam, John and Ron suggest a minimum of a 4 on a 5-point scale. Students who take AP literature and composition and score a 4 or above on that exam might receive credit for a general education literature course.

We also agree that there should be more focus, both in high school and college, on writing that reflects an awareness of the rhetorical situation it is written for. Such writing will involve students in a mental conversation with the audiences they are writing for and, in doing so, will be less likely to produce the kinds of unexamined theme writing that they have often settled for in the past. Here we find ourselves differing, at least in emphasis, from David Jolliffe's comments in his chapter in this collection. As we understand it, he believes that, on the whole, AP language and composition courses are superior to college courses because they are about "the principles of rhetorical theory" (64) that will help students develop the ability to "critically read texts of all kinds ... as rhetorical artifacts, as the instantiation of a rhetor's efforts, in a particular rhetorical situation, to achieve meaning, accomplish a purpose, or create an effect with a reader or group of readers" (64). Jolliffe contrasts these AP courses with college writing courses; in speaking of them, Jolliffe expresses some concern as to exactly what "the content of the typical college composition course is" (65). Here we differ from Jolliffe. While we are happy that AP language and composition teaches the principles of rhetoric, we will not be satisfied with that: We want to see that students understand and implement those principles in their own writing, and that entails writing with a clear sense of audience.

A third area of agreement for the three of us—and a surprising finding in this set of essays—concerns the need for additional attention to issues of sourcing. We were not expecting to find the number of unsupported claims that we found in this, admittedly very limited, sampling. If this sampling is in any way indicative of how sourcing is being handled, then students must be encouraged to think about, and make their readers aware of, where they are getting their information.

A final area of agreement involves issues of writing process. All of us teach writing as process; failure to do so might result in having our union cards revoked, so we had better say that. But we really do believe in (and teach) writing as process. It is clear to us (not so much from these papers as from our overall experience) that some teachers still pay a good deal of lip service to "process," without creating an environment in which real revision occurs. If the student isn't challenged to think critically, to see his or her writing as an internal conversation in the process of the development of a piece of writing, then the various drafts being produced are exercises in editing and polish.

One issue is not clear to us at this point. Before we discuss that matter, though, we should note something that is clear to us. As veteran readers of the AP exams and consultants for the College Board, both John and Ron have long noted that the kinds of argumentative writing taught in high school AP courses differ from the argument taught in many college writing courses. Even though high school AP teachers are advised to prepare their students to deal with argumentative topics, the argument essays on the AP exam have been consistently of the thesis and support variety. That is, students may be asked to write about an argumentative topic by examining the arguments on both sides of that argument or by proposing a compromise for competing sides of an argument. However, they are not asked to stake a position on a controversial topic and then defend that position for an audience that takes the opposing viewpoint. As a result, they do not have to deal with counterarguments to the position that those on the other side of this issue would take.

This kind of argument is the focus of the second course, ENGL 1102, at UNC Charlotte and at many other colleges and universities around the country. As long as it is confined to a second-semester course, one that students may not exempt, there is no major conflict as to whether AP language and composition should deal with such arguments. Given the connection between maturation level and thinking required by this type of assignment (as detailed by Perry and by Basseches), it would seem to be a good idea not to introduce such arguments to the high school AP program.

But the larger question for the three of us, one that we are still very much discussing, is the role that such pro and con arguments should play in a second-semester college course. Ron and John find it difficult to separate the development of critical thinking from the kind of thinking this argument entails. Deborah is of the opinion that there are other approaches—such as a focus on visual rhetoric in the second required composition course—that have the potential to help students grow just as much as writers and critical thinkers as does a focus on argument. Clearly this is an issue we need to continue to explore.

In closing, we would like to discuss two issues that the editors of this collection specifically asked us to address after we completed a draft of this chapter: (1) the question of just what it means to be ready for a college writing course in general and, specifically, whether the students in our study are ready for college writing courses; and, (2) the issue of whether students taking dual-enrollment courses in high school should be exempted from college writing courses.

We turn to the question of readiness for college first. To do so, however, we need to differentiate between being "ready" for a college writing course and being exempt from one. We tend to feel that all three of the students whose work is represented in this essay are "ready" for college writing. But none of them shows the kind of rhetorical awareness that we want to see developed in a college writing course. Therefore, we do not believe that high school students should be exempted from college writing courses. The students whose work we have discussed here are still writing what we see as teacher-directed prose. Of course, that may be a fault of the assignment in the reflective literacy assignment, which raises the issue of whether personal writing provides a sufficient indicator of mastery of the skills a first-year writing course should develop. We are not convinced that it does.

Finally, we would like to thank all those teachers who helped us gather essays for this project and all the students who agreed to let us use their essays. We are excited to be a part of what we hope is the beginning of an important conversation between teachers at the high school and college levels.

Works Cited

Basseches, Michael. *Dialectical Thinking and Adult Development.* Norwood, NJ: Ablex, 1984. Print.

Heaney, Seamus. "Blackberry-Picking." *Opened Ground: Selected Poems, 1966–1996.* New York: Farrar, 1999. Print.

Jolliffe, David A. "Advanced Placement English and College Composition: Can't We All Get Along?" *What Is "College-Level" Writing? Volume 2: Assignments, Readings, and Student Writing Samples.* Ed. Patrick Sullivan, Howard Tinberg, and Sheridan Blau. Urbana, IL: NCTE. 2010. 57–76. Print.

Perry, William G., Jr. *Forms of Intellectual and Ethical Development in the College Years: A Scheme.* San Francisco: Jossey-Bass, 1999. Print.

Minding the Gaps: Public Genres and Academic Writing

PETER KITTLE
California State University, Chico

ROCHELLE RAMAY
Corning Union High School, Corning, California

Practically any English teacher at the high school or college level has experienced the frustration of running into a colleague who, apparently, feels duty bound to complain about the quality of academic writing produced by students at the school. Such interactions often turn into uncomfortable discussions wherein we end up feeling cornered and defensive about our teaching practices. The "we," by the way, that provide the voice for this article are Rochelle Ramay, English department chair at Corning Union High School, Corning, California, and Peter Kittle, English education professor at California State University, Chico. The two of us have worked together in a variety of pedagogical and professional development contexts through the auspices of the Northern California Writing Project since 2000.

It was early in our work together that we began informally examining this phenomenon of defensiveness, the issue arising after Ramay endured a rather fiery diatribe on the collapse of US education from an uncle at a family event. Why, we wondered, did it seem so easy for us to be put on the defensive? What alternatives might we envision that would allow us to move such conversations in a different, more productive direction? This gap between our classroom practices and the perceptions of our students' work, whether judged by colleagues or the general public, is one that we are trying to bridge within the scope of this chapter. However, in recounting how we address the issue of defensiveness, we are also describing the development of reflective teaching practices through teacher inquiry, professional development, and cross-institutional collaboration—the growth of teacher leadership, in short. But leadership is empty without a worthwhile and important focus and purpose, and, in our case, "academic writing" proved to be our touchstone. Scaffolding our teaching so that students experience a continuum that moves coherently from high school- to college-level writing has been our agenda as collaborators, reflective practitioners, and professional development presenters.

A Few Words about Academic Writing

As teachers of English, we both care deeply about our students' ability to write for a variety of audiences and purposes. Academic audiences and purposes, clearly, are included in that variety. But the term *academic* is a fraught one, and we would like to spend a little time examining the various ways it is used.

For some, *academic* has a pejorative connotation. Images arise of pipe-smoking Professor Tweedy, absent-mindedly wandering a college campus while engaged in a minutiae- and jargon-laden argument with an equally minutiae-obsessed colleague. *Academic* as an adjective has become synonymous with *irrelevant* and *unimportant*. The phrase "It's all academic, anyway" signifies that any points that have been made are, in the long run, irrelevant. This derogatory use of *academic* relies on notions of elitism rooted in seeing higher education as an ivory tower, safely removed from the concerns of the "real world" and the general public.

Such dismissals of academic concerns have some validity. The increasingly competitive atmosphere in postsecondary education, where faculty fight to pursue and publish innovative research in increasingly specialized disciplines, has led to ever more esoteric topics with little readily discernible, real-world value. Some conservative organizations, such as the Collegiate Network, give yearly Campus Outrage awards that highlight the perceived disconnect between town and gown; such inflammatory (and often context-deficient) depictions of academe only contribute to the notion that scholarly work holds little significance for the general public.

But we recognize that such work, despite its often arcane focus, represents the various ways that scholars explore matters of great personal interest as well as considerable disciplinary import. That is to say, researchers choose topics because the study engages them, they already have prior knowledge and are passionate about their subjects, and they have colleagues who care about the issues under discussion. These are the aspects of academic writing that we would like to reclaim: personal and professional engagement with topics, and connections to real audiences who share concerns and assumptions with the writer.

Some academics are already working to remedy the disconnect between the university and the public and private sectors. Jeffery Di Leo, writing in *Inside Higher Ed*, notes the fact that "academe privileges highly specialized modes of discourse, whereas the public-private world favors generalized ones" (n.p.). Arguing for a return to the notion of public intellectualism first advocated by Emerson in the mid-nineteenth century, Di Leo identifies a current need for "intellectuals [who] are always already involved in the public and private spheres as well as in the academic spheres and others" (n.p.). The melding of academic interests with public concerns is what we would like to see happening in the writing of our own students as well. However, we struggle with the tension between the varied needs and expectations of public and academic audiences.

We wonder, for instance, whether particular genres that are regularly classified as "academic"—the formal-register essay in particular—are the only avenues open to students for exploring ideas and being public with their academic inquiries. The emphasis on accountability in the No Child Left Behind Act has resulted in an increased prominence of standardized written forms in the public school sphere—a prominence that does not lend itself to effective college-level writing. Formulaic writing—exemplified by the Step Up to Writing program used by elementary schools, the Jane Schaffer system adopted by many secondary schools, and that old standby, the five-paragraph essay—ends up becoming the de facto genre for academic expression in too many educational settings. Such formulaic structures claim to simply guide the writer, sometimes even dictating the numbers and types of sentences in each individual paragraph. The attraction of such writing lies in its easy "teachability." The formula is clean and clear for the writer to compose and for the teacher to score; the "genre"—persuasive essay, expository essay, literary response essay, and so forth—is checked off from a lengthy list of required standards, and the class heads toward the next one, until all of these "genres" are covered. The fundamental problem is that these "genres" never invite the writer to consider that someone, besides the teacher, might take an interest in the writer's ideas.

Channeling William Blake, Bruce Pirie argues that such writing puts "mind-forged manacles" on students who are forced "to make unwilling material fit into three obligatory body paragraphs" (77). Lorraine Ouimet seeks to remedy this in "The 'Ins and Outs' of Public Intellectualism," noting the challenges of "striving to find a way to guide students in the crafting of 'legitimate' academic writing and argumentative skills without imposing . . . a prescribed, restrictive, and ideologically loaded style of writing and thinking" (51).

The challenge, then, becomes finding means of meshing three inextricable (but all too often treated as disparate) elements: the inherent engagement of public intellectual discourse, with writers addressing real problems for real audiences; the academic skills necessary to read, research, and write about shared issues for the public; and the presence of a fostering educational environment that not only values students' voices but provides public opportunities for those voices to be heard. While few teachers, parents, or administrators would directly object to student projects that incorporate those three elements, such groups might question the role this type of work plays in the preparation of students for not just standardized writing exams but more broadly for the kinds of analytic literacy required for proficient college-level writing.

Patrick Sullivan, in the essay that framed the driving question in *What Is "College-Level" Writing?*, suggests that a "primary goal" of college writing is "to introduce students to an ongoing conversation that is multilayered and complex" (16–17). The role of audience in this ongoing academic conversation, as argued by Gadda and Walsh, "requires that each writer create and define significance for the reader, and that the writer cite and explain evidence in a way that will make the reader understand and, if possible, accept the significance defined" (3). These attributes are echoed in *Academic Literacy: A Statement of Competencies Expected of Students Entering California's Public Colleges and Universities*, composed by a joint committee of faculty from the University of California, California State University, and California Community College systems (Intersegmental). That document further suggests that college-level writers should avoid "formulaic patterns" in their writing because such patterns "discourage critical examination of the topic and ideas" (22) under investigation by student writers.

In the remainder of this chapter, we outline writing pedagogies at the high school and college levels that require exactly this kind of rigorous academic thinking and expression but in forms that we believe allow our students to engage intellectual issues in genres with public, rather than formulaic, tendencies.

A Place to Start

Consider the following paragraph, written by Rochelle's high school student, Mallory, during the first few weeks of her first year:

> I am a sister. I have a older sister and a younger sister too. I am the middle of the girls. Often I am mistaken for my older sister Casey. We think we look nothing a like. Yet everyday it seems like I am reminded that I look like her. I admire people who don't think we look alike. Not that it's a bad thing to look like her don't get me wrong. But when someone tells me I look like her its hearing the same joke over and over. I love having sisters to talk to and play with. But I often consider dying my hair brown just to see if I look like my younger sister Bethany.

This snippet of text demonstrates many things about its writer's abilities. Mallory knows how to write a full paragraph with a variety of sentences in it. She demonstrates a good vocabulary and provides the reader with some details about herself and her sisters. She uses transitional words and phrases to move through the ideas she's trying to communicate. For a high school student at the beginning of her first year, she appears to be a competent writer. She stays on topic, has a governing idea, and provides some information to flesh out that idea. In the assessment-driven world of contemporary education, a teacher whose students produced work like this might justifiably be compelled to accept a paragraph like this as an end product and move on to the next mandated standard.

We acknowledge that Mallory is a competent writer, and, in general, this text is representative of work produced by other beginning ninth-grade writers. We are also very reluctant to use a deficit model for discussing and evaluating student work. That is, we prefer to look for what a writer's capabilities are, rather than focus on elements that are unrefined or absent. Nevertheless, we see the text as rather weak in terms of the writer's ability to think about and depict complex ideas in writing. Because she is writing with no set "form" or genre to help her shape and marshal her ideas, Mallory compresses the subject, rendering her ideas in ways that are overly simplistic and superficial.

Within the span of a few weeks, Mallory wrote a new piece about her family that showed considerable improvement. Her second piece, reworked and revised, had a clear sense of purpose, met the expectations of an audience Mallory knew and understood, employed a compelling combination of anecdote and research, spoke from an authoritative position, and created a voice that synthesized authority and wit. How did this transition occur? And what are the implications here for her teachers, for her school, and for Mallory herself? How will the changes she made as a writer follow her as she moves through high school in preparation for college-level writing? These are the questions that underlie our inquiry into bridging students' writing from simple competence to the compelling articulation of complex ideas.

Learning from "My Turn"

One of our fundamental beliefs about writing is that it is best learned within an apprenticeship model like that articulated by Lave and Wenger. As they note, apprenticeship models are often employed when "high levels of knowledge and skills are in demand" (63), such as law and medicine. Apprenticed learning occurs in situations where actual practitioners of a craft employ their skills to achieve particular ends. In our writing pedagogy, this means that writing occurs in a context wherein students learn from examining and interacting with "real" writing in a variety of forms.

Newsweek magazine is "real" in this sense. The weekly magazine sits on racks at the grocery store and in school libraries; some of us actually pay for subscriptions and receive it in the mail. Whether students read it regularly matters little; it is an embedded part of their public sphere. One section in particular, the "My Turn" weekly guest column, is particularly useful for teaching writing. In these guest editorials, the writers use their own knowledge and experiences to explore topical issues in ways that actively convey that relevance and significance to the reader. Let's look a little closer at the particular genre attributes of the typical "My Turn" essay and see how the writers accomplish this goal. We reference one particular column here—Robert E. O'Connor's "Has Basketball Become Hockey on Hardwood?"— that Rochelle has used effectively in her high school classes.

First of all, the layout of the page jumps out. Bold typography tops the page, dominating three columns of text framing a large, central picture of the author, usually posed in a way that suggests something about the subject matter of the piece. The guest writers, as the pictures' nonglamorous nature makes obvious, are everyday people, the kind of people who may hail from a city we've never heard of, such as Hamburg, NY, or Cochranville, PA. In our model column, the photo shows O'Connor standing next to his seated son, Jim. O'Connor is wearing a suit and tie, while Jim wears a basketball jersey and holds a basketball. They might be any father and son from anywhere in the United States.

The text in the headline, subheads, and picture caption provide quick insights into the subject and structure of the piece. The title, often framed as a question, poses something thoughtful and intriguing. "Has Basketball Become Hockey on Hardwood?" immediately showcases the central question the essay will explore, while the subhead elaborates on the subject: "When rough play is considered fair play, kids like Jim get hurt. At least football players wear helmets." The photo caption reads "BAD DREAM: I can't remember who won, just his tears as the physician pushed his small bones back into alignment." Together, these immediate elements of text and photograph are poised to engage us as potential readers. Perhaps we have been wondering about the same issue, and finding the topic we've been wondering about printed in a national magazine draws us into reading what this particular person believes about it. We are invited to compare our views with his. These prominent words and image hold power; the writer wants us to keep going. We see a face and then we hear a voice. The writer and the reader are nose to nose. It's an essential, electric moment. If the writer flinches, the reader vanishes.

This example illustrates the impact of a writer poised in anticipation of a reader's response and reaction. Of course, as we read this essay we don't normally think about the ways O'Connor caught our attention or the craft he employs to fashion his article. But, as readers, we know that if he misses his mark and doesn't deliver on his promise to help us think about the violence in high school basketball, we'll move on to another section in the magazine. The stakes for the writer are high.

O'Connor, like most published "My Turn" authors, does deliver. His piece begins with an extended anecdote, poses some questions raised by the story he tells, cites some statistics from the Centers for Disease Control, hypothesizes and generalizes, and finally draws some conclusions about why basketball seems to have increased in violence in recent years. As O'Connor works his way through the piece, he uses narrative to establish some common ground with his readers and to set up a scenario, employs research to support his assertions, suggests possible reasons for the situation, and anticipates likely consequences for the trend he outlines. His writing is purposeful, clear, concise, and reasonable. He writes for a real, national audience, anticipating the demands of that audience each step of the way.

This crucial relationship between what readers demand and what writers deliver is the missing component of "school genre" writing, in which there is rarely a dynamic and critical audience anticipating what the writer might present. For ninth graders, inexperience with anticipating a critical reader's demands—an expectation that the writer will support a complex (and possibly controversial) claim through a variety of rhetorical strategies—can lead to flat, lifeless, and dull writing, no matter how accomplished the writer's skills may be. Without purpose and audience, and we mean here an audience of critical and informed readers, writers stall. Without purpose and audience, writers' lively interactions with academic ideas are replaced by lifeless formulas simply because the writers don't know what else to do. And, often, neither do their teachers. We know, having been in this frustrating situation ourselves (Kittle, "It's Not the High School Teachers' Fault" 136–8).

Unpacking and Composing "My Turn"

Preparing students for composing a "My Turn" essay begins with familiarizing them with the genre. Because *Newsweek*'s readers, unsurprisingly, tend to be older than ninth graders, the beginning of instruction for this starts with orienting student writers to some actual "My Turn" essays, beginning with O'Connor's "Hockey on Hardwood" piece. The first time students encounter this text, we simply read it aloud so everyone hears the entire essay. Students find the article compelling and so are primed for discussing and analyzing the piece. Several questions bubble up. What is O'Connor's claim? Where does it show up? How does he begin his essay? Why didn't he begin his essay with research? Where does he put his research? What does he want the reader to think about? With these questions guiding them, students begin their actual work: It's time to take the essay apart to understand its construction. In other words, students practice reading the genre while adopting a writer's point of view.

Armed with colored pencils, students take on the essay by reading for the writer's craft. They mark up aspects of the text, color coding for fact and opinion, the writer's stories, other people's stories the writer tells, examples of research, cause and effect, claims, calls to action, loaded language, and generalizations. Working with a partner, students might first mark up the essay's use of support and its claims, highlighting the writer's own stories in red, the stories of others told by the writer in green, examples of research in orange, and claims in yellow. By doing this, two important things happen: first, students collaboratively come to an understanding of the various attributes of the text; second, students' coloring of the text creates a visual representation of the relationships among the different types of support and the claims made by the text.

This latter element becomes more important as students color-code a variety of "My Turn" columns. Students begin to recognize that specific elements appear in most published columns, but they also notice that, depending on the column, those elements show up in varying quantities and locations. For instance, the writers' claims in "My Turn" columns often don't appear until near the end of the piece, rather than at the end of the first paragraph—the spot students have been told repeatedly is the *only* place for a thesis. By making these variations in textual structures visible through their use of color-coding, students are able to map out the writers' choices. Students do not see writers who unthinkingly follow a recipe; instead, they see authors who strategically employ a number of choices to express their ideas in ways that will be engaging and effective to their readership.

The importance here is that students are supported in deeply reading these essays, not once but several times. They become better at purposeful reading, and they recognize that reading texts in different ways, for different purposes, productively adds to a reader's understanding not just of the text itself but also of the ways the text conveys its meanings to readers. By making the essay's attributes visible, students learn to conceptualize the genre more fully and are ultimately positioned to move from consumer to producer as they write a "My Turn" column themselves. In their own writing, as they raise an issue and need to find the best way to achieve their intentions, students have schema ready at hand to help them make wise choices for structuring, supporting, and organizing their claims.

Let's return now to Mallory, the student whose early ninth-grade writing we have already examined. For Mallory to succeed academically, she must understand the relationships between form and function. Accustomed to personal narrative and isolated "school genre" writing experiences, a writer like Mallory can see how the form and structure of "My Turn" not only invites her to use her experiences purposefully but also guides her to take on an issue of personal relevance and familiarity, analyzing and elaborating on the significance of that issue for herself and her audience.

In her first-year English class, Mallory's initial work wasn't particularly distinguishable from those of her peers. She struggled most with finding focus and intention for her writing. Mallory not only wanted to do well, though—she *expected* to do well, but even with her strong motivation, she didn't know how to express her thinking effectively on the page. What she needed was something to help her bridge the gap between what she knew and cared about and the ability to write about her ideas in an engaging way for a real audience. Her "My Turn" essay, reprinted in its entirety, gives evidence of how Mallory crossed that bridge.

My Turn
Are People Getting Too Original?

Mallory Vader

My brother and his wife were about to name their baby Ellie. I couldn't let that happen.

In about a month, my brother and his wife are going to have a baby. I'm very excited but also a little worried. Not worried about the delivery or the health but the name. A while back they were discussing names for the baby; they wanted to name it Ellie. Ellie is not so bad, but when you have the last name Vader to follow it, that changes things a little bit. Ellie Vader. When they told me that was the name they had chosen, I was ready to laugh until I saw the serious looks on their faces. I quickly replied with the nicest thing I could say, "That's original."

We quickly started to put new ideas in their heads of different names. Finally they cracked—they started to consider other names. Then came the name Mattie, the name we had all been waiting for, the one that would change their minds.

I was so excited when they told me they had changed their minds I just about jumped for joy. I was just getting ready to think of a good nickname for her, because the name you give a child really affects them I think.

One study done in 1945, looked at 1,682 case histories of children treated in a mental health clinic in New Jersey. Kids with unusual first names were more likely to have moderate or severe emotional disturbances, compared with kids with more traditional names.

So what's the matter with these guys? Don't they understand that by naming their child something weird their child is in for a lifetime of mocking and teasing? Sometimes I think they just don't get it and according to the mother she thinks it would be "so cute." Yeah, right.

Fortunately we got them to change their minds. Not to say anything bad about the parents or anything, I thought they were pretty normal people. They're both college students at Chico State. While Matt goes to work, Julie stays home to put their new house together to make it into their home. So what motivated them to the weird side? I think they were shooting for originality. Which brings me back to the question, are people getting too original? I'm all for being original, I just think they need to think things over. I don't want my niece getting teased. Though I guess it really depends on her personality. I once met someone named Robin Hood. His name didn't seem to affect him one bit. Though being named after such a cool super hero would be kind of fun. But being named after something that travels up and down in big office buildings and hospitals is not quite the same. I was going to start calling Julie the Ellie Vader to see how she likes it. Maybe she would see how it feels; maybe it would make her never want to use that name again. I can only hope and pray for that.

When my mom turns out the light at night and tells me to pray for a healthy baby, I can't help but think how mentally unhealthy it could have been with a name like Ellie Vader. So now when my mom says that, I thank God that my brother and his wife changed their minds.

How do names affect children these days? Is it just a name that doesn't affect them? I think the name you have will always affect the way you live and the way you are treated. So while my brother and his wife did change their minds, I can't help but think they might use that name for the next child. I don't think they're trying to be mean. They are just being a little too original.

In Mallory's "My Turn," she takes the topic she was first exploring in the earlier piece—family—and turns it from a commonplace subject into an inquiry that challenges her to think and write differently. In Mallory's initial piece, she was writing about a subject some people—those whose siblings look like them, particularly—might find interesting; however, she isn't doing anything in particular to engage readers or help them think of ways that the subject matter might be relevant to them. However, in "Are People Getting Too Original?". she takes pains to structure her piece in ways that not only will engage readers in the investigation of a problem that she faces but that she also discusses in a way that helps expose its relevance to her readers. As with the published "My Turn" columns, Mallory's essay incorporates the purposeful use of anecdotes (her own story concerning the name Ellie; her encounter with Robin Hood) and research (the study on names and mental illness) to investigate why her future niece's name was so important to her.

By paying attention to the elements present in a successful "My Turn" essay and incorporating them into her composition, Mallory accommodates not only her own inquiry but her readers' interests as well. Using the story of her niece's name shows us, as readers, why the issue matters to Mallory. Including her research findings shows readers that Mallory's concern isn't a trivial one, even though her piece has a light tone. The example of the "real" Robin Hood acknowledges that an unusual name doesn't necessarily guarantee an unhappy outcome. Her inquiry leads to the claim that people are moving toward a tendency to be original just for the sake of it and that the consequences of such behavior aren't always considered as closely as they should be. Together, these inclusions anticipate readers' questions: Why does the writer care about this issue? Why should I care about this issue? Do others think differently about this issue? What is at stake in this issue?

In most school genre assignments, these questions about readership are part of the instruction. The importance of anticipating arguments that counter the writer's claims, in particular, is often emphasized. However, what differentiates the work done on the "My Turn" projects is that, unlike most student assignments, there was a genuine public audience for the students' pieces. Mallory's piece, along with all of the columns composed by her fellow first-year students, was published in a schoolwide literary magazine. The entire school community, composed of ninth through twelfth graders, teachers, and administrators, anticipates the magazine's debut each year. Mallory and her peers, well aware of this readership, found motivation for choosing compelling topics, composing intriguing titles, utilizing purposeful organization, and writing with voice and articulation. These young writers aimed for that same relationship with their audience as O'Connor, author of the "Hockey on Hardwood" column, had with his audience.

It is our contention that the growth in Mallory's writing is due, in large part, to her experiences with public writing for an audience that both appreciated and supported her thinking. Her academic engagement with a topic was shaped for an audience that cared about her insights, and Mallory's knowledge of this readership's demands spurred her academic drive and stimulated her intellect. Mallory's move from the beginnings of a personal narrative that merely reported a thin (albeit nice) story to a final composition, with its focused analysis of anecdotes and use of research, demonstrates the shift that transitioned her from a simple storyteller to an accomplished academic writer who is well prepared to be a successful college-level writer. Her finished piece demonstrates the efficacy of using the "My Turn" genre as an "investment strategy"—a term Patricia Lambert Stock uses to describe teaching practices that "prepare students to enter discipline- and field-based conversations . . . [and] invite students to write about and relate their prior texts—the languages and experiences that they bring with them to school—to subjects they are beginning to study" (108).

Transitions, Echoes, and Resonances

Mallory was once again one of Rochelle's students during her senior year, and we are happy to report that the lessons learned her first year were not lost. One of the genres taught to college-bound seniors at Corning High is the timed academic essay, using the University of California's Academic Writing Placement Examination (AWPE; formerly called the Subject A exam) as the model. The AWPE provides students with a brief academic reading (usually fewer than one thousand words) and a writing prompt related to the ideas in the reading; two hours are allotted for reading the piece and constructing the response. It is one of many standardized assessments of writing that attempts to measure students at the transitional stage between high school and college. One of the practice tests administered to Mallory asked her to respond to an excerpt from Doris Lessing's "Group Minds," a work that questions the ability of people to exercise free thought in group contexts. The prompt was straightforward: "How does Lessing propose that we guard against the influences of our 'group minds'? What do you think of her proposal? To make your essay convincing, you should discuss specific examples drawn from your own experience, your observation of others, or any of your reading—including, of course, 'Group Minds' itself."

Mallory's response to this prompt, written in a single two-hour sitting, is titled "My Mind Is My Own," and in it she takes a position that reinforces some of Lessing's points while questioning some of her conclusions. Her opening paragraph summarizes the key ideas at issue:

> "I am a citizen of a free society, and that means I am an individual, making individual choices" . . . or at least that's what we'd like to all say. We as a society tend to think that along with our many personal freedoms, of course, we're free thinkers as well, never conforming to what others think, say, or do. This thought in our minds, however desirable, tends to be proven wrong in most of us. This idea, explored by novelist Doris Lessing in the excerpt from her lecture "Group Minds," that most all of us claim to have our own opinions decided by us, is frequently disproven, and most of us aren't even aware of it.

Here, Mallory has oriented the reader to the central ideas that will be discussed. Knowing that her audience comprises educators who have particular expectations of timed academic essays, she uses a quotation as a hook and introduces by name both the text to which she responds and its author. She also decides to use *we* in the text as a way of rhetorically connecting the audience and herself.

In her second paragraph, Mallory carefully examines one of Lessing's examples concerning the influence of the majority on a small minority. Agreeing that those in the minority often do bow to the majority's wishes, Mallory adds that such submission does not happen "without questioning the decision first." Her next paragraph continues to modify Lessing's ideas:

> Lessing goes on to talk of how to be aware of these tenden-cies to change our minds, saying "you must be on your guard against your own most primitive reactions and instincts." This is where I begin to disagree with Lessing, remembering what happened in the experiment that she spoke of earlier in which there was "a period of exasperation, irritation, even anger." Are these things not the most primitive reactions? Instead I think it would be most beneficial to be aware of and listen to those most primitive reactions instead of "be on your guard against" them. We all know in the back of our minds what we know to be true and right. It is just a matter of being strong willed enough to push through the majority.

Rather than accept at face value the conclusions Lessing draws, Mallory suggests a different interpretation. The "primitive" sense of "exasperation" felt by those in the minority, according to Mallory, is valuable in that it alerts us to "what we know to be true and right" and so can help us resist majority-driven inequities. She goes on, in the following paragraph, to cite an example from her own life that reinforces her assertions:

> In thinking about this I'm reminded of a day in my child-hood. It was my little sister Bethany's 3rd or 4th birthday, and a tradition in our family we all look forward to is the birthday person gets to choose the meals for the day. Usu-ally these meals consist of only the best, the things we only can ask for once a year. So it was lunchtime on Bethany's birthday and what do you think she chose . . . peanut butter and jelly sandwiches. To say the least my older brothers and sister and I were shocked. We tried desperately to talk her out of normal old PBJ, but she wouldn't budge. So that day we had PBJ for lunch, exactly what Bethany, the minority, wanted. . . . I'm sure at the age of 3 or 4 she wasn't aware of how majorities can change the minority's mind, but she didn't need to be. . . . It may not have been easy standing up against four older siblings, but she did it.

As she did in her very first writing from her first year, Mallory goes back to her family, and particularly to her sister Bethany, as a way to think through the idea. By doing this, she strategically employs the strategy of incorporating carefully chosen personal examples to flesh out an academic idea. This also serves to provide a transition to her concluding paragraph, in which Mallory synthesizes her thinking by comparing Lessing's ideas with her own thoughts and experiences:

> Lessing makes some valid arguments that I agree with to the point that yes, minorities in groups are easily swayed. I however do not agree with how she interprets the information we've collected on the issue, and how she suggests to approach these situations. We must be aware of pressures on us to conform, but also aware of what our minds are telling us. My mind is my own, and I intend to use it.

As more seasoned academic readers and writers ourselves, we recognize that these final thoughts in the paper actually reflect the very faith in individual strength that Lessing is attempting to critique in her speech. At the same time, we see that Mallory has not reached her conclusion haphazardly or by accident. Rather, she has used the same inquiry-based heuristic that served her when she was writing for her classmates as a first-year high school student. Here, however, she has refined her writing to incorporate a more formal register and assumed a more academic stance as a writer.

College Connections

Students from Corning Union High School, where Rochelle teaches, and small rural high schools similar to it from around northern California, are feeder schools for California State University, Chico (CSUC), where Peter teaches. The CSUC First-Year Experience Town Hall program mirrors, in significant respects, the attributes that make the "My Turn" assignment meaningful to the high school students in Corning. The town hall meetings, held toward the end of each semester at CSUC, allow students in first-year composition to showcase their research to a public audience. In upper-division writing classes at CSUC, students compose multimodal documents that incorporate video, still images, voice narration, and sound effects in ways that also take academic inquiry into a public realm. Such projects allow students "to tell a compelling story while using rigorous academic thinking as a lens for helping their projects' audiences understand the significance of the points made by those stories" (Kittle, "Student Engagement and Multimodality" 168). The "habits of mind" supported when students compose in public genres such as "My Turn" columns, in short, lead them to proficiency in the kinds of thinking, reading, and writing expected of students in college-level courses.

While the "My Turn" assignment represents a particular implementation of an assignment that scaffolds effective academic writing, we also recognize that not every piece of writing assigned to students can mirror a published magazine column. Nor should it. However, we have been able to extract several common elements in our various assignments. Note that these elements are not strictly distinct; rather, they bleed into one another:

- *Student investment.* Students need opportunities to write about issues of importance to them. Assignments should be crafted to allow for students to connect their own thoughts, experiences, and attitudes to the course content. If we want to encourage student interest in and respect for our subject matter(s), this is one way to begin to make that happen.

- *Genre immersion.* Whatever genre students are expected to produce must be studied in depth. Numerous examples should be read and analyzed to reveal the structures and traits that characterize the genre. Students should have chances to practice replicating particular aspects of the genre before being expected to produce complete drafts.

- *Complex audiences.* In conjunction with the genre immersion, students should have regular opportunities to examine the ways that particular audiences impact writers' choices. Rhetorical devices, types of argument, and forms of support that compel one type of audience may be ineffective to other audiences. Students too often assume that the teacher is, and will always be, their only audience, but effective writers must understand audience as a complex, rich entity.

- *Focused research.* To effectively and fully represent their arguments to a specific audience, student writers must understand how to find, analyze, and marshal support for their assertions.

Students should study and recognize the ways a genre uses researched support and leverage that knowledge in their own writing.

◆ *Purposeful revision.* Revision should manifest in assignments as a complex, ongoing, and recursive process. It should be explicitly tied to genre and audience, with the express purpose of helping the writer meet the characteristics of the former and the expectations of the latter.

◆ *Public intellectualism.* As often as possible, students should be encouraged to take their knowledge, arguments, and research into the public realm. This can be as complex as the publication process of the "My Turn" articles or as simple as brief "paper talks" given to the class (or even within small groups in a class). Giving student intellectual labor a public reception, however minimal, reinforces the tenets of the reclaimed notion of "academic" writing we argue for throughout this chapter.

Building Bridges

We began this chapter by looking at the notion of teacher defensiveness when confronted with claims about poor student writing performance. We attribute at least part of that defensive behavior to the remarkably private space of the classroom. Despite the many imperatives that arrive in our curricula, teachers too often simply close the door and teach their own private way, believing (with apologies to Las Vegas) that what happens in the classroom stays in the classroom. Our belief is that the same attribute that makes our students' work increasingly compelling—its public nature—is also essential to bridging the problem of defensiveness in our own profession.

The evolution of the teaching practices in this chapter came about in part because we were collaborating on writing practices that we were making public. At the same time as these practices were developing in our classrooms, we were planning and implementing extended professional development programs focused on academic literacy, as well as presenting at local, state, and national conferences. True, we were addressing our own need to be more open and descriptive about our practices to satisfy the naysayers we occasionally encountered. At the same time, though, our work was undergoing a kind of public, face-to-face (and occasionally contentious!) peer review process as we shared our models of reflective practice with teachers we encountered during inservice sessions and on conference panels. We knew that our fellow teachers would want to know about our own classrooms, our struggles, our findings, and our successes.

Our colleagues constituted, for us, a very particular audience with very specific expectations. Knowing that audience and their expectations, in turn, changed the way we thought about our practices. It was a recursive system that led us to collaborate more, consider how to represent our work to those beyond the classroom door, and be as descriptive and public about our practices as possible. As it did with our students before us, the investment strategy operates to engage us through addressing our own concerns while simultaneously giving us a "vested interest in the construction of a knowledge base" (Stock 112) whose benefits spread well beyond ourselves.

Works Cited

Di Leo, Jeffrey R. "Public Intellectuals, Inc." *Inside Higher Ed* 4 Feb. 2008. Web. 24 June 2008.

Gadda, George, and William Walsh. "Analytical Writing in the University." *Teaching Analytical Writing*. Ed. George Gadda, Faye Peitzman, and William Walsh. Los Angeles: California Academic Partnership Program, 1988. 1–22. Print.

Intersegmental Committee of the Academic Senates. *Academic Literacy: A Statement of Competencies Expected of Students Entering California's Public Colleges and Universities*. Sacramento: ICAS. 2002. Web. 13 Nov. 2007.

Kittle, Peter. "Student Engagement and Multimodality: Collaboration, Schema, Identity." *Teaching the New Writing: Technology, Change, and Assessment in the 21st-Century Classroom*. Ed. Anne Herrington, Kevin Hodgson, and Charles Moran. New York: Teachers College Press, 2009. 164–80. Print.

―――. "It's Not the High School Teachers' Fault: An Alternative to the Blame Game." *What Is "College-Level" Writing?* Eds. Patrick Sullivan and Howard Tinberg. Urbana, IL: NCTE, 2006: 134–45. Print.

Lave, Jean, and Etienne Wenger. *Situated Learning: Legitimate Peripheral Participation.* Cambridge: Cambridge UP, 1991. Print.

Lessing, Doris. "Group Minds." *Prisons We Choose to Live Inside.* New York: Harper Collins, 1987. 47–62. Print.

O'Connor, Robert E. "Has Basketball Become Hockey on Hardwood?" *Newsweek* 24 Mar 2003: 11. Print.

Ouimet, Lorraine. "The 'Ins and Outs' of Public Intellectualism." *Thought and Action: The NEA Higher Education Journal* 17.1 (2001): 51–60. Print.

Pirie, Bruce. *Reshaping High School English.* Urbana, IL: NCTE, 1997. Print.

Stock, Patricia Lambert. "Toward a Theory of Genre in Teacher Research: Contributions from a Reflective Practitioner." *English Education* 33.2 (2001): 100–14. Print.

Sullivan, Patrick. "An Essential Question: What Is 'College-Level' Writing?" *What Is "College-Level" Writing?* Eds. Patrick Sullivan and Howard Tinberg. Urbana, IL: NCTE, 2006: 1–28. Print.

Making the Leap from High School to College Writing

MERRILL J. DAVIES

I sat across the table from my ten-year-old grandson—a bright, exuberant fifth grader enrolled in what I consider to be a good public school. In response to some comment I made, he asserted, "We need to know this for the CRCT!" (the state's criterion-referenced competency test).

"Is that what your teacher said?" I asked, laughing.

"Oh, yes!" he responded. Then he went off on a tangent, as he often does. "You better learn this, for it may be on the . . . CRCT. You students are doing so well. You'll do great on the . . . CRCT. You need to get lots of rest, so you'll do well on the . . . CRCT." He went on and on, jokingly mimicking his teacher.

While I'm sure he may have been exaggerating, his "tirade" made a point to me that, even as a fifth grader, he saw it as comical that all his learning seemed to be focused on passing a standardized test. I tell this story because it seems that learning in the K–12 classroom has become so focused on testing that the learning itself is seen almost as a by-product, not the real goal. Even the teaching of writing in high school, as compared to college, is permeated by the need to get ready for the standardized writing test in our state, not about fostering self-expression, developing strong writers, and promoting related language skills.

To explore the differences between high school writing and college-level writing for this project, I worked with two writing teachers, one in college and one in high school. Both were highly committed to the teaching of writing in their respective schools. My goal was to examine artifacts from each writing class and to determine how high school teachers are preparing students for college-level writing. Working collaboratively, we designed a common writing activity, and each teacher assigned it to one of her classes. This assignment focused on the general topic of what it means to be a "community." Each teacher was free to adopt teaching strategies appropriate for their particular teaching situation and to adjust the writing prompt to fit their particular circumstances, if necessary. This chapter describes what I discovered from this collaboration.

Lara Whelan is an associate professor in the Department of English, Rhetoric, and Writing at Berry College in Rome, Georgia. This assignment was the first of four in her English 101 class—an introductory English course at Berry. Their task was to write an analytical essay defining "community" (Figure 6.1). Seventeen students completed the assignment. The topic was first introduced on August 31, and the essay was due on September 24, giving students more than three weeks to complete the assignment. During the time between the assignment and the due date, students spent a total of nine days on some aspect of this project. They read articles on community; they discussed groups that are and are not communities; they generated lists of community characteristics; each student brought a working thesis to class; they wrote sample paragraphs and discussed development; they conducted peer reviews. When they submitted their papers, they had no opportunity to rewrite; they were assigned a grade. Out of the seventeen students, five received a grade of B, eleven received a C, and one received a D.

Linda Templeton is a teacher at Cartersville High School, Cartersville, Georgia. She is associated with the Kennesaw Mountain Writing Project (an affiliate of the National Writing Project). She assigned the "community" essay to her tenth-grade college preparatory class of twenty-three students (making only a few minor changes in the instructions). Templeton decided to use this assignment to help prepare her students for the state-mandated graduation writing test. Templeton explained:

> The main objective for this writing assignment will be to prepare students for the writing portion of the graduation test, which they will be facing at the beginning of the next semester. Without practice and preparation, students cannot be expected to do well or be held accountable for standardized testing that monopolizes education at this time. In addition, this first writing assignment will establish a benchmark

---

ENG 101/Whelan

Essay #1: Community

Due: September 24

Write an *analytical essay* (without introduction or conclusion) that addresses the following question for an audience of your peers:

> **What is the nature of "community"?**
> Another way of looking at the question: What IS community? What makes a community a community?

The purpose of this essay is to help your peers think about community in a way that they may not have before, as well as to help your peers understand how you interpret the term.

If you don't have an answer right away, some of the following questions may help you 'invent" one:

- What are the component parts of a community – of what is it made?
- How are members of a community selected, or how does one become a member of a community?
- What limitations are there on community – e.g. size, membership, location?
- What isn't a community – i.e. are any groups excluded from being considered a community, and why?
- What causes a community to come into being? How do communities form?
- What effects does a community have, or expect to have, on its members? On its environment?
- What effect do its members expect to have on the community?
- Can you think of examples of situations in which your answers to any of the previous are true?
- ***More importantly, can you think of examples of situations in which your answers to any of the previous are false?*** How do you incorporate those situations into your thinking about community?

FIGURE 6.1. *Berry College, community assignment for English 101.*

for future writing assignments, giving me, the teacher, a place to begin writing instruction.

Because the assignment was a practice test, students were asked to discuss the nature of community and to persuade their audience that their view of community was the correct one. They were given no instruction before the day of the writing prompt in order to accurately simulate a testing situation. After students completed their essays under test-taking conditions, Templeton used a workshop approach with them during the following ten days of class, meeting with students individually to discuss how they had done and to work on revisions. Only two students earned a passing grade on their timed first draft. Everyone else was given suggestions, with no grade assigned. Those students were allowed to revise and resubmit their essays during the next week and a half—as many times as they needed to in order to meet the standards required. After the week and a half, they were assigned a grade.

Templeton used the rubric from the state assessment. It consists of four domains: content/organization, style, conventions of written language, and sentence formation. Each domain is rated on a scale of 1 to 5, with 5 being the highest. The grading rubric for the college essay was specific to that particular assignment and had ten criteria, with each being given a separate letter grade.

Now let's look at one of the college papers. This essay (Appendix 6A) received the highest mark among Whelan's students.

In contrast to the grade given on the preceding essay, Whelan's assessment of the next essay was a D+ (Appendix 6B). As you will see from the rubric, several areas of the paper were completely unacceptable. Whereas the first student's paper received above-average grades on paragraph development, this student received failing grades in the areas of development and adequate support.

One of Templeton's high school students wrote five drafts of his paper before the week and a half was up. Following are the first and last drafts, along with Templeton's comments.

Draft #1
Community

Do you live in a community? Many people like living in them and some others do not. When I think of a community, I think on it as a great place to live and grow up. All communities are not great and happy though. Communities consist of people, homes, and many other things.

No one word can explain a community. The size range on them can vary also. Some communities can be very large and others can be small. Communities in citys are diffrent also. Take Cartersville, for example, there is not one sole community in the city. That can be good, but could also hinder the city. Some communities get along, but there is always the few that do not.

People make communities. They build the houses, the stores, and whatever they need. Not all communities work, but most of the time they do. Different neighborhoods can be separate communities. If you lived on the east side of town that could be one communitiy and so forth. Communities can be separated by race, religion, or what school or where you work. Communities are not always close together either. A boarding school and its' surroundings are a very good example of a close community. The only way to make a good community is to all be together for the right thing.

Many people have their own opinion about what a community can be.

Communities are how some people get along through life. The help from other people can make them better in life. There are many examples of different communities on television and that shows how life really can be.

Responding to the first draft, Templeton noted that this student's thoughts seemed "random" and questioned what he considered to be the thesis of his paper. In the process of revision, Templeton also gave him verbal feedback, and the student was offered peer feedback, as well. In drafts two through four, the student was encouraged to "be more specific by expanding ideas," "give specific examples for support," and pay more attention to wording his thoughts. His last effort at the end of the week and a half is as follows:

Draft #5
Community

Many people like living in communities and some do not. When I think of a community, I think of it as a great place to live and grow up. All communities are not great though. Some have problems with discipline and law enforcement. There is no real meaning to what makes a community, but my outlook on it consist of people helping people and everybody getting along.

My thoughts of a community are of family, friends and even strangers getting along. People control a community's needs and wants. People also help make a community strong or even weak. Some communities have problems though and are not perfect. I think about that and picture my perfect community to be the way I live: safe, friendly, and clean.

To me Cartersville contains many communities. We have neighborhoods such as the Waterford and Mission Estates. Within these neighborhoods people get to know each other, by having barbecue's and parties. Where people and their friends hang out is a part of a community, too. For example my friends and I hang out at baseball and Taco Bell. We call that our community.

I think the community I am a part of now is very strong, but could be stronger. We should do whatever it takes to clean up and make our community great. If our community improves, we could set better examples for other communities.

Everybody has their own outlook and thoughts on what makes a community. I think of mine where everybody gets along and there are law abiding citizens. My community is even fairy-tale like with everything perfect. I love my community and where I live. People may not love theirs, but they can always make a difference.

On the final draft, Templeton commented: "I like how your essay improved with each writing." She suggested some changes in wording and pointed out some mechanical errors but recognized that the student had made improvements. This student was given an A for his last draft.

These two writing instructors have much in common. They both believe it is necessary to lead students to process their ideas, develop a controlling idea, support their ideas with meaningful examples and illustrations, and present them in a logical order that readers can follow. They both expect their students to use effective and correct language. Both instructors indicated that they struggle with getting students to provide specific examples to support their general ideas. One of the major differences in their approach, however, is based on their respective school circumstances.

The pressure to prepare students for a state test figured into the way Templeton made the assignment and assessed the writing. Since the state test focuses on *persuasive* writing, she used that term in the assignment instructions. She omitted Whelan's instructions to *not* write an introduction and conclusion, because those elements are expected on the graduation test. Although the state rubric simply says, "evidence of a sense of order that is clear and relevant," most teachers feel that an introduction and conclusion is expected. The biggest difference in the two assignments, of course, was the fact that Templeton gave the prompt with no instruction or discussion of the topic before the students wrote, as they would receive on the state test. The instruction and rewriting came later.

In addition to the problem of preparing for the graduation writing test, high school teachers have to think about time spent on writing not related to literature, since most of their courses are composition and literature. Because of this combination, teachers are always trying to balance instruction in the two areas. Often, the writing instruction is either omitted or limited to writing about literature, and little time is spent on actual writing instruction. Assessment is focused not on writing skills but on whether the student understands the literature.

I don't think what I'm saying here necessarily conflicts with what Patrick Sullivan says in his chapter in this collection, "What Can We Learn about 'College-Level' Writing from Basic Writing Students? The Importance of Reading." It is often true that in college, as Sullivan states, "writing must be judged primarily by how well students read." What I'm saying is that when we focus on literature as secondary teachers, we are often looking for a mastery of literary terms or some other skill rather than focusing on the writing itself. From what I have observed, Templeton is probably an exception in the amount of writing instruction she gives students because of her association with the National Writing Project.

Unlike Templeton, Whelan focuses entirely on writing skills. At Berry College, students are required to take two semesters of composition. The first one focuses on expository writing. Students learn to create an analytical thesis, develop paragraphs explaining how or why, and use appropriate transitions from one idea to another. The second semester includes more rhetoric and is more resource or source based, and students learn persuasive techniques. After these two semesters, students choose any 200-level literature course, including Introduction to Literature, which is genre based, or British, American, or World Literature.

In my conversations with these two writing instructors, I came to a few conclusions that might lead to further exploration into what is going on in high school and college classrooms. Basically, I was encouraged by both these instructors. Their dedication to writing instruction is impressive. My question is how can we increase the likelihood that students moving from high school to college will have a smooth transition in developing their writing skills?

First, let's look at the two papers that were given the best grade in each class. My first observation is that the tenth grader's writing tends to be much more general, with few specific examples. The closest he comes to specific references is the paragraph in which he mentions the name of his town, a couple of communities, and Taco Bell. In contrast, the college student's essay includes specific "communities" in which she has functioned, such as her college dorm, a seminar class for first-year students, and her basketball team.

In addition, the college paper achieves a certain cohesiveness through a discussion of communication that leads to bonding in order to achieve desired goals. The high school essay lacks this cohesiveness. Rather than define community, the tenth grader seems to assume that community mostly has to do with where one lives; he discusses it in terms of how well it works and sets forth no particular criteria with which to define its effectiveness.

Finally, the college essay is much more sophisticated in its sentence structure, competency in grammar, word choice, and overall effective writing. In fact, even the college essay that was judged ineffective by the college professor demonstrates much more competency in these areas.

We might say, of course, that the college student is a more advanced writer than the tenth grader. She's had more experience. But only two years. We're talking about a second-semester tenth grader and first-year college student (first course in writing). We also must remember that the college student did not receive an A on the paper.

So how do we make sure the high school student is advancing properly? Those of us who teach high school English want to know if we're on the right track, if we are doing all we can to prepare our students for the college writing experience. I'd like to suggest something that might help both the high school teacher and her student (and probably the college teacher, too). At the high school level, we might do better to change our focus from a complete essay (which they do have to write on all those assessment tests!) to a focus on logical thinking, effective sentences, and effective paragraphs.

If students can write one effective paragraph, they can write several effective paragraphs. In our hurry to get students to the point of writing a whole paper, we often don't have time to work on the particulars. In my creative writing classes, I often asked students to "write the best sentence you've ever written." It was amazing how hard they would try to write one really good sentence! It was a challenge, but it was within their reach. Focusing more on good sentence structure and strong paragraphs is also an advantage to the teacher—it's much easier to assess one paragraph for each student than to assess a whole paper. In dealing with only one paragraph, we would be able to give students the feedback that Steven Schmidt mentions in his chapter in this collection, "Moving the Tassel from the Right to the Left," as being so critical to his continued growth as a writer (267–279). Students do have to deal with writing a whole essay for some of the tests, but in the long run, we may help them more by focusing on the parts than the whole. It seems that we may have the sequence backward. If we high school teachers, with our limited time to spend on writing, could do a really good job of teaching students to write effective sentences and paragraphs, then maybe the college professors could build on that and be able to put *their* focus on the whole composition. What seems to be happening is that we require high school students to write whole compositions again and again, but we don't have the time to help them improve their individual paragraphs. Writing whole compositions in this manner may also, unfortunately, encourage students to adopt some particular formula (such as the five-paragraph essay) for producing an essay, with little reflection or thought, as Edward White points out in his chapter in this volume, "My Five-Paragraph-Theme Theme" (137–141).

Having said that, I believe some administrative problems that are beyond the teacher's scope of influence may need to be addressed as well if students are to be properly prepared to be strong writers. Those in charge of curricula should work toward putting composition back in the curriculum as a separate course. At one time it was in Georgia's state curriculum, required in the eleventh or twelfth grade, but it is no longer there. As long as literature and writing are combined, some teachers will focus primarily on literature and not on writing. What little writing *is* done is in response to literature.

Another issue that needs to be addressed is communication between high schools and local colleges. There are many ways in which we could improve communication. High school teachers could invite college English teachers to come in and talk to students about what will be expected in their college English classes. Colleges could organize events where high school teachers could meet English professors and discuss the teaching of writing. Effective communication between high school and college teachers can be accomplished. Someone just has to initiate the process.

Appendix 6A

B+ Student Essay

A community is a group of people that first establishes good communication between its members which in turn allows a special bond to form. That community then uses the bond to form a loosely organized structure that is able to form common goals to make a positive impact on the surrounding environment.

[handwritten: who]
[handwritten: among the members,]
[handwritten: good]

Setting goals is a key component in the process of turning a group of people into a community. Many groups can form and accomplish nothing, but a true community looks to do something productive with the time that it spends together. Short term goals also help to keep the group focused on the main goal the group wants to accomplish. My dorm room is a good example of a group taking this step in the process of building a community. At the beginning of summer, my three roommates and I found out we would be in one room together. We were all afraid that having four girls in a room would not work out if we did not have certain guidelines to help us get along. The first night we moved in, we sat down and talked about all of the things it would take for us to reach our goal which was to survive our freshman year together.

[handwritten: relate examples specifically to claims.]

To reach the goals the group has set, there should be some form of organization. That organization helps the group move in a more unified direction toward the common goals. The leaders of the group oversee the actions of the members and make sure they are all working as hard as they can to reach those original goals. The members then know what they need to accomplish and what it takes to get there. My basketball team displays this kind of organization. After all of the players on my team met and played together a few times, several players emerged as the leaders. These girls were the ones that understood the concept of working together as a team and making sure everyone stayed involved on and off the court. This organization is very loose, but the main purpose of leaders is to help guide the team and make sure everyone stays on the same page while working to towards a unified purpose. Organization can also be seen in my first example of our dorm room. All of the girls in my room sat down and defined how we wanted the rooming situation to work. We wrote out the rules and responsibilities on our roommate contract and signed the bottom to ensure that there was some organization in the room. I have to keep my area of the room clean and take out the trash every week as my part of the contract.

[handwritten: OK - now a second example would help explore this idea of a bit more depth.]

continued on next page

Appendix 6A *continued*

People in a community need a special bond in order to organize. As members of the group get to know each other better, they feel more connected. The individual members begin to learn more about the ideas and thoughts of others in their group. The longer a person spends getting to know another, the stronger the bond becomes because more intimate details are revealed through longer conversations. Time builds a trust which strengthens the bond and allows members to feel closer to each other and share deeper thoughts with on another. Organization comes out of this bond because each individual wants the bond to last, and the group needs guidelines to help it succeed. My freshman seminar class displays this kind of special bond. Everyone in our class really gets along because we have spent so much together. Through a swimming party, dinner at our advisor's house, and group discussions, we have all shared personal experiences that have enabled us to get to know the others in our group. This has allowed each of us to develop a friendship with our classmates that will last throughout college. Our basketball team has already worked in this way, too. The more time we spend running, practicing, and eating meals together, the stronger the bond between us grows. As we learn more about each other, we feel more comfortable sharing more personal details from our lives. As a result, we have all become friends.

Bonding grows out of good communication. Without communication, there can be no community because the group needs to interact before any of the other steps can take place. People need to meet and talk to each other to establish an initial connection. When members of the group communicate, they learn the basics about each other, and whether or not they will be compatible. In our dorm room, it was very important that we laid the foundation of good communication when we first met. That communication led to a much stronger our bond. Because of this, we made a contract that allowed us to have organization to reach our common goal of getting along throughout the school year. If we had not first established a way of communication, none of the other steps could have followed. Our basketball team also had to establish that initial communication. Without it, our team would never have been able to form the friendship that we have, nor formed leaders that would guide us toward the common goal of winning games.

Many groups form and have communication, a bond, organization, and goals, but if they do not make a positive impact in someone's life, the other qualifications do not matter. Communities have been blessed with friendships and purpose; therefore they should share that with others by doing anything they can to help those less fortunate. Making a positive impact is important because that is God's plan for all Christians, and it is a part of the Berry College motto of "Head, Heart, and Hands." God has given us the purpose of ministering unto the world. Most non-Christians even have the moral initiative "to treat others the way they want to be treated"

continued on next page

Appendix 6A continued

especially in times of need. Living in Dalton, there were many examples of groups that

displayed every characteristic except this one. Hispanic gangs have formed, and they go around

terrorizing the public mainly through gang initiation weekend. Each group does have

communication, a bond, organization, and the common goal to kill innocent people for fun just to

initiate new members into the group. This in no way resembles a community because a gang

harms others for amusement. Gangs like to abuse those around them instead of using their God-

given talents to help others. An example of a true community is the service organization, Anchor

Club, which I was a member of in high school. All of the girls in the club were friends; we had

leaders, and the goal to make a difference around our school and city. We volunteered at school

events and took food to the elderly in nursing homes. Each service project was a chance to bring

joy into someone's life.

This ¶ is better but still doesn't quite explain why the positive impact is necessary – it's mainly relying on assertion still

Criteria – each worth 10%	Level of Achievement
Thesis provides a defensible and relevant response to writing problem and clearly establishes relationships among and between ideas	B+
Focus idea of each paragraph gives purpose to the paragraph and develops **one** key idea in the thesis	A
All paragraphs have **developed** their focus idea	B−
Paragraphs are coherent and unified; no ideas extraneous to thesis or focus idea or repetition of ideas already developed	B
Transitions between paragraphs tie old idea to new idea coherently without relying on "crutch" words	B+
Quality of support is adequate for thesis/purpose/audience; the essay as whole provides sufficient support for the thesis statement	B
Purpose of essay is appropriate to writing problem – helps readers understand your perspective on the issue at hand	A
Audience is considered throughout – formality and tone is appropriate for target audience	A−/B+
Quality of sentences: sentences are not awkward/cliched/confused	B
Editing: grammar/punctuation/spelling is effective and correct	A
Essay grade:	B+

Meeting the above criteria at an **average** or **minimum** level of achievement equals a "C" grade.

Appendix 6B

D+ Student Essay

A community is a group of people who have something in common that support each *[and]* other in some way because they are all working towards a common goal. Out of communities, *[something?]* friendships and support groups are formed.

To start off explaining what a community is, I should first explain what makes a group a community. A group of people are just a bunch of people. They do not have to have anything in common. For a group to become a community they must have something in common. *[first]* It could be the fact that they live in the same area, have a certain type of disability, or simply like to play video games. Something has to bring them together. *[OK – analyze how the commonalities might bring them together. Note your examples actually illustrate your point.]* *[transition?]*

[not predicted by thesis] To be considered part of the community group, they must be communicate with the rest of the community. It doesn't matter how they communicate, but communication without communication, nothing can be solved or changed. If the members of the community do not communicate, how can it be said they are working towards a common goal? Nothing can get done *[said already]* if they are not communicating in some way. Internet communities are probably some of the most *[What makes them successful?]* successful communities for the simple reason that they communicate extremely well. Someone *[how is it related to comm.?]* *[haven't really talked about this yet, so you're getting ahead of yourself]* cannot be considered part of the community if he does not communicate or take part with the *[Is this a different idea re: participation?]* group. For instance, Bob who lives in the back of the neighborhood, never goes to any of the neighborhood meetings. While he may live in the neighborhood, he cannot be considered part of the community because he doesn't help them achieve their goal. Their goal may be anything from getting a neighborhood watch together to building a neighborhood pool. But, since Bob excluded

[relation to communication? This seems to be about participation…]

himself from these meetings, he is not a part of the community.

Just talking to each other isn't always good enough. They have to listen to each other. *[Members also]* While arguing and yelling may be considered communication, it does not help the community *[Why not? This it is completely undeveloped.]* move forward in accomplishing their goal. That means that sometimes it is necessary to compromise. *[transition?]* *[new criterion]*

When being around people for enough time, which is what happens in a community, friendships and support bases naturally begin to form. The community members begin to realize that by helping each other, they are helping the group, and ultimately helping themselves and what they believe in. *[How? No development…]*

continued on next page

Appendix 6B continued

Most of your ¶s assert rather than develop your claims. In addition your 2nd ¶ adds a new criteria not predicted by your thesis & assumes another (goals) that you don't develop elsewhere.

To be a true analytical essay based on the ideas here, you'd need a structure like this:

① Communities must have a common goal (¶ tells why)

② The goal develops out of something the members have in common (¶ tells how)

③ In order to achieve the goal, members must elect to participate (¶ tells why)

④ Communication is the primary means of participation (how/why)

Criteria – each worth 10%	Level of Achievement
Thesis provides a defensible and relevant response to writing problem and clearly establishes relationships among and between ideas	C+
Focus idea of each paragraph gives purpose to the paragraph and develops **one** key idea in the thesis	C/D+
All paragraphs have **developed** their focus idea	F
Paragraphs are coherent and unified; no ideas extraneous to thesis or focus idea or repetition of ideas already developed	D/F
Transitions between paragraphs tie old idea to new idea coherently without relying on "crutch" words	C−
Quality of support is adequate for thesis/purpose/audience; the essay as whole provides sufficient support for the thesis statement	F
Purpose of essay is appropriate to writing problem – helps readers understand your perspective on the issue at hand	D
Audience is considered throughout – formality and tone is appropriate for target audience	B−
Quality of sentences: sentences are not awkward/cliched/confused	B−
Editing: grammar/punctuation/spelling is effective and correct	B
Essay grade:	D+

Meeting the above criteria at an **average** or **minimum** level of achievement equals a "C" grade.

Works Cited

Schmidt, Steven. "Moving the Tassel from the Right to the Left." *What Is "College-Level" Writing? Volume 2: Assignments, Readings, and Student Writing Samples*. Ed. Patrick Sullivan, Howard Tinberg, and Sheridan Blau. Urbana, IL: NCTE. 2010. 267–279. Print.

Sullivan, Patrick. "What Can We Learn about College-Level Writing from Basic Writing Students?: The Importance of Reading." *What Is "College-Level" Writing? Volume 2: Assignments, Readings, and Student Writing Samples*. Ed. Patrick Sullivan, Howard Tinberg, and Sheridan Blau. Urbana, IL: NCTE. 2010. 233–253. Print.

White, Edward M. "My Five-Paragraph-Theme Theme." *What Is "College-Level" Writing? Volume 2: Assignments, Readings, and Student Writing Samples*. Ed. Patrick Sullivan, Howard Tinberg, and Sheridan Blau. Urbana, IL: NCTE. 2010. 137–141. Print.

II

THE IMPORTANCE
OF WRITING ASSIGNMENTS

My Five-Paragraph-Theme Theme

EDWARD M. WHITE
University of Arizona

Since the beginning of time, some college teachers have mocked the five-paragraph theme. But I intend to show that they have been mistaken. There are three reasons why I always write five-paragraph themes. First, it gives me an organizational scheme: an introduction (like this one) setting out three subtopics, three paragraphs for my three subtopics, and a concluding paragraph reminding you what I have said, in case you weren't paying attention. Second, it focuses my topic, so I don't just go on and on when I don't have anything much to say. Three and only three subtopics force me to think in a limited way. And third, it lets me write pretty much the same essay on anything at all. So I do pretty well on essay tests. A lot of teachers actually like the five-paragraph theme as much as I do.

The first reason I always write five-paragraph themes is that it gives me an organizational scheme. It doesn't matter what the subject is, since there are three parts to everything you can think of. If you can't think of more than two, you just have to think harder or come up with something that might fit. An example will often work, like the three causes of the Civil War or abortion or reasons why the ridiculous 21-year limit for drinking alcohol should be abolished. A worse problem is when you wind up with more than three subtopics, since sometimes you want to talk about all of them. But you can't. You have to pick the best three. That keeps you from thinking too much, which is a great time saver, especially on an essay test.

A portion of this essay was published in *College Composition and Communication* 59.4 (2008): 524–25 and is used here with the permission of the National Council of Teachers of English.

The second reason for the five-paragraph theme is that it makes you focus on a single topic. Some people start writing on the usual topic, like TV commercials, and they wind up all over the place, talking about where TV came from or capitalism or health foods or whatever. But with only five paragraphs and one topic, you're not tempted to get beyond your original idea, like commercials are a good source of information about products. You give your three examples and zap! You're done. This is another way the five-paragraph theme keeps you from thinking too much.

The last reason to write this way is the most important. Once you have it down, you can use it for practically anything. Does God exist? Well, you can say "yes" and give three reasons or "no" and give three different reasons. It doesn't really matter. You're sure to get a good grade whatever you pick to put into the formula. And that's the real reason for education: to get those good grades without thinking too much and using up too much time.

So I've given you three reasons why I always write a five-paragraph theme and why I'll keep doing so in college. It gives me an organizational scheme that looks like an essay, it limits my focus to one topic and three subtopics so I don't wander about thinking irrelevant thoughts, and it will be useful for whatever writing I do in any subject. I don't know why some teachers seem to dislike it so much. They must have a different idea about education than I do.

I wrote this little jeu d'esprit while flying back to Arizona from Florida after serving as a table leader for the 2007 Advanced Placement English test. I had been part of an army of readers scoring about 280,000 exams, each containing three impromptu essays written by high school students—many of them trained to write five-paragraph essays in order to pass writing tests. I had been disheartened by how many good writers I saw writing badly. It was clear that this training in producing five-paragraph essays often had little to do with writing as a form of discovery and reflection, not to speak of developed argument. But what else can we expect of high school seniors writing an impromptu essay in forty-five minutes? Many of these 280,000 students had obviously been trained to write five-paragraph themes, and who can blame either the teachers or the students for that? Still, I was troubled: Why did so many of the AP essays show so little of what we teach in first-year writing courses, despite the obvious competence of the students in the techniques of essay production?

I know that there is much to be said for teaching the five-paragraph theme, from the teacher's as well as the student's perspective, and I tried to have my theme enumerate them. Though a formula, it is an organizational scheme—and it is better to have some organization than none at all. We know that an essay needs to be built around assertions and that some kind of evidence for these assertions is necessary. The writer of this five-paragraph theme doesn't appear to have any sense that writing could encourage reflection or discovery; the formula doesn't exactly prohibit it, though this writer appears to be among the many who feel it renders such matters unnecessary. Above all, this writer appears to know that the five-paragraph theme allows every student to turn out something "that looks like an essay," and this important fact meets our obligation as teachers to get as many of our students as possible through the incessant testing of writing. It is even possible, as a few AP students demonstrated, to use that formula to turn out some real writing, and I'm sure some very good English teachers have used the five-paragraph formula to help students get started. But by and large, formulas don't much engender thinking; indeed they actively discourage it.

Finally, what troubled me most as I wrote this five-paragraph theme was what happened to me as a writer when I knew the only purpose I was writing was to pass a test. I organized my thoughts, such as they were, edited my work carefully, even imagined the teachers who would be grading my work. Would I have passed the test? Probably. And yet most of what I value about writing is missing here: reflection, understanding of the issues, awareness of other perspectives on the topic, and an understanding of the relation of writing to thinking.

We see plenty of students like this in our first-year composition classes, whether the college is a "selective" one or not. Our job is to make sure students like this have "a different idea about education" by the time they leave our class. That is not only a pedagogical problem embedded in the curriculum of most such courses but an issue that rhetoricians for the last two thousand years have wrestled with. How can we teach the rudiments of an organized argument without trapping our students in a limited formula? The five-paragraph theme is the most recent version of writing from models, learning through copying formats, developing templates—a concept with a long pedagogical history. Used well, this form of rote learning teaches important skills that students learn to use in many different ways; used badly, it dries up the imagination, substitutes form for substance, and teaches that writing is not a matter of discovery or thought but just a matter of filling in the blanks.

If we choose to use the five-paragraph theme to teach the concept of organization and development of ideas, we need to be sure that competing heuristics with the same goals are also part of what we teach. Thus, we should also spend some time with narrative structures that respond to assignments calling for telling about a personal experience and what it means to the writer— and, possibly, the reader. The first draft of such a paper will have a simple chronological structure, detailing the experience. But revisions will find ways to open with the reasons the experience mattered, include those ideas throughout the narrative, and conclude with some suggestion that readers should be interested in the writer's reflections, which are not merely personal.

Or we could present, as another alternative, the structure required by a comparison/contrast assignment, derived from two readings: In what respects do these writers differ or agree, and what conclusions on the topic do you draw from that comparison? Now we need a structure that allows the writer to discuss each reading in some detail, then moves to another section describing their agreement, another on their differences, and finally a developed argument about what matters about the two positions and where the writer has come to stand on the topic.

Such an expanded idea of organization needs to deal with the exigency that calls forth the writing—that is, some reason besides getting a grade for producing a text. Only then can we approach formats and formulas that might help with organizing ideas. I was lucky enough to find such a teacher in first-year composition, and he turned me into a writer—and changed my life. I'd like to think that college-level writing will continue to offer such challenges and opportunities to all the students passing through our classes.

Powerful formulas help students get going and often help them to pass tests—but at the cost of creativity or really thinking about what they say. I would like to argue here that formulas—and especially the five-paragraph essay formula—should be regarded by teachers as a way station on the path to more real writing. This formula should be used only to meet short-term goals. Unfortunately, I think most students are happy to stop with the formula, so teachers should avoid it whenever possible.

The Thirty-Eight-or-So Five-Paragraph Essay (The Dagwood)

Alfredo Celedón Luján
Monte del Sol Charter School

Introduction

On the first day, I tell the juniors and seniors in my Mexican American/Chicano(a)/Latina(o) literature class that they are writing a "thirty-eight-or-so five-paragraph essay" for their final paper. And, even if they haven't yet written a single tangible word, I tell them that they began writing the paper yesterday. They have to think like writers for this assignment, not just as students fulfilling a task, I tell them. They already know stuff.

Each student entered the class with applicable knowledge and actual developed skills: what she or he can do without the guidance of a teacher (Vygotsky). The experience of sensing the environment, of formulating coherent thoughts, and of putting them down on paper is behind them; the content of this course is ahead of them. They will be transitioning through Vygotsky's "zone of proximal development" (84–91), where they will acquire additional knowledge and advance their writing skills.

They live in the present and in the region we will be studying. They have intimate knowledge of the Southwest, especially northern New Mexico, primarily Santa Fe. I tell them to put their antennae on for the semester and to pay *real close* attention to where they live, where they cruise, what they eat, what they hear—the bilingual code switches that happen daily in conversation, on street signs, in the literature, in our class itself.

The material we cover begins with Luis Alberto Urrea's *The Devil's Highway*—nonfiction that reports a riveting story of twenty-six men who crossed the Mexican border in 2001; we thus begin the course with the contemporary issue of immigration. After reading Urrea, we go backward in time to Elizabeth "Betita" Martinez's essay, "Be Down with the Brown" (1998). After Martinez, we read some pre-US oral traditions of the Spanish and Mexican periods in the Southwest from *Mexican American Literature* (our anthology). In this folklore segment of the curriculum, we read "El Corrido de Gregorio Cortez/The Ballad of Gregorio Cortez" from *Mexican American Literature* and watch an excerpt of the film (same title, which is based on a book about Cortez titled *With a Pistol in His Hand*). Then we move forward to excerpts of journals written by Spanish explorers of the Southwest in the sixteenth century: Alvar Nuñez Cabeza de Vaca, Fray Marcos de Niza, and Junipero Serra. We follow this with some twentieth-century nonfiction and fiction, including works by Jorge Ulica, Nina Otero, Josefina Niggli, Sabine Ulibarri, Sandra Cisneros, Gary Soto, and Tomás Rivera.

We also read a Mario Suarez excerpt that uses *capirotada* (a bread pudding dish) as a metaphor for the Chicanos of his fictional town, El Hoyo. We read Rudolfo Anaya's *Bless Me, Ultima*, of course—it is, after all, the quintessential coming of age story of Antonio, the protagonist, but it is also the coming of age of modern Chicano literature, and it takes place in northern New Mexico. Later, we read some nonfiction, fiction, and poetry of the contemporary period; we end the class with the Chicana/o activist literature of the '60s, linking us back in full circle with Betita Martinez and "Be Down with the Brown."

1/5abc + 1/5a + 1/5b + 1/5c + 1/5cba = 5/5abc = 1 essay

I remind my students that essentially their paper has been in process their whole lives, being prewritten through their sensory perceptions of the New Mexican culture and Southwest terrain. Structuring the paper so that it has the elements of the five-paragraph essay is, in part, the writing component of this class.

I emphasize that I should not have to tell them to start taking mental and physical notes now. The rubric for the paper is being presented to them as I speak. Most of them immediately take out their notebooks and writing utensils and begin taking notes, if they haven't already. The others wait until I execute my "Get it?" pause, and, if they still don't pick up on the hint, I repeat: "Your paper started being written yesterday. The rubric is being presented to you now, as I speak, so . . . (*pause*) . . . get your writing utensils out *pronto* quick, for crying out loud."

Teaching, learning, and writing the five-paragraph essay makes perfect sense. It does. Edward White shows us why in his tongue-in-cheek "My Five-Paragraph-Theme Theme" in this collection. He uses the five-paragraph essay structure, he says, because the form gives him an "organizational scheme" (137)—an introduction, body (three *and only three* subtopic paragraphs), and conclusion (a reiteration of the three *and only three* subtopic paragraphs for the purpose of repeating, reminding, and clarifying the three *and only three* subtopic paragraphs)—and because it makes the writer "focus on a single topic. . . . [W]ith only five paragraphs and one topic, you're not tempted to get beyond your original idea" (138). You (the writer) can use it (the formula) for anything, and you're bound to get a good grade. "[T]hat's the real reason for education [*wink*]: to get those good grades without thinking too much and using up too much time" (138).

Indeed, when I was in elementary, junior, and high school, the essay was called a theme or composition. In college and graduate school, it was a paper. For me, writing academic papers was excruciating, especially since I was a stamped and approved procrastinating/wait-until-the-last-minute/*carpe mañana* (a term copyrighted by George Adelo Jr.) writer for most of my academic life. Perhaps I had spent too many hours trying to construct the simple, perfect thesis statement—that miraculous sentence that would serve as the underpinning of my essay and guide my reader (the teacher) through the five-paragraph junkyard of my thoughts. In retrospect, I ask myself, "Self, did learning the five-paragraph essay formula help you prepare for college-level writing?"

My self answers, "Do you want the good news or the bad news first?"

"The good news."

"The good news is . . . you passed English."

"*Órale*. What's the bad news?"

"The bad news," says my self, "is that your paper looked and sounded like every other paper in the class. It was a template, *ese*. And it bored your teacher to death."

No wonder my five-paragraph essays were bland and riddled with "college-level mistakes." I had learned to construct the thing, but I did it by formula: $1/5abc + 1/5a + 1/5b + 1/5c + 1/5cba = 5/5abc = 1$ essay. Everybody had the same formula! We hadn't really learned to develop or rewrite or revise our thoughts. Oh, sure, we had learned to correct most of our punctuation mistakes, but we hadn't yet discovered the pleasure and pain of grappling with words. We hadn't learned that we could bend, break, or invent words, and we hadn't discovered the art of shaping thought sequences.

The five-paragraph essay structure taught us to write quickly and safely without taking much risk. Sure, it taught us a canned writing technique, and it helped prepare us for high school and college writing. It didn't, however, guide us to produce *real* writing—writing with voice and rhythm—writing that doesn't count words or paragraphs. It didn't prepare us for college-level curiosity; you know—the "thorn in the flesh" that stirs you awake at 2:13 a.m. to look up the meaning or spelling of a word in the dictionary or to find its etymology or part of speech. It didn't teach us to turn our writing inside out and upside down or to "love it like your own best friend" and "edit it like your own worst enemy." It taught us to write words, and we worked our *como se llamas* off trying to come up with the 250, 500, or 1,000 that were required, but it didn't teach us to cut whole sentences or paragraphs. That would have been a ludicrous suggestion because every single word, including *and*, was, after all, in our final word count. One of the most difficult tasks in the 250-word essay was to avoid making *and* the 250th word. The formula for essay writing was an implement for completing a composition—an assignment—a task; it was a tool, like a shovel, for *completando la tarea*. Five-paragraph, college-level essay writing didn't make us wonder if a passage was transitional, even if it did teach us how to create transitions with words like furthermore, consequently, for instance, conversely, finally, then.

The Dagwood

Then, in 1986 I took "Making Yourself Up," a post-seventeenth-century English literature course that focused on first-person narrative, taught by Professor Jim Maddox at the Bread Loaf School of English. He offered the option of writing a pastiche for a final paper. Aha! . . . enter a creative writing alternative to the traditional paper. Yay! Well, first I had to look up *pastiche* in the dictionary. I tried to write one that summer, but I had limited experience with post-seventeenth-century English lit, so I couldn't quite pull it off to my satisfaction. However, the idea of composing a pastiche lingered.

Then, in 1990, I participated in "The Writer's Eye," a National Endowment for the Humanities institute at Brandeis University, sponsored by the Brookline Public Schools in Massachusetts. The reading list was eclectic: *Crito, One Hundred Years of Solitude, Gulliver's Travels, A Room of One's Own, Sacred Emily, One Writer's Beginnings,* among other texts. We had to write a paper for the institute. The pastiche idea had been percolating for four or five years, and this became the perfect opportunity to write one. I wrote "Camarada's Travels," a bilingual log that imitated Jonathan Swift's *Gulliver's Travels* via Tofe Camarada's adventures through Waltham, Boston, Harvard Square, Fenway Park, the trains, and some of the texts that were covered in the institute. My title page and introduction to Chapter I, as well as the remainder of my paper, mirror Swift's satirical tome:

TRAVELS
into several
Remote Nations
of
THE WORLD

By Captain Lemuel Gulliver

A Voyage to BROBDINGNAG

London:
Printed in the Year MDCCXXVI

CHAPTER I
The author gives some account of himself and family. His first inducements to travel. He is shipwrecked, and swims for his life. Gets safe on shore in the country of Lilliput; is made a prisoner, and carried up the country.

TRAVELS
into
A Remote City
of
AMERICA

By Capitan Tofe Camarada

A Voyage to NEHRDIA

New England:
Printed in the Year MCMXC

CHAPTER I
The author tells about himself and his family. He tells why he likes to travel. After flying across America, he wakes up in his residence hall and disburthens himself. He joins the institute on the hill, where the International Lounge is located. He meets the NEHRDS.

By coincidence, *Gulliver's Travels* is a post-seventeenth-century English text, but this time the literature lent itself to a parody of my summer of adventure in Waltham, "a remote city in America." I could connect the book to my personal life; this, I had learned in a Reading in the Content Area course back in the '70s, is called the "applied level" of reading. (Later, I learned more about reader response theory through Judith Langer's "envisionment-building" strategies in *Conversations in Literature*.) This time, however, I felt like my pastiche was successful and began to think of it as a potential writing exercise for my own students.

The assignment did not materialize until I had found a southwestern book that I thought my students could imitate, even though it was Native American, not Mexican American. After reading Leslie Marmon Silko's *Storyteller*, I thought, "Okay—here's a regional text that can be mirrored. Its narrative style meanders down the page and is presented in multigenres: biography, autobiography, essay, poetry, article. It has the elements of a five-paragraph essay: an introduction, body, and conclusion. Yes, this would work."

In class, I tell my students that they will compose their paper, not as a culminating essay when the class ends but as a theme that is being developed over the course of the semester. I hand out an excerpt of *Storyteller*, and I tell them they should read it, but, more important, they need to look at the method in which the text is formatted, how it's being presented—from poetry to prose and back again as it saunters down the page.

COTTONWOOD *Part One: Story of Sun House*

Cottonwood,
        cottonwood.
                It was under the cottonwood tree
                in a sandy wash of the big canyon . . .

                        . . . "you will know,"
                        he said
                        "you will know by the colors

                        Cottonwood leaves
                        more colors of the sun
                        than the sun himself . . ."

When the light
        from the autumn edge of the sky . . .

        . . . "But what if . . ."

COTTONWOOD *Part Two: Buffalo Story*

. . . When it got so dry
nothing was growing . . .

. . . It was all because
one time long ago
our daughter, our sister Kochininako
went away with them.

                        * * *

THE TIME WE CLIMBED SNAKE MOUNTAIN

> Seeing good places
>   for my hands
> I grab the warm parts of the cliff
>   and I feel the mountain as I climb.
>
> ... don't step on the spotted yellow snake
>   he lives here.
> The mountain is his.

* * *

> When I was thirteen I carried an old .30-30 we borrowed
> from George Pearl. It was an old Winchester that had a steel
> ring on its side to secure it in a saddle scabbard. It was heavy
> and hurt my shoulder when I fired it . . . (63–77)

Silko's *Storyteller* is the model for my students' final paper. They will not write their essay, as I did years ago—by writing an outline or by painfully trying to formulate a perfect thesis statement. Instead, we will build a "Dagwood essay"—modeled after the big, multilayered sandwiches that Dagwood Bumstead, from the comic strip *Blondie*, was fond of. Students build an essay from the inside out, starting with the sandwich meat, condiments, and veggies, and then later pressing it together with their choice of bread ends.

Building an essay sandwich from the inside out may seem preposterous, but why not try? I venture to say that most of us have made a sandwich by holding the fridge door open and looking first for the goodies inside, then pulling out the ingredients— meat for some; vegan for others; cheese; then slicing the tomatoes, cucumbers, and onions . . . laying the lettuce and bean sprouts on the counter, putting out the mustard and mayo and vinegar . . . toasting the wheat, sourdough, or rye bread using one slice as a base on which to spread the mayo and a splash of vinegar. Then we stack our stuff on it. Then we put the top piece on after spreading the mustard on it; we cut the sandwich in half, put the garnish, including a jalapeño and a *guerito* (a yellow hot pepper), on the side and presto: the Dagwood sandwich. Geez, this looks a bit like the Subway or Quiznos counter!

In my class, the students will construct the Dagwood paper from several pieces of writing, most of which will have already been proofread, edited, and graded. Each piece of writing the students compose over the semester is archived in a computer file so that it will be easy to copy and paste into a draft that will become an essay/pastiche/puzzle comprised, like *Story-teller*, of multigenres. In our case, it will contain essays, poems, self-biographies (autobiographies written in the third person), quizzes, shorts, notes, journal entries, and reader-, viewer-, and listener- responses. As we approach the end of the quarter and again at the end of the semester, I ask students to find seven to ten pieces of writing that are thematically related and to string them together so that they make chronological, historical, poetic, or some other kind of sense.

"It's a Great Five-Paragraph Essay, but It's Forty-Two Paragraphs Long!"

"You will write a five paragraph essay that will be approximately thirty-eight paragraphs long," I tell my students that first day. When I ask them to brainstorm on the parts of the five-paragraph essay, they regurgitate: "Introduction . . . "

" . . . Body . . . "

"Conclusion."

Some say, "Beginning . . . "

" . . . Middle . . . "

"End."

As devil's advocate, I ask, "But that's three parts; why is it called a five-paragraph essay?"

Most of them fall silent for a moment. Eventually one will say that the first paragraph contains a thesis statement and introduces three main points. Another will say that each paragraph has a topic sentence that supports the introductory paragraph, and the fifth paragraph summarizes or reiterates.

"Can't that be done in fewer than five paragraphs?" I ask. "Can it be done in more than five?"

A lively discussion results. Arguments go both ways and include the assertion by some students that five paragraphs means five paragraphs and that's that. 5 = 5. Fine. Others maintain that it can be done in more or fewer than five paragraphs. Some don't care; either way is fine.

My work is cut out for me because I will try to convince them that five paragraphs is a framework, not a hard-and-fast rule. One doesn't count paragraphs in a five-paragraph essay any more than one counts the number of words in a 300-word theme. This revelation came to me midcareer, when I was an adjunct instructor of first-year English at Santa Fe Community College (SFCC).

In the writing segment of the curriculum at SFCC was the essay, of course. *Models for Writers* was our composition book. The students read sample essays by notable authors and used them as models for their own writing. In Section I, "The Elements of the Essay," is Chapter 1, the thesis lesson; it includes Helen Keller's "The Most Important Day"—a perfect representative piece of the well-written essay. Hold on. Isn't it also Chapter 4 of Keller's autobiography, *The Story of My Life*? Yup.

Nevertheless, it's an excellent example of the five-paragraph essay controlled by a perfectly crafted thesis statement. Every sentence, thus every word, in the essay/chapter is logically linked to this thesis: "The most important day I remember in all my life is the one on which my teacher, Anne Mansfield Sullivan, came to me." The succeeding paragraphs are buttressed by solid topic sentences and parallel structure, and the transitions are seamless. But it's nine paragraphs long! Hmmph. Try to sell that at the five-paragraph essay store. If I were marking that essay, would I deduct points because it exceeds the five-paragraph limit?

When we read Martinez's "Be Down with the Brown," we notice that her five-paragraph essay, included in Howard Zinn and Anthony Arnove's *Voices of a People,* is forty-two paragraphs long. Her essay describes the "blowouts" at the East Los Angeles schools in 1968, when activist students strategically walked out of the schools for several days, demanding an equal and relevant education, including respect, coursework, Chicana/o teachers, and other civil rights. "Be Down with the Brown" also compares the young activists of the '60s to the contemporary teenage activists of the '90s. I repeat, it's a great five-paragraph essay, but it's forty-two paragraphs long!

The Devil's Highway itself is a five-paragraph essay that is three hundred or so pages. It is the nonfiction account of the fate of twenty-six immigrants who cross the border in 2001. The book opens with a scene that happens near the end of the story. The story begins with the end:

> Five men stumbled out of the mountain pass so sunstruck they didn't know their own names. . . . They were drunk from having their brains baked in the pan, they were seeing God and devils, and they were dizzy from drinking their own urine, the poisons clogging their systems. (3)

Then one of the passages earlier in the book gives an insider's view of a Border Patrol SUV. Though I'd seen Border Patrol vehicles on the highway in southern New Mexico, Arizona, and California, I never knew what one looked like on the inside:

> The Explorers are nice. You go out there four-wheeling in an SUV that has been retrofitted by felons in a Texas prison. . . . The Explorer has a cage behind the back seat, and a mounted radio down between the front seats, and a shotgun rack behind your seat. . . . The trucks weigh ten thousand pounds. . . . [They] have two standard features that everyone finds indispensable: a killer AC unit and a strong FM radio. . . . [T]he air conditioner is a lifesaver—literally. . . . [T]he FM keeps morale elevated. . . . Van Halen and Led Zeppelin bleed through the call-ins. . . . (24–25)

Brandon Vandiver, a senior, points out that one of Led Zeppelin's famed tunes is "Immigrant Song." This teachable moment launches us into a discussion of immigration other than that of Mexican immigrants. The song, Brandon tells us, is about the North American invasion by the Norse and their journey to Valhalla. Bianca Madrid then throws in the immigrant song to which she listens: Jae-P's "Latin Invasion"—a hip-hop tune that tells of Latin immigration to every community in the United States. I download the songs. We listen. "Our only goal will be the western shore. Ah, ah. We come from the land of the ice and snow . . ." ". . . *la tortilla vende mas que el* Wonder Bread . . ." We discuss. This dialogue leads us to Teresa Palomo Acosta's poem "My Mother

Pieced Quilts," a narrative poem of migrant workers told through the fabrics in a literal yet metaphorical quilt, and to "Geraldo No Last Name," a vignette from Sandra Cisneros's *The House on Mango Street*, and this leads to "The Circuit" by Francisco Jiménez.

All along I've been assigning several consecutive pieces of writing that I hope lead to close readings of our assigned texts. I tell my students that they each have deep familiarity with something in northern New Mexico, especially Santa Fe, akin to the inside information that Urrea has of the SUV. I ask them to write a paper that shows their up-close-and-personal perspective of what most people see only from the outside. In this stretch, they also write parodies of their favorite migrant songs or poems—pieces they feel speak to immigration. "Imagine yourselves in that Border Patrol SUV cruising across the desert at 30 miles per hour . . . what song are you listening to?" I ask. Write the lyrics.

After reading, discussing, and writing seriously on the issues of immigration in *The Devil's Highway*, we watch Cheech Marin's *Born in East L.A.*, a satirical film that includes slapstick and hyperbole on immigration issues and also parodies Bruce Springsteen's "Born in the U.S.A." I ask my students to write a viewer-response parody of that as well.

Conclusion

I argue that in structure, if not in number, the pastiche is a multigenre five-paragraph essay. It has a middle, beginning, and end. I conclude with a sample of what I consider college-level writing that I believe supports my premise. It is a pastiche written by Bianca Madrid.

The Other Side/El Otro Lado

by Bianca Madrid

Bianca Madrid
(1991-)

Bianca Gardenia Madrid Huerta was born in Chihuahua, Chihuahua, Mexico on September 13, 1991. She moved to

Santa Fe, N.M. when she was five years old and has been living there ever since. She currently lives with her dad Samuel, her mother Gardenia, her little brother Sammy and her little sister Britsy. She is a junior at Monde Del Sol Charter School and will be graduating in 2010.

Since Bianca was a baby, her mom would read books to her. As she became older she got more interested in books because the stories were really interesting to her. She still remembers the first time she went to the library and rented her first book. The book is called *Stellaluna,* she doesn't remember the author, but that was and still is her favorite picture book.

She has loved writing but only when she wanted to. During her elementary and junior high years, she didn't really like to write papers that were assigned to her. She would do them but not with a lot of enthusiasm. But there were times when she had assignments that had something to do with her personal life. These she liked because she was able to express herself. She also really liked writing short stories because she was able to let her imagination free. Ever since, Bianca has been doing a lot of writing. Some of her writing has gotten published in books as examples of college level writing. [Note: Bianca's work is cited in "The Salem Witch Trials: Voice(s)," in the first volume of *What Is "College-Level" Writing?* (Luján)] She also got an article published in the *Sustainable Santa Fe Guide* of 2009. She loves writing poetry. That wasn't published, it was performed, because Bianca thinks poetry has a deeper meaning to it when it's said with the right feeling.

Bianca continues writing. She likes to express herself that way. Her goals for writing are to improve her spelling. For Bianca writing is like dancing; they both have a melody. Writing and dancing are forms of expression.

* * *

In my Latino Literature class we have been learning many things about a very serious topic: immigration. We have been looking at this topic in different ways. We have read books, stories, heard songs and watched movies. We took some quizzes and wrote some parodies on a couple of songs. We also wrote journals about our surroundings. We took notes and wrote an autobiography.

In the first couple of weeks we read *The Devil's Highway* by Luis Alberto Urrea. It is a book that tells the stories of 26 men that were crossing the border from Mexico to Arizona. It talks about their journey and the tragedy that happened when they were crossing. On their way to America, 14 died. We did two quizzes about the book. The first test we took was on September 10, 2008:

1. What does the inside of a Border Patrol SUV look like?

The Border Patrol drives white Expeditions with a green line going across it. On the line it says "Border Patrol." They have bars that divide the two front seats from the rest of the vehicle so that they won't be in danger with the immigrants.

2. What is OTM?

OTM is "Other Than Mexican." The Border Patrol uses that term for people they find in the desert that are not Mexicans. They can be immigrants from another country or people that just like the desert a lot and are visiting. One example of the OTM's is when the Border Patrol finds the Arabs in the desert.

3. What is a tonk?

A "tonk" is the sound that is made when a flashlight hits someone's head. The Border Patrol calls the immigrants Tonks because the Border Patrol would hit them on the head with their flashlights.

4. What do people who die in the desert look like?

The immigrants that die in the desert get really black from being sunburned. Their lips get all cracked up and big, and their eyes get full of dust. Their postmortem packages might have their watches, a little Mexican money, sometimes ID, and other stuff that they would be wearing.

5. What does *mordida* mean in the book?

It means bite, that they each get their part in the deal, a piece of the cake.

* * *

After the test we wrote a paper called "Inside Out." In this paper we got to write about something that was personal to us, something that not everybody gets to experience. I decided to do my Inside Out paper about immigration, but not about crossing the border because people know about that because so many people write about it, but not a lot of people know what happens after they cross the border.

Inside Out

Immigration is a big issue in the U.S., and we all know that. At some point or another we have all heard about the things that immigrants go through when they are crossing the border: deaths, the rapes, and the things stolen. It's hard, but do people really know what happens when they do make it to the other side of the border? The journey doesn't end when they make it to "The Promised Land!" It starts there.

Being an immigrant myself and having the chance to be part of the immigrant community, I've heard many stories. Some people come to the U.S. without a single penny. Nothing. All they have is themselves and the clothes they are wearing. They come here to work, but most don't have work or a place to stay. The people in the park downtown, across from the Guadalupe street, don't have a place to sleep. People in my family went through that.

Others get here, and after a few months, or even days, they get deported. After that they need money more than ever because most of them are in debt from the first time they crossed. Then the only way they can pay that money is by coming back. But when that happens, they then owe money from the first time they came, and they owe the second time, too.

In other cases some people don't get caught. Some people get to stay in the US for years and years, but during those years they live in constant fear. It's fear that someone in the family might get deported. It's even worse when illegal immigrants have kids here. The kids go to school and sometimes go home, and their parents aren't there, and the next day either! Why? They were deported while they worked!

Once the word gets out that *La Migra* is on the streets of Santa Fe, it's a mess. Parents don't go to the store because *La Migra* is there. Students don't go to school because they are afraid that the Migra will be outside of the schools. Even though it's against the law, it has happened. There are a lot of people that don't know about this, and it happens in their own community.

So many things went through my mind when I was writing this paper: my past, present, future—the borders—my family here and in Mexico, the moments that I missed over there, and the moments they missed here, all because of a border. And for that, a new journey has begun every day.

* * *

On September 24 we had to answer some questions about the book. They were five discussion questions at the end of the book. They were mostly about our opinions. These were my answers:

1. It is true that every family in the United States came here from somewhere else. My family came to the U.S. from Mexico. It all started a long time ago. My great-grandparents, my grandparents—my family has been coming to this country for years. There's always fear in the family when someone is going to cross the border, even when they are crossing legally. We are always aware that in the trip something can happen. It's hard when family members leave, but things have to happen in order to do something better in life. That's my family, and many other people's stories.

2. There are many other borders that are not physically visible. In the story another border that existed and divided the people was the wall of *coyote* and *pollitos*. The coyotes had more money, and they were the ones leading the *pollitos*. Therefore, in their mind they were superior. They wanted their money and nothing else really mattered. The people with less money were seen as almost nothing. If they were getting lost, the *coyotes* would leave them there and just wouldn't care.

3. There are many other borders that divide people. Some of those borders are age, race, economic situations, religion, cliques, style, culture, background, and many more. These borders should be broken or bridged. There is no point in looking at the differences when at the end we are so similar. It doesn't matter if we are rich or poor, young or old, or anything else. We can put our differences aside and look at the good things that bring us together as one community.

4. For me, Jesus Antonio Lopez Ramos, A.K.A. Mendez, was neither a villain nor a victim in the story. He was in between. He wasn't a villain because if he would've wanted, he could've left the desert since the beginning. But he didn't. He got lost with them. But he wasn't a victim because he didn't share his water, but then again, who would if it would probably be the only way of surviving.

Even though he didn't mean to kill them, he shouldn't have taken them like that if he didn't know what he was doing.

5. The theme of survival applies to the Border Patrol because they save people who are crossing the border to a possible death. That isn't always the case, but in this story it was. The *coyotes* do this work so that their families can have a better way of life. It also applies to the *coyotes* because they are the ones responsible for making sure that the people with them survive. I don't know to what extreme I would go to feed my family, I don't think anybody really knows until they go through that.

* * *

We then heard different types of music. The purpose of this was to see how we felt depending on the music played. That led to writing lyrics of our own. The lyrics had to do on some kind of story about immigration. Oscar Romo, Adrian Lara, Fabiola Perez, and I worked together to write our lyrics:

We came here to improve.

Our country got messed up.

Tell me what you're trying to prove by throwing all my people out.

You say we took your job,

You're already living the American dream.

That's why you put us down,

But your family had to start the same as me.

And if you would know your history you would know,

That your flag wouldn't just be red, white and blue,

It would have brown in it too.

We helped your economy, and that's a fact.

And now you want to throw us out, man that's fucked up.

Now you're putting up a wall, to keep us out.

But you need to understand that it isn't just my country's fault.

You think putting up the wall will keep us from coming.

Stop and think twice because you're just wasting a lot of money.

because no matter what we'll keep on coming.

You need to take another second and think, about your life.

It wouldn't be the way it is,

If other people wouldn't be working hard.

Working hard for nothing in the *maquiladoras* this country put there.

And all for what?

So you can live the American Dream,

To make this the promised land.

Our parents suffered to come to el "Norte."

Sometimes they got caught and sometimes they didn't.

Generations before you, your family went through something similar,

Admit it!

We may have brown skin but we're gonna light the way to success.

So don't even stress, because you can't shatter our dreams.

And you know I'm right when I say,

Santa Fe wouldn't be what it is without some tortillas and beans!

* * *

Quiz #2

1. What was the tower in the desert designed for?

The tower was designed by an agent of the Border Patrol. The tower had a sign that said that if they walked beyond that time they weren't going to be able to survive. They weren't going to find water beyond that point. It had a button next to it so that the people would press it and help would arrive in a while.

2. The Counsul Flores Vizcarra said, "It isn't the desert, coyotes, or the *Migra* that kills the immigrants, what kills them is the politics on both sides of the border."

* * *

We also read Betita Martinez's "Be Down with the Brown." She wrote about organized protests that young Chicano/Mexicans did. They were tired of being oppressed, and they wanted to change that. They were being stereotyped because of their race. The school saw them as drop-outs and the troublemakers. They were walking out of school all together. This happened in different parts of the US, but mostly in California. They were really stereotyped by the gangs, so they traded in their colored bandanas for brown ones to represent their unity. I really liked her article because she described what the people's goals were and what they did to accomplish what they wanted! It showed the strength of the community and how, even though a lot of people doubted them, they still didn't give up.

* * *

One of the last things we did this quarter was watch a movie. The movie was *Born in East L.A.* It was a satire of the immigration issue. Rudy was born in East L.A., and he got deported because he forgot his wallet at his house and he didn't have a way to prove that he wasn't illegal. Then he got sent to Tijuana, Mexico, and he had to find a way to come back. It pointed out the issue of crossing the border, but he made it look funny by coming up with different ways of crossing but he would always get caught! Then we wrote a parody of the song *Born in East L.A.*, which was a parody of "Born in the U.S.A." They were imitating the song's flow and rhythm, but the words were different. This is my song:

I Grew Up in Santa Fe

I grew up in Santa Fe.
Came to a new town.
A million things all around.
Missing my family and friends too much.
Just remembering while I grew up.

[Chorus]

I grew up in Santa Fe
I grew up in Santa Fe
I grew up in Santa Fe
I grew up in Santa Fe

Still a child when I came.
After so many years I'm still the same,
Rolling around in streets with skates and bikes.
Safe in my neighborhood from the oppressing Whites.

[Chorus]

Things changed a little in school.
I had to keep my cool.
Calm down and toughen up.
If not, I would've gotten beaten up.

[Chorus]

Most of my friends went through the same thing.
And now we remember and think,
All the stories we have,
All from growing up, all from the past.

[Chorus]

Living in the shadows of this great city.
And it's such a pity,
That we work so hard and get so proud.
And at the end get shut down.

[Chorus]

So far, so close to my homeland.
I grew up in Santa Fe.
And my culture still in my veins.
I grew up in Santa Fe.

* * *

After that we started the new quarter. We wrote journals about Santa Fe. We were pretending to be explorers in our town. We were supposed to write about things in Santa Fe that we were noticing, things that now had meaning for us.

Journal #1
November 5, 2008

Dear Journal,

Today was the first snow of the season. I thought it was going to snow yesterday because the sky looked so sad, so gray. The wind was whispering that snow was *en camino*. Fall was leaving to rest, until next year. This morning, when I stepped out of my house, I felt the cold winter air touch my face and hands. *Era una caricia del viento.* I knew winter was coming up. On my way to school I remembered last year's snow. It was great helping my little sister make her first snow man! WOW! I wonder what surprises this winter will hold for us.

Everything was the same at school, except for the fact that it was super cold. I hurried to get to class so I wouldn't be outside freezing for too long. When I got to my Latino Literature class, I was listening at our teacher Alfredo talk about our journal assignment. I looked out the window that is in the corner behind Alfredo's desk.

I noticed the sky get darker and darker through the window. Then the snow storm burst out. It was crazy! There were leaves flying all over the place. They were dancing with the snow flakes. That was the sign that fall was turning into winter. *Pero la tormenta termino.* All the signs and the emotion over this fabulous event were over after only a few minutes. The sky cleared again. It seemed as if the sky was giving us a little clue about life. Something new was starting. I guess we'll know in time.

Journal #2
November 9, 2008

Dear Journal,

Today my friend asked me if I could go with him to *El Santisimo* in the Guadalupe Church. That is the most sacred room in the whole church. It can never be alone. So people offer to go there for one hour once a week, so that just in case nobody feels like going, there will be someone there. My friend's parents signed up and go every Sunday from 9pm-10pm. They asked their son (my friend) to go, and he asked me to go with him. I didn't really notice anything in my surrounding until I got out of *El Santisimo*. As we were walking back to the car, I turned back and looked at the Guadalupe Church. The light brown building looked so beautiful in the angle it was in because it stood out in the dark night. The sky behind it was starless, and the weather was perfect. It wasn't cold and it wasn't hot; it was calm. On the way to my house I was looking at the streets of *La Plaza*. The cracked-up sidewalk and the antique buildings. Those streets had never seemed so long. I asked my friend to put down the volume of the radio, so I could listen to the streets with my heart. It was completely silent, but I could hear the history of *las calles de Santa Fe*. Through the streets of *La Plaza* I could almost see the people who had walked through there before. I realized how much I haven't seen and may never see of *La Plaza* that I go to almost every week. *Ese sera por siempre el misteeri de una ciudad que parece estar abandonada durante la noche.*

Journal #3
November 10, 2008

Dear Journal,

Esta Neveando!!!!! This morning I woke when I heard my dad tell my little sister that it was snowing. I got really happy because I like how Santa Fe looks when it puts on its winter coat. I like the view of the snow on the roof tops and on the piñon trees. I got up and went straight to my window. I stared out the window. My neighborhood was covered with snow. It was still snowing when I went to the window, so I watched the snowflakes fall on everything. Then I noticed my brother outside. He was taking the snow off his car with a broom. Kush, kush, kush . . . the sound of the broom taking off the snow made this strange noise. I could feel the cold through my window. I got the chills so I went to my room to find something that would be warm so that I wouldn't be cold during the day. When I went outside to take the snow off my car, I was surprised to feel that it wasn't as cold as I thought it would be. That's one of the reasons why I love New Mexico. Each day's weather is a surprise. I guess that its nickname fits it right because this is the Land of Enchantment.

Journal #4
November 11, 2008

Dear Journal,

In the gathering today I didn't really learn anything new from our speaker, Greg Mortenson. The gathering just refreshed my memory. I already knew that in places all over the world schools get bombed, girls aren't getting the education that they deserve, and that there are a lot of kids that are more privileged and want to change these problems. But what really impacted me was that we are focusing on making the other side of the world a better place when our neighbor countries are going through something similar. Don't get me wrong though, I'm really happy that people are doing this kind of work. It really improves the world we live in. It just made me realize that it's my job to work on this side of the world.

In Mexico and in the southern countries little kids are working in factories so that they can survive. Every day they're out selling candy and cleaning car windows when the cars stop. Girls get killed and disappear every day because they are out late on their way home from work because they can't get another job because they don't have an education. This could be different if they would have a school like we do here in Santa Fe.

Journal #5
November 12, 2008

Dear Journal,

Lusiernagas en una noche sin luna. That's what Santa Fe looked like when I was coming back from Albuquerque. I love how this little city looks. It's always beautiful. It's not in other places. This place is awesome. It looks great during the day and during the night too. During the day there are so many things and color that make Santa Fe look so magical. The mountains that look blue from far away and sometimes have white peaks because of the snow bringing a fresh theme. And the yellow desert with the green *piñones* that show the sense of life. Everything fits together. And at night . . . WOW! Every time I'm coming back to Santa Fe from Albuquerque, Española, or Hyde Park, I love to see the lights of the city. Yellow, orange and sometimes blue street lights decorate the city. And then there are the orange and red lights from the cars that move around and bring a kind of rhythm to the lights. They shine, sparkle, and one by one illuminate the road to my *casita*. I've always wanted to take a picture of that view. Both during the day and during the night. I want to do this so that I can show other people what I get to see every day. *Algun dia lo hare, pero por ahora prefiero contemplar la belleza de Santa Fe.* Everybody should have the chance to see something so beautiful as this city.

Translations

en camino = on its way

Era una caricia del viento = It was gentle touch from the wind.

Pero la tormenta termino = But the storm was over

Las calles de Santa Fe = The streets of Santa Fe

Ese sera por siempre el misteeri de una ciudad que parece estar abandonada durante la noche = That will forever be the mystery of a city that seems to be abandoned during the night.

Esta Neveando! = It's snowing!

Lusiernagas en una noche sin luna = Fireflies in a night without moon

Casita = House

Algun dia lo hare, pero por ahora prefiero contemplar la belleza de Santa Fe = Someday I'll do that, but for now I prefer to contemplate the beauty of Santa Fe.

* * *

Notes: 11/12/08

The kinesthetic sixth sense allows us to react to what is happening to us—like we're able to catch an object when it is thrown at us.

Use other senses for it.

Makes us aware/alert.

Everybody has it.

This is the speed of our reaction.

It is important to listen to all of our senses.

All five (possibly six) senses are important.

Pay attention to our surroundings.

How it smells, looks, sounds, feels, possibly tastes, and what we are aware of.

Code Switching

Code switching is good.

Gives a different feeling to the writing,

It's an important form of expression.

Changes power of meanings in some occasions.

* * *

We also had more reading and more quizzes. These are a couple of them. They were both in November. They were stories from writers that had different styles but were Mexican American. The first quiz is "An Extraordinary Touchdown" by Jorge Ulica; the second one is "Bells of Santa Cruz" by Nina Otero, and the third one is "My Grandma Smoked Cigars" by Sabine Ulibarri.

Quiz: "An Extraordinary Touchdown"

1. Given what you know about fiction, tell as much as possible about the lady as you know.

Could she be a nonfictional character? The fat lady is big and at first seemed nice when she gave the guy the ticket. But during the game she changed slowly. She started being mean to the guy. After the game was over she would kick her victims in the lower backbone if they were cheering for the opposite team. That's how she would try to kill them—the same way she killed her husband. She could be a nonfictional character. Maybe not to that extreme but there could be a woman that hits people because they don't agree with her. And there are people who seem very nice but are actually very crazy people.

Quiz: Bells of Santa Cruz

1. Why do the bells of Santa Cruz have a different sound from other bells?

These bells have a different sound from other bells because those bells were made with love stories. That church didn't have bells, so Spain made bells for them. These bells were made by jewelry that the people in a village in Spain gave them. Dona Teresa put in her cross of gold (necklace), and the ring that her love, Don Angel, gave her before he left to New Spain. This meant a lot to her because they were going to get married when he returned from New Spain, but he was killed in an attack by the Indians. She never fell in love again, and when the Spaniards recovered Santa Cruz and rebuilt the church, they needed bells, and they were made in Castillo where Dona Teresa lived and died waiting for her love.

Quiz: My Grandma Smoked Cigars

1. The grandma smoked cigars because they were a symbol. They represented the boss s*el patron*). After her husband died, she was in charge of everything. She would also leave lit cigars in ashtrays all over the house because the smell reminded her of her husband.

2. The jar of holy water on the window sill was the irony of ironies because everything burnt down except for that. That could represent two things. It could represent religion, the idea that no matter what, evil (hell/fire) can't defeat heaven (in this case the holy water). Or it could also represent the strength of his grandmother, and how she managed to get through every hard point in her life, like her husband's death, her son-in-law's death, and the burning of the house without showing many signs of damage.

* * *

After that we had to write a paper about a dish that represented some part of our community. I chose to write about my family because it's a big part of my community, and a very important part too. The plate I chose was *chile colorado con papas*. I chose this plate because it's a great combination of two very different things, such as both sides of my family.

Chile Colorado con Papas

My family is like *chile colorado con papas*. It's meat with *chile* and potatoes. Both sides of my family are completely different. One side is like *el chile*, and the other is like *las papas*. It seems that they couldn't go together but they do.

The side that is like *chile colorado* is crazy—not crazy like they belong in an asylum but crazy as in fun to be with. They always spice things up with some music, jokes, or simply talking and laughing. They're great, just like the *chile colorado!*

The other side is just like the *papas*. They are so simple, but at the same time there's so much that goes with them. For example, everyone is different, *ninguna papa es igual,* no potatoes is the same. They are unique, every single one of them. And just like *el chile colorado,* they add flavor to the plate!

My family goes together, and one wouldn't be the same without the other. *Chile colorado con papas* is a delicious plate. My family is a small part of my community just like the meal, and it needs the drink and *tortillas, ensalada,* and *postre* (dessert) on the side.

* * *

We did a lot of work this semester in my Latino Literature class. We learned about immigration, the risks and the point of view of the *migra, los coyotes,* and *los pollos.* We also learned about our surroundings, our community, and our town. We learned to be more aware. We also learned about different types of writing. But in my opinion, the most important thing we learned was to discover ourselves as writers.

Works Cited

Acosta Palomo, Teresa. "My Mother Pieced Quilts." *Infinite Divisions.* Ed. Tey Diana Rebolledo and Eliana S. Rivero. Tucson: U of Arizona P, 1993. Print.

Anaya, Rudolfo. *Bless Me, Ultima.* New York: Grand Central, 1999. Print.

Cannon, Jenell. *Stellaluna.* Sandpiper, 1997. Print.

Cisneros, Sandra. *The House on Mango Street.* Vintage, 1991. Print.

Jae-P. "Latin Invasion." *Esperanza.* Univision Records, 2005.

Jiménez, Francisco. *The Circuit: Stories from the Life of a Migrant Child.* Boston: Houghton, 1997. Print.

Keller, Helen. *The Story of My Life*. New York: Dell, 1961. Print.

Langer, Judith A. "Conversations in Literature." *www.learner.org/ workshops/conversations/envisionment/index.html*. Web.

Led Zeppelin. "Immigrant Song." Atlantic Records, 1970.

Luján, Alfredo Celedón. "The Salem Witch Trials: Voice(s)." *What Is "College-Level" Writing?* Ed. Patrick Sullivan and Howard Tinberg. Urbana, IL: NCTE, 2006. [41–57.] Print.

Madrid, Bianca. "Youth Allies for Sustainability." *www.earthcare.org*. Sustainable Santa Fe. Web. 31 Oct. 2009.

Marin, Cheech, writ., dir., and perf. *Born in East L.A.* Universal Studios Home Video, 2003. DVD.

Paredes, Américo. *With a Pistol in His Hand*. U of Texas P, 1970. Print.

Rosa, Alfred, and Paul Eschholz, eds. *Models for Writers: Short Essays for Composition*. Boston: Bedford/St. Martin's, 1986. Print.

Silko, Leslie Marmon. *Storyteller*. New York: Arcade, 1989. Print.

Springsteen, Bruce. "Born in the U.S.A." 1984. *brucespringsteen.net*. Web. 31 Oct. 2009.

Swift, Jonathan. *Gulliver's Travels*. New York: Penguin, 1983. Print.

Tatum, Charles, ed. *Mexican American Literature*. Boston: Harcourt, 1990. Print.

Urrea, Luis Alberto. *The Devil's Highway*. New York: Little, Brown, 2004. Print.

Vygotsky, L. S. *Mind in Society: The Development of Higher Psychological Processes*. Cambridge: Harvard UP, 1978. Print.

White, Edward M. "My Five-Paragraph-Theme Theme." *What Is "College-Level" Writing? Volume 2: Assignments, Readings, and Student Writing Samples*. Ed. Patrick Sullivan, Howard Tinberg, and Sheridan Blau. Urbana, IL: NCTE. 2010. 137–141. Print.

Zinn, Howard, and Anthony Arnove. *Voices of a People's History of the United States*. New York: Seven Stories, 2004. Print.

What Is College-Level Writing? The View from a Community College Writing Center

HOWARD TINBERG
Bristol Community College

Promoting a "Hybrid Literacy"

As Muriel Harris notes in her chapter in this collection, college writing center personnel often develop a kind of practical wisdom related to college-level writing—and about the features in assignments that lead to successful student engagement and writing (183–206). After all, writing center tutors often spend years witnessing student efforts firsthand to engage college writing assignments and meet faculty expectations. As such, writing centers offer researchers a unique window into the everyday life of college-level writing.

Like other multidisciplinary writing centers, our college's writing lab invites students to bring writing from any course for which writing is assigned. As Tony Cimasko reminds us in his essay that appears on our companion website, college writing varies considerably depending on the course or major. Assignments that come to our college's writing lab often vary dramatically, depending on genre, purpose, and intended audience. While about half of the writing comes from the required two-semester English sequence of college writing and writing about literature, the remainder represents a range of disciplines and programs with a concentration coming from the social sciences, including human services. Given the mission of community colleges to provide comprehensive preparation both for entry into the workplace and transfer to four-year colleges, it is not uncommon for students to be assigned substantial writing in courses that are career centered. Such assignments aim to endow students with a kind of hybrid literacy: exposure to the forms of written and spoken communication available in the professional setting while requiring students to demonstrate competence in standard academic prose. By the same logic, it is not unusual for students in the required English composition courses to be asked to write in genres used in the larger working world, such as advocacy pamphlets, trend analyses, and news reporting. Within career areas at community colleges, in other words, writing instruction often places emphasis on what Michael Carter calls "ways of doing" as much as "ways of writing" or "knowing" (388).

What exactly do we mean by "hybrid literacy"? A close look at a single assignment required of students in Human Services 51, Principles and Methods of Interviewing—a course required of students in the human services program—provides a window into this concept. Students often come to our writing lab with this assignment. What we offer here is a tutor's perspective, beginning with the instructor's detail assignment and rubric. We will then consider a complete paper written by a student in response to the assignment. Here is the complete assignment, as given to students:

Human Services 51—Term Paper Requirements

Basically, you can propose to do just about anything related to interviewing skills, methods, or techniques; communications; or the helping process in general. Regardless of what specific topic you choose, the following requirements will apply:

◆ Your topic must be discussed and approved (in writing) by the instructor in advance. A form will be provided for you to submit your topic.

◆ Documented evidence relating your work to materials from the course text, video, lectures, and/or classroom exercises must be presented. At least three other outside sources besides your course textbook (other textbooks, journals,

---

magazine articles, interviews with practitioners, internet-accessed materials, etc.) must also be integrated into your paper. No more than one web-based source can be cited.

◆ The main body of your paper should be no more than seven typed (font size 12), double-spaced pages.

◆ You must format the paper with a separate title page (listing your name, course title, date or semester, and instructor's name) and a separate References list at the end of the paper, per standard APA format. These additional pages are not counted in the seven-page limit.

◆ Any sources beyond your own ideas, thoughts, or comments should be cited following the standard APA format.

◆ A required first version (actually a complete paper in final form) must be submitted by your announced due date. You will not be graded on this first version of your paper. Your ultimate grade will be determined by the required version which you will turn in. Your original version, with instructor comments, must be resubmitted with your final paper version.

◆ Because of the required revision component, composing and saving your paper on a computer or word processor will make your revisions much easier to do. Computers are available on campus at no charge, except for obtaining your own disk on which to save your work.

◆ YOU ARE STRONGLY ENCOURAGED TO MAKE USE OF THE BCC WRITING LAB TO HELP WITH YOUR WRITING SKILLS, and you will be given extra credit on your paper if you do so. Because writing, record-keeping, and case documentation are important parts of all human service work, your grade will reflect your writing and organization skills, as well as the content of your paper.

You are free to develop your own topic, but possible examples for the paper include, but are not limited to, the following:

◆ Researching a specific method of interviewing or communication or helping skills (a traditional "library" or research report)

- Describing and elaborating on the specific technique(s) of helping that a human service agency or program employs, including an interview with an appropriate staff member

- Critiquing the method of helping (formal or informal) described in a book, movie, or other "nonacademic" source and relating it to your course

- Developing a "training manual" or "mini-text" on interviewing skills and techniques for a hypothetical group of inexperienced human services students to use

- If you have any personal involvement in a formal helping relationship (past or present), critiquing your own and/or the other person's performance with specific examples

- Presenting three process recordings (plus background information and supporting materials) that each capture a five- to ten-minute helping interaction between you and a "helped," annotated with your own critical comments

- Participating in and writing up your findings in a special "quality control" project connected to a specific local social services agency (this is a *limited* option available to only a few students; the specific agency is already selected)

Late submission of the first or revised version of your paper will be penalized, as noted on your course syllabus.

Good luck! I sincerely want this assignment to be a positive (and fun?) learning experience for you. Please see me anytime to discuss your ideas and suggestions as to how you will personalize this paper and make it "your own."

This assignment requires students to conduct an interview and then incorporate the interview in some form of extended writing. We'll get to the forms of writing that are possible, but for now it's important to note the instructor's goals here: to demonstrate skills compatible with academic writing (using research in a purposeful way, employing conventional citation format, composing drafts) and with writing in the profession of human services ("record keeping and case documentation," as well as developing listening and observational habits important to the field).

In a separate handout, the instructor produces a lengthy rubric and scoring grid, the latter of which supplements written comments on students' drafts. Somewhat conventionally, the rubric is divided into "organization/presentation," "writing skills," and "content." The first two categories include formatting, grammar, punctuation, and mechanics. Under "content," the instructor lists the following:

- the general theme or topic of your paper or project is weak, or relatively unrelated to this course

- you need to more directly relate your topic or theme to this specific course content or assignment

- [you] need more specific integration of course text, video, lectures, class discussions, and/or exercises

- please include and integrate some additional outside source materials (books, other texts, Internet articles, professional journals, etc.) in your paper/project, as the assignment directions specified

- you must cite and properly document any and all sources (using proper APA format, etc.) that do not represent your own opinions, thoughts, and ideas or generally known facts

- there is no evidence of the required interview and/or textbook that this assignment called for

- more of "you" is needed in the paper or project; too much reliance on outside sources

- offering some opinion(s) or relating this to your own personal experience(s) would help

- a conclusion or some type of summary is needed to better "tie things together" for the reader

- the conclusion or summary you have offered is too weak

- paper is too long for the topic you've chosen; edit down to approximately _____ total pages (main body only—not including title page, bibliography, etc.) to make it more concise

- paper is too short for the topic you've chosen; expand on some of the points

---

Much emphasis is placed on integrating source materials, but it's worth noting the balance that is required between incorporating other voices in the writing and keeping the student's voice and ideas in the paper. While such a balance may indeed be valued in a college composition course, we suspect that it is less likely to be considered important by disciplines outside of English composition and rhetoric. Yet it makes a great deal of sense to find it in a human services course, given the field's attempt to balance an understanding of individual needs with the laws and dictates of a community. To personalize this research process and paper is in some sense to enact the professional attachment and detachment required by the profession.

The list of written genres available for students similarly reflects the "hybrid literacy" expected of the student. Keywords suggest skills long practiced in the academy: "researching . . . describing . . . elaborating . . . critiquing." In fact, each of these choices requires students to engage in all these academically sanctioned behaviors. But note as well the processes and forms associated with the human service agency: "training manual . . . process recordings . . . quality control." It's important to note what students are *not* asked to write: forms and processes of writing existing in the classroom only. Human service professionals, for example, would be expected to make "process recordings" and take careful notes of any interaction between them and the clients served. What students learn here goes beyond "essayistic literacy" to include the practices necessary to assist others in a human services context.

The list of available options given in the writing prompt sends some very strong signals to students about their writing. First, not one size fits all. The list provides wide-ranging options in terms of genre: interviews, critiques, training manuals, process recordings, and something called a "quality control" project, which we speculate may take the form of an internal memo or planning document. Second, the writing topics are designed to bridge academic convention with workplace literacy, as noted earlier. Third, clear efforts are made to link the assignment with the objectives of the course (to master interview methods while at the same time to learn more about the unique demands of the human service environment). Fourth, in at least two of these suggestions, the reader is clearly constructed and realized (new employees at an agency or an administrative staff at a local service agency).

Note the role of the instructor in all of this. Written approval from the instructor is required, presumably with feedback given regarding focus and logistics of the topic selected. Revision is required, and drafts are annotated by the instructor. A rubric is provided that clearly describes the criteria for success. Visits to the writing center are strongly encouraged through the granting of extra credit. We know from having tutored students with this assignment that the instructor comments on a range of features in the writing, from lower to higher order concerns—from sentence-level matters such as subject-verb agreement to matters of organization and appropriate use of evidence. But we also know that the instructor intends that his students become editors of their own writing (the instructor places a stop sign about a third of the way through a draft, having commented to that point, after which the students are on their own).

Student Writing Sample

To assist students working on this assignment, the instructor sent to our writing center a copy of a paper that he deemed successful. Modeling student success, he feels, is an essential step for his students, many of whom haven't written in these forms before. Not afraid to frontload "visions of the possible," as Lee Shulman phrases it, the instructor offers concrete evidence that success is indeed reachable. The paper that we'll be focusing on here is titled "Speaking to Children: A How-To Guide for New Employees of St. Joseph's Home."

At the start, the writer constructs her fictional reader and enunciates her purpose:

> Welcome to St. Joseph's Home. Here at St. Joseph's you will encounter many different types of children. Each child will be different, with each child having his or her own experiences and issues. Because of the uniqueness of each child, no two interactions with a child will ever be the same. However, there are some basic principles that will guide you through each interaction.

Students writing in an academic context face these two central and related challenges: How do they write to a reader who essentially already knows what the writer might give her? What application can the writing have outside the classroom if the writing is done in a form privileged only in the academy (the essay)? These obstacles are not unique to the college setting, of course, since high school writing—which typically requires explication of literature in the form of an essay—features the same limitations. But what is noteworthy here is that the student writer, given license by the instructor, is freed to write to a meaningfully defined reader (new employee at St. Joseph's), in a practical genre (training manual) for a clearly articulated purpose (to train the employee how to work with kids at the home).

From the first body paragraph, the writer establishes an informal and relaxed tone:

Qualities of a Helper

Just as you encounter different types of children, the children encounter different types of staff. Try to imagine, just for a minute, being a resident. What type of staff person would you want to work with? Would you want someone working with you who yells at you? Would you want to work with someone who lies, or who has no patience? My guess is you answered "no" to all these questions. The qualities that children look for and the qualities that are most influential in affecting the behaviors and feelings of others are: self-awareness, cultural awareness, honesty, and an ability to communicate (Ohun, 1997, as cited in Murphy and Dillon, 1998). In short, kids want you to be open, honest, knowledgeable, and empathetic.

Think about someone in your life that you have found helpful. What characteristics of that person did you find most helpful?

As the poet Wordsworth might remark, here we have a man speaking to men (or woman to women). The mode is nearly conversational; the attitude, with its balancing of expertise and tact, engaging. It's hard to underestimate the impact of form and function on the writer's level of comfort here. "Try to imagine . . .": For a moment, the writer assumes two important roles—storyteller and mentor. And it all makes sense, given the rhetorical situation dictated by the purposes of the training manual. Note how even the very academically conventional move of citing sources (technically correct in its distinction between firsthand and second-hand information) fails to disturb the illusion created by the writer. Perhaps if the writer had "played it by the book" and used a signal phrase within her own sentence to introduce the quotation, the effect might have been different. But that choice wasn't made, nor, apparently, was the instructor insistent on that technical point.

The facility with language—not in a showy way but rather in a serviceable way appropriate for an accessible manual—is noteworthy throughout but especially in the following section:

Empathy

> First it is important to understand that empathy is not sympathy. Sympathy is what I feel toward you; empathy is what I feel as you (Murphy and Dillon, 1998). Empathy is not just what I experience as me in your shoes but rather what I experience as you in your shoes (Murphy and Dillon, 1998). You must be able to put yourself in the place of the child. When a child yells at you, or swears at you, or even tries to hit you, it is imperative that you can appreciate where this anger comes from. The child's attack is not personal; do not take it that way.

The balanced phrasing here is noteworthy: "empathy . . . not sympathy. Sympathy is what I . . . empathy is what I . . . yells at you . . . swears at you . . . tries to hit you." The shift in mood in the last sentence lends a quality of surprise and unpredictability. Such a shift would meet some skepticism in a formal piece of academic prose (not to mention the use of the imperative at all). Here, the move works. The writer has constructed a relationship with her reader that allows for a gentle chiding.

Indeed, in the next passage, the writer goes on to assume a limit to the reader's empathy, following that admission up with practical advice:

> Many people find it easy to be empathetic when they share a common bond with the child. It is easy to relate to a child who has lost a parent if you have lost a parent. It is not as easy to put yourself into the place of an abused, neglected child if you have been raised with love and nurturing. To develop empathy in this situation you must do what Murphy and Dillon call

"getting into the role" (Murphy and Dillon, 1998). You must take on the dynamics of the child's experiences and history.

Again, the tone appears quite complex, as does the implied relationship between writer and reader and the function of the writing itself. In contrast with conventional classroom writing, here, genuine information—information needed by the reader to perform a task—is being provided. Far from being acknowledged as already knowing the subject of the writing (as often occurs in classroom-based writing), the reader here is constructed as needing to acquire new and sometimes difficult new knowledge. The writer, then, becomes the repository of expertise, which the reader would do well to attend to:

> Looking at the child as he or she speaks and giving the child your undivided attention says to the child you are listening and understanding (Lovett 1996). You can also convey this attention through supportive sounds, such as "ohhh," "uh-huh," "I see." These sounds show the child that you are listening and they encourage the child to continue speaking. (Murphy and Dillon, 1998)

But where does the writer's expertise in fact come from? In short, why should the reader grant authority to the writer? This is an essential question affecting all college-level writing. How does a student writer construct an authoritative self in the writing? In part, that question is resolved in the design of the assignment itself: Here the instructor has required students to become researchers themselves, interviewing a staff member at an agency. Students are discovering knowledge and not simply relying on others to provide it to them secondhand or thirdhand. Students become empowered as a result of visiting the worksite and incorporating the original research into their writing. In part, also, that authority comes from the form in which the writer is working, the genre, and expected action derived from the choice of genre (Bazerman; Miller; Russell). Certain forms of writing, such as a training manual, carry with them a potential for genuine action outside the getting of a grade.

Of course, authority is granted as well when the writer demonstrates, in the writing, a depth of usable knowledge, as happens in this passage (in a section labeled "Giving Directions"):

When giving directions you must be very clear. There can be no ambiguity in any direction that you give. One way to ensure your directions are clear is to break down the direction into small pieces. "John, go take a shower" might be a clear enough direction for you. However, that statement might be too much for John. An alternative could be, "John, it's shower time. Here are your towels. I'll get your hygiene supplies and bring them to the shower." This strategy of breaking down tasks can be useful in every aspect of your job.

Implied in this set of directions is knowledge of the home's residents. If this were a formal research paper, the writer might simply have offered an exposition of the residents' history and challenges. But the form and purpose of this paper, as we've described them, necessitate a different take: to use that knowledge for the purpose of training new staff members. That said, there can be no doubt that the writer understands these children (including their nonverbal communication):

If you see Tommy sitting in the living room with his shoulders raised, tapping his foot and his eyebrows lowered, you should understand that without speaking a word Tommy is telling you that he is angry and anxious. If you know her mother is not coming to visit this weekend, and you see Betty walking down the hall, shuffling her feet, she is screaming for you to go talk to her.

As we read through this document, it becomes evident that the self being constructed here is not merely the writer's but the reader's as well. Clearly, a level of self-awareness is required to work productively in this environment:

Often, when addressing behaviors or giving consequences, the child will get upset and begin to yell or act out. At this time you must "respond not react" (Applestien, 2000). You must remain calm, always tending to your own actions and reactions. This use of self is important to remain calm and focused on the child's behavior (Murphy and Dillon, 1998) . . . Open your ears, your eyes and your mind. Listen for not only what is being said but the true meaning behind it. Stay alert to any hints the child might give you as to underlying issues.

Suddenly, we are reminded of the task given to a student who must write in a college literature course about a poem or novel: Pay attention not only to what appears on the surface but also to those meanings that are merely implied. Indeed, an important feature of college-level writing, whatever the discipline, is to give evidence of critical reading, whether of a poem, a lab experiment, or a historical or psychological event. Here, of course, the reader is exhorted to turn her critical gaze both on herself and her charge. Conventionally academic behavior is translated to the workplace.

Conclusion

The writer has exhibited facility with translation throughout the piece, providing a strong model for her reader to emulate. It is possible to write well in school and in the workplace, simultaneously. A college-level "hybrid literacy," as we have been calling it, can be achieved. The possibilities start with an assignment that encourages (1) genre exploration, especially genres not found in the classroom; (2) research relying on original sources; (3) the creation of a realistic reader or audience; (4) a functionality in the writing that transcends the giving and getting of grades; and (which follows from all these components) (5) the possibility of an authoritative writerly self in whom we have every reason to believe and not merely to judge.

Works Cited

Bazerman, Charles. "Systems of Genres and the Enactment of Social Intentions." *Genre and the New Rhetoric*. Ed. Aviva Freedman and Peter Medway. London: Taylor and Francis, 1994. 79–101. Print.

Carter, Michael. "Ways of Knowing, Doing, and Writing in the Disciplines." *College Composition and Communication* 58.3 (2007): 385–418. Print.

Cimasko, Tony. "A Little More Relevance." Sullivan, Tinberg, and Blau. Web.

Harris, Muriel. "Assignments from Hell: The View from the Writing Center." *What Is "College-Level" Writing? Volume 2: Assignments, Readings, and Student Writing Samples*. Ed. Patrick Sullivan, Howard Tinberg, and Sheridan Blau. Urbana, IL: NCTE. 2010. 183–206. Print.

Miller, Carolyn R. "Genre as Social Action." *Quarterly Journal of Speech* 70 (1984): 151–67. Rpt. in *Genre and the New Rhetoric*. Ed. Aviva Freedman and Peter Medway. London: Taylor and Francis, 1994. 23–42. Print.

Russell, David R. "Rethinking Genre in School and Society: An Activity Theory Analysis." *Written Communication* 14.4 (1997): 504–54. Print.

Shulman, Lee S. "Visions of the Possible: Models for Campus Support of the Scholarship of Teaching and Learning." *Teaching as Community Property: Essays on Higher Education*. San Francisco: Jossey-Bass, 2004: 203–17. Print.

Assignments from Hell: The View from the Writing Center

MURIEL HARRIS
Purdue University

S amuel Johnson may have originated the phrase, "The road to hell is paved with good intentions," but from the perspective of a writing center tutor, the road to hellishly bad papers is often paved with well-intentioned assignments. Okay, not as pithy as Johnson's aphorism, but much student writing can and does go astray when assignments prompted by good intentions are not well constructed. As a result, students coping with such assignments often head for their campus writing center looking for clarification, assistance in interpreting what the assignment is about, or feedback about whether their draft meets the requirements of the assignment because they aren't sure what the assignment has asked them to do. In some cases, such students haven't learned to read assignments. Without that ability, they aren't likely to be able to produce college-level writing. But while some students falter with college-level writing because they can't read the assignments critically—a topic for another day—there are other students who can't respond appropriately to the assignment because it isn't well constructed. In a workshop handout I developed long ago, I used to call these poor examples of assignments "AFHs: Assignments from Hell."

Unfortunately, as someone who has spent many years tutoring in a writing center, I am not alone in realizing that tutors have to deal with far too many sadly deficient papers that are the outcome of weak assignments. Derek Owens describes this problem as follows: "To put it bluntly, many—and probably a great many—of the writing tasks our tutors and clients discuss are train wrecks. Too many of the assignments they work on are unimaginative, uninspiring, predictable, and ill designed—overly vague or excessively picayune" (153). Owens, a writing center director, vents a level of frustration that afflicts writing center tutors, too— and for the same reason. Many of the "train wrecks" that tutors see in writing centers are the result of poor assignments—muddy, overly long, confusing, or vague. Often, assignments can be all of these at once. In my years of sitting with students at tutoring tables, I have also heard students' confusions, frustrations, and misunderstandings, and I have seen what hinders their ability to respond appropriately to assignments. In the belief that bad examples are good teaching tools (in the sense of seeing specific things to avoid), I offer this introduction to what can go astray with assignments as seen from my perspective as a tutor and writing center director.

Anticipating Teacher Expectations

It's important to begin this discussion with the understanding that many students read assignment sheets and interpret them through the filter of their previous experience with English teachers— a vitally important variable that current instructors, of course, cannot control. Although an assignment may be clear, strong, and focused, students will often shape their reading of assignments based on what they think is hiding behind the words on the assignment sheet. Even if they've been told what the criteria are for grading, they are prone to interpreting such information in idiosyncratic ways. Some of their misperceptions about grading arise mysteriously during their years in secondary school and carry over into college, and some don't originate until they enter college. It's hard to pin down exactly how such grading schema get embedded in students' minds, but they are there and they need to be recognized when we read student papers.

Much of this confusion comes from students' internalized beliefs about "good writing." One idea that prevails in secondary schools is the conviction that longer papers are always better. They have no doubt heard endless lunch table chatter about sets of papers being graded by tossing the pack down the steps to see which reached farthest down. The ones at the very bottom, of course, get the A's. Thus, if there isn't some general expectation of length given in the assignment, some students who write long, rambling papers are simply adhering to the rule that "more is better." A well-intentioned teacher who doesn't want to set what she or he sees as arbitrary or artificial limits may inadvertently allow some students to pad, add more, or drift off into whatever else can fill more pages because such students are working on the assumption that they are enhancing their grade. When comments come back about unneeded digressions, unnecessary information, or wordiness, these students may assume some other mysterious criterion is in play.

There are other expectations that lead students astray, such as assuming that they are required to be creative or to have "fresh new ideas." Many students, in fact, are adamant that some teacher, somewhere in the past, spelled this out unequivocally as the single, lone criterion for all good writing. Students who perceive the absolute need to come up with "new ideas" struggle to be original, but their time and effort generally would be better spent elsewhere. A variation of this is the student who is making a strong connection between a text and his or her analysis but looks hopelessly at the tutor and shrugs: "She's a smart instructor. She knows that already, so I can't just repeat what she knows."

Since contradictory myths can coexist comfortably, some students have told me that the obvious lack of attention to grammatical correctness doesn't matter since, in high school, they were graded "on ideas," not grammar. Another prevalent myth is not that "ideas," creativity, or length matters but that grammatical correctness is the predominant standard by which papers are judged. A paper might be poorly organized and in need of significant clarification and development, but if all the commas are there in the right places, the student "knows" it will get a good grade. This will be where that student expends the most effort. A superb example of this was a student who once appeared at a tutorial and showed me a draft that had a long succession of short, clipped sentences, arranged in staccato fashion on the page. I assumed we'd want to talk about sentence variety, but the student had no interest in that topic. Finally, after much discussion, he explained that because he feared comma mistakes (a deadly sin instilled somewhere in his past), he kept his sentences short.

Most often the unspoken assumption about the importance of grammar among some students derives from dreading that the teacher will slash and burn her or his way through the paper, wielding a red pencil in a hunt for any possible error (sometimes graphically described as "bleeding all over my paper"). Tutors know how pervasive the fear of grammatical mistakes is and have to struggle with students who come in half an hour before the paper is due because they want it proofread, thereby ensuring a decent grade. Such students are not anxious to know how the tutor reads and interprets the paper or in listening to discussions that will lead to insights into how to develop ideas. Despite some instructors' grading sheets that indicate that grammatical correctness will count only 5 or 10 percent, such students continue to seek out the writing center to be sure there are no misspellings, no punctuation mistakes, or heaven forbid, a fragment (shudder!). Any conversation the tutor tries to initiate about clarity, organization, or some other obvious problem with the paper is unimportant for such students. They *know* what counts. Attempting to debunk these myths and misperceptions with a class can provoke an interesting discussion and help to disperse the unspoken notions about writing that often inhibit student growth and learning. Teachers can mitigate these mistaken perceptions that can flaw papers by providing students with clear and succinct grading criteria and then discussing those criteria in some detail. When an instructor works intensively to clarify what actually does determine the grading process, more students will respond to those criteria instead of what they think the hidden criteria are.

Clarifying Those Standards

Although teachers do attempt to indicate criteria for how papers will be graded, generalities, abstractions, and ambiguous word choices often weaken communication between students and teachers. It is also very confusing if there is no indication regarding which parts of a grading rubric are more important than others. In this case, students are given no guidance as to where best to expend their energies. Consider the following example (slightly altered in topic from the original but not in the rest of the wording):

Analyze the problem of gender in *Hedda Gabler* and *Uncle Tom's Cabin*. Remember to consider other relevant factors such as race, social conditions, economic class, and author's nationality. I expect clean, tightly written, interesting prose that is free of literary jargon. If your thinking is sloppy, the paper will be sloppy, and I grade accordingly.

In the instructor's mind, the student's "thinking" is important, so the main point of the paper has to be something that is not "sloppy" and is "cleanly written." But what's "clean" writing or "sloppy" thinking? What does the student focus on for the topic? What is the instructor's hierarchy for what is more important than some other element in the assignment? The assignment stresses gender initially, but there is that added note about "other relevant factors." So must the point to be made be in the context of all those other concerns? Will a student be able to craft a topic sentence or introductory paragraph that's unified if the instructor expects all of these factors as part of a "tightly written" essay? Or does "tightly written" possibly mean that critical thinking will tie it all together? Or that the paper will develop its points briefly and cogently? Since there's no word limit, how long would a "tightly written" paper be? And given the known variety of human taste as to what constitutes "interesting prose," what would that mean? What makes prose interesting? Any group of instructors could have a serious two- to three-hour discussion that might lead to a definition or a consensus of opinions.

Delineating criteria is so complex that a number of other problems can creep in when we indicate how papers will be graded. When the various aspects of a paper are determined numerically (e.g., 20 percent of the grade will be determined by how thoroughly the topic is researched), students whose goal is simply to get through a course are likely to browse through the numerical level of various criteria and focus on what will get them the most points. Sadly, a teacher who has emphasized researching, for example, may not want correct formatting of the bibliography to consume the student too much, so that may be rated as merely 10 percent of a grade. But the unspoken assumption in the teacher's mind is that she wants her students to learn how to document sources. The lackluster student may choose to ignore the requirements of a works cited list because it's not worth it to him or her. Tutors often try to talk to students about how they might revise some aspect of a paper only to hear students say that in terms of grading, whatever the tutor had suggested they work on is not important. Such students don't see the need to labor over all aspects of a piece of writing. They don't feel the need to craft a well-written document. They simply go for the points that count the most (especially if they've procrastinated in getting the assigned paper done and a chemistry test is looming on the horizon). Setting up criteria that are weighted in importance is clearly a way to help students see what truly is important and what is being stressed in any particular assignment, but they need to hear that the whole set of criteria is important and that even something that will only count for 5 or 15 percent is important, too. A paper is a composite of many writing abilities, and it helps to explain that they all must work together to form the satisfactory paper.

Students care about their grades, and giving them understandable, concrete criteria, as complete as possible within reasonable limits, can result in papers more consciously aimed at the effective, clear, literate prose we are trying to help them learn to write.

Stressing Form over Substance

There are yet other aspects of grading standards for assignments that can cause problems. Kim Ballard, the writing center director at Western Michigan University, reminds us how overemphasis on formatting can consume too much of students' energies and writing time:

> I've noticed that instructors who struggle with assignments tend to write assignments based on how they want a docu-

ment to look—which is crucial to them—not on (a) the writing goals the task is supposed to help students grapple with or learn or (b) the way the task fits into a particular discipline.

For example, the assignment will be full of details about margins, fonts, and length. The teachers may have a full chart of the types of mechanical errors they don't want to see in the paper. Yet the assignment may say little about how the writing task supports

(a) the goals of the course

(b) the abilities the assignment is intended to help students learn

(c) the history of "errors" or "poor writing" that the teacher has experienced and has written his or her assignments against.

Certainly it helps to clarify format if that is among a teacher's goals. And visual literacy makes format important. But, again, there is a need to clarify the hierarchy of which criteria are more important than other criteria. Too many details about how a paper should look broadcasts by the sheer percentage of instructions on the page that this is what really counts. This is evident in the following example from a high school world history class that had been studying the Incas:

Answer the following essay question using the documents provided in class as the main source of evidence.

Question: What happened at Cajamarca?

Format: Essays must have such things as double-spaced, 1-inch margins, 10 point font, name in left corner, and class period in right corner of first line, title on second line, no longer than two pages, stapled in upper left corner.

Language: Essays are to be written in formal English observing the stylistic conventions outlined in Strunk, William Jr., and E. B. White, *The Elements of Style*. The library and writing center should have copies. Formal written English is serious in tone; frivolity is out of place. Pay particular attention to the following:

a. History is always written in the active voice and past tense.

b. Slang is not appropriate.

c. Avoid personal pronouns.

d. Use quotation marks only around the actual words in sources and not as a means of emphasis.

e. Do not use parentheses in a short paper.

f. Numbers under 100 must be spelled out.

g. The first time a person is named in a paper the full name must be used; subsequently his last name should be used.

Running Off in All Directions

When constructing a writing assignment, instructors with excellent intentions sometimes don't stop at stating the focus in terms of the purpose, audience, topic, and so on. They also want to offer students questions to think about and heuristic prompts to help develop the paper. All those questions and suggestions for directions to go in can congeal, in students' minds, into a hydra-headed quest that could lead in multiple directions. Such overloaded assignments wind up confusing students who don't know what to focus on. Here, for example, is such an assignment (as elsewhere, this is a slightly altered version):

I want you to reflect on the exhibit by [the photographer], in the exhibit on brutality in Tibet. Please visit the URLs below to find out more about the photos and photographer [two websites are provided]. Then, visit the following websites that focus on other atrocities [two more websites are listed].

Do a search on your own to find out and look at photos that describe other attempts at suppressing the local population. Think about the other countries we discussed in class. Then, you are to write a short paper on your thoughts on [the photographer's] exhibit knowing what you now do. Why did you like or did not like the exhibit? What did you think of the mixture of color and black and white images? The sizes? Why do you think the United States did absolutely nothing to stop the brutality when they knew exactly what was happening, when we rush to other country's aid for lesser problems?? Why do you think that these things STILL continue throughout the world? Your report is to be single spaced, with no bigger than 10 point type!!!

If that instructor wanted a well-defined topic, would a writer focus on the visual aspects of the exhibit? The global situation in relation to what is pictured there? The United States' response to that country's plight? The human condition that causes people to commit such brutality? The likelihood that humans are prone to brutality toward each other?

In her article about assignments, Irene Clark discusses a classic example of an assignment from a first-year college writing course that also illustrates the trait of charging off in all directions at once. Clark offers the following example of such an assignment:

In the popular television show *Star Trek: Deep Space Nine*, what do the writers and producers wish to suggest about society? Do the different races of aliens have analogous groups in our contemporary society? What image does the show provide of law enforcement? Of racial tendencies? Of moral leadership? What ethical message does the show give its viewers?

Clark then goes on to explain the problems with such an assignment and the various student interpretations of it:

This assignment prompt is likely to be confusing to students because it contains too many questions. Unaware that one of the generic requirements implicit in many college writing assignments is to construct a thoughtful position on a problematic issue, novice students are likely to answer all the questions without connecting them, resulting in a disjointed and undeveloped essay that lacks focus and unity. Some, aware that a writing assignment constitutes a type of "test," might even retell the plot of various episodes of the show, as a means of demonstrating knowledge, a phenomenon that is particularly characteristic of responses to assignments concerned with literature or film. In contrast, more knowledgeable students would be able to read through the poorly defined assignment—or at least be able to ask pertinent questions about its goals. These students would realize that it is really the first question that the essay must respond to, and that the subsequent questions were designed to prompt the development of content.

Jeanne Simpson succinctly offers the following advice: "Don't blather on and on. Write a set of good instructions, just like instructions for assembling a bicycle, because that's what the rhetorical task really is." Clarity, brevity, and specificity are goals to keep in mind when composing that most difficult of writing tasks—writing a good assignment.

Assuming Student Knowledge

We know and acknowledge the diversity of our students' backgrounds, linguistic abilities, cultural knowledge, and other differences. But sometimes that awareness recedes when an assignment is written, and problems can arise when the instructor forgets to consider whether the class shares common knowledge. This is particularly evident when some of the students in the class come from immigrant backgrounds, are nonnative speakers of English, or are international students. Sometimes, the age gap between the instructor and the students shows up in assignments about things students can't really know much about. Other times, the whole class has different cultural assumptions or are from different ethnic, economic, or geographical settings. Consider the topics for following three assignments (the whole assignments are not included here, just the topics):

1. American attitudes about mixed race schools have come a long way from the old segregated schools to present-day integration. Think of other major changes in Ameri-

can attitudes and actions over the last ten or twenty years. For example, think about how explicit films have become or how attitudes towards teen pregnancy have changed. Another example is how Americans have become so much more conscious about their health. Select one major change that you're interested in and discuss a personal experience of yours in noticing this change or that relates to it.

* * *

2. Much has been made about the homogenization of America due to big box stores, chain restaurants, the elimination of regional differences due to these influences, etc. The short stories we've read in class about work and how it was defined years ago show us how different our views of work are now. Do you see a similar homogenization in how we earn our livings now as compared to the types of work our grandparents did? Discuss.

* * *

3. [For an ESL class's first assignment] Describe your first day in the United States and a few of the differences you noticed between your home country's culture and the culture that prevails in this country.

The third example assignment is a frequent one. It assumes the writer has knowledge the reader lacks and therefore should be a fairly easy assignment in a beginning ESL class. When I met an ESL student in a tutorial who had a similar assignment, she needed help in finding a topic. She was a conscientious, motivated student but was utterly lost in terms of thinking she had sufficient awareness of the culture of the United States to make any valid comparisons. She could describe a number of vivid memories of her arrival at a US airport, but she had no knowledge of whether what she noticed was typical of such airports or whether it reflected anything about our culture. For example, among the memories she shared with me was one about the shops in that airport. She couldn't decide if the expensive, elegant shops there were indicative of US stores in general, if US airports cater primarily to wealthier people, or if the shops hoped to sell to tourists passing through (that is, is the assumption that most US travelers who fly from one place to another are able to buy such items?).

The first two assignment summaries require, among other things, some knowledge of the culture of the United States in the recent past. Moreover, the term *homogenization* in the second assignment assumes that students understand in some specific way what is meant by that term. Consider, for example, an immigrant student now in college, struggling to leave the confines of a neighborhood where other immigrants from her or his country have congregated and where, if *homogenization* has any meaning, it's that the stores and people mirror the culture she or he came from. But this does not only apply to those new to this country. At the large midwestern land-grant institution where I tutored, some students who came there from very small towns or farms had little close acquaintance with highway exits where restaurants and hotel chains line the streets leading from the off ramp. Their parents might have welcomed the arrival of a box store fifty miles away, but it caused little or no change in their towns. What can *homogeneous* really mean to them?

Assuming Shared Views

When constructing assignments, we tend to work from what our own values are, what interests us, and what we hope will interest students. But biases have a nasty way of sneaking in so that students who don't share such views are likely to respond to what they think will please the instructor, the "give them what they want to hear" axiom. That can result in writing that is not genuine because students are smart, pragmatic, and interested in their grades. They play to their audiences, or, if they choose not to, they may decide to argue their way out of the viewpoint embedded in the assignment and hope the instructor will honor that. Consider the following assignment:

> Select two ads from current magazines or TV ads and analyze them in terms of how they manipulate our emotions and how they overlap or coincide with the values of the power structure in our society.

Not every student in whatever class was given that assignment may be busy rebelling against the "power structure in our society." It's likely that some students hope their college degree moves them up the ladder of success toward entry into whatever power structure the instructor perceives to be out there. For those students who view the college degree as a successful entry into the jobs they want, there's no conflict. It would be an interesting bit of research to survey first-year college students to see how they actually view the ads they read, particularly when they're interested in learning how to update their iPods and iPhones, which cell phone to buy and what its plan offers, what the latest advances in cosmetics are, and which hot new band's music they need to buy or download.

Intimidating Novices

In some courses, instructors may want their students to write up to the level of the authors they have been reading or use those authors as models. Modeling is a long and honored tradition, but asking students to write to models can, depending on the model, require extensive examination of the model's writing and also extensive practice in writing to that model. It's not clear how, without substantial preparation, students will respond with the level of writing called for in the following assignment:

> Read Ahren's "The Great American Football Ritual" and Cleaves's "Blood Lust." Using these essays as models for your own writing, choose and define an activity (such as a sporting event, proms,

IMing friends) as a symbol of some aspect of American society. Make sure your essay reveals more than just something about the activity; it should cause the reader to think critically about the society which produces and enjoys that activity.

Under the rubric of "intimidating novices," I include those assignments in which the instructor's word choices can cause the ordinary writer to quake before the expectations laid out for him or her:

Show in a precise manner how Dillman's definitions and relationships agree with your own. Use vivid, concrete examples to illustrate your understanding and to expand your reader's insight. You are expected to be in control of your subject, to think with analytical skill, not to pad with unnecessary words, and to display a mature understanding which synthesizes class work, discussion, and reading.

We can also intimidate students when we revert to the jargon of our field but haven't spent class time explaining terms we are comfortable with to students who do not yet have those terms in their lexicon:

For this five- to seven-page formal paper, write an extended definition of the global village drawing on the essays read in class. Select at least two of the readings to use in your analysis and close reading. Choose readings that are in conversation, that are intertextual. From the texts, generate your own original claim, your own argument about how the writers imagine, deploy, use, and define the conjoined world we now live in.

Your paper by necessity will include a very brief synopsis of your chosen readings and will demonstrate your ability to close read each text. However, this assignment asks more from you than a compare-and-contrast paper. Remember that this paper is about your claim, your analysis, your ideas about what your readings are arguing, doing, critiquing, saying, or showing. Also remember that you are not just summarizing or repeating what your writers have written. You will be expected to critically analyze your texts and persuasively articulate how they reveal something significant about the globally connected world in which we live. Keep in mind your exigencies and your stakes for your paper.

A Potpourri of Other Problems

When I asked the writing center people who read *WCenter*, the listserv for those involved in writing center work, about the types of assignments they and their tutors found problematic for students, they provided a variety of examples. Some noted that students are especially bewildered by assignments that are so short they lack almost all the necessary information. Carol Mohrbacher offered a great example of this: "One of our grad tutors tried to help a student who brought in an 8 1/2-by-2-inch strip of paper that simply said, 'Write a four-page essay using descriptive language.'" From a tutor's perspective, it is difficult to know if one- or two-sentence assignments are prompted by good intentions, mistaken perceptions about students' preferences, or lack of knowledge about what an effective assignment is.

At the opposite end of the spectrum is this assignment, recommended to me for this essay by Pamela Childers, that would require the writers in the secondary school class in which it was assigned to be masters of incredibly concise prose in order to respond to the topic within the required two pages:

Causes of World War I Essay

If you could narrow down all of the many causes of World War I, which event, incident, development, or person would be most responsible? In a well-argued, well-written essay of at least two full pages in length, define based on what you have learned in class and from your textbook, what one factor contributed most to armed conflict. Explain why your choice was more decisive than all of the others and choose at least three less decisive factors and explain why your choice played a more pivotal role in creating war. This exercise will take the place of a traditional class exam and is based on pages 272–327 in our textbook. Each student will present their opinions to the class during our second meeting next week (the day the papers are due) and will submit their papers at the end of class. The successful 2- to 3-minute presentation of your ideas will account for 20 percent of your grade on this project. Please see the accompanying rubric for the presentation component of this project.

To further compound the question of length of assignment are those that run on for a page or two—or sometimes three, usually single-spaced. (For an example of such an assignment, see Appendix 10A.) While there may be students in these classes who will wade diligently through the dense prose, some will falter after the first few paragraphs and fail to notice some important part of the assignment buried in a long paragraph on another page.

While some instructors note that reading an assignment closely should be a skill students must learn, others offer different perspectives. In a listserv discussion for writing program administrators, *WPA-L*, Ryan Skinnell offers the following:

> I think many students, myself included, believe assignments should function like directions. They should tell me the basic process and what to expect as a final product. Too much information can be as daunting as too little. I work under the assumption that the test is supposed to be the writing, the thinking, and the revision—not reading the prompt. Therefore, in my opinion, assignment sheets should have as little information as possible while still encouraging the type of writing I hope to get.

Trixie Smith noted that in a previous institution she worked at, some students who came to their writing center never had written assignment sheets because one faculty member always gave his assignments orally. Some students only had confused recollections of what the assignments entailed.

Kathryn Nielsen-Dube offered a different problem—the topic that causes students personal discomfort. The example she offered was as follows:

> About two years ago a female student arrived in the writing center with an assignment from her FYC course. The instructor was a young, male adjunct. The assignment was to write a personal descriptive essay about a body part (of their own) that they did not like. Students were to state what the body part was and describe it effectively with plenty of descriptive details; then, the assignment went on to ask students to explain why they did not like the body part using examples of how it affected them physically and mentally. I will never forget the affect of this student as she told the tutor (with me present) how horrible the assignment had made her feel.

Finally, another topic designed for all the wrong reasons led Jeanne Simpson to offer the following:

> Okay: worst assignment ever. A teacher assigned her twenty freshman students in a summer class (six weeks) to write a ten-page documented paper on penguins. Why? Because she had determined that there were apparently no penguin papers on file among the frats (this was before the Web shops where papers are easily bought and downloaded). The sole criterion for the topic was to avoid plagiarism. There was no discernible purpose, other than to prove an ability to write a documented paper. Worse, the instructor had not consulted with any librarian, so the library was suddenly overrun with students wanting all there was on penguins. Nothing was put on reserve. Books vanished and students despaired. My only consolation (I had to tutor one of her students) was that this teacher would to have to read twenty unavoidably wretched papers. But she would, of course, blame the students, never imagining that her assignment was the real problem. A complete waste of time.

Conclusion

My hope is that, viewed from this perspective on types of assignment problems, along with some examples, problematic assignments can be signposts for what we want to avoid. (See Appendix 10B for a set of guidelines summarizing some questions to ask when constructing assignments.) There are other ways to ensure that an assignment will enable students to write effective papers. Some instructors suggest previewing the assignment with writing center tutors or the directors in the writing center on their campus, or even with the class; others create the assignment together with the class. Numerous methods exist and are limited only by the creativity of the teacher.

Reminding ourselves of positive ways to ensure good assignments is, of course, important, though I continue to also believe in the power of the bad example. Seeing how something can malfunction—and looking at how to make it work—can provide much-needed clarity. As we create assignments, we can recognize that there are hurdles, mistakes, omissions, lack of clarity, and mistaken assumptions that we are all prone to, which can result in papers we don't want to read and students don't want to write.

Appendix 10A

Example of an Overly Long Writing Assignment

DEFINING THE VIRTUAL NEW WORLD OF THE INTERNET

In this course you have been reading, writing, thinking, and exploring different conceptualizations and articulations of the Internet. This should now lead you to thinking more deeply and critically about what this new space is, might be, and could be through the lenses of history, science, popular culture, and science fiction. Some have defined it as an imaginary space in which computer users travel when surfing the Net, and as such it is a far more generic term for the Internet than just the World Wide Web. The concept of the Internet may also include that imaginary place where online communication takes place and a virtual world which provides a heuristic to explore our inner beings. The ideal, the myth, the interstices of reality and imagination is, however, much more, and you may or may not agree with some of the conceptual formulations that are made.

This cyberspace is amazing, complex, full of potential, scary, imaginative, physically elusive, and so, finally, what is it? Is it the land of the free and the home of anyone and everyone willing and able to jump in? Is it the land of the lost and the home of the dark, dangerous, and deviant? Is it a place where dreams are lived, an avenue of commerce, a place for humans to reach across the globe to make contact? Is it all of the above? All of the writers you have read so far have offered their hopes, fears, praise, and cautions for cyberspace. They recognize that the technology and its concomitant stories are important, part of what is to come, and ultimately a reflection of ourselves as a culture, a world, a species. All of the writers then are trying to map, to imagine, and to define cyberspace. But think also about the inter-textual spaces that lie between these authors, especially the as-yet unexplored potential they haven't treated. In turn, inform your discourse with some understanding of the persona and stylistic turns used by the writers you have read.

For your five- to seven-page formal paper, you will write an extended analytical definition of the world/space of the Internet, drawing on the short stories and essays read in class, plus class lectures and discussion, but focus most on the readings. Select at least two of the readings to use in your analysis and close reading. Choose readings that are in conversation. From the texts, generate your own original claim, your own argument about how the writers imagine, deploy, use, and define this space. Think about the following questions when you sit down to make your claim as they may help you come to a conclusion that you can then argue:

◆ Do the writers imagine and define the Internet similarly? How? Why is that important?

◆ Do the writers conceive of this space radically differently? How? Why is that important?

◆ What are the writers' arguments? What role or function does this virtual world play in life, in culture, in the text? How and what does the virtual world tell us about the world?

- Explore the recurring motifs, and draw on arguments that move through logos, pathos, and ethos for appeals.

- Do the writers critique the creations that the Internet has made spaces for? What are the consequences or dangers of virtual worlds on the Internet?

- How are these virtual worlds described? Materialized? Used? Why is that important? Consider the imagery employed. Are there paradoxes in the imagery that further the argument?

- Ultimately, what can you argue with your writers' arguments about the virtual spaces? Why is that important? Be self-reflexive.

Your paper by necessity will need to include a very brief synopsis of your chosen readings and will demonstrate your ability to closely read—and attend to—each text. However, this assignment asks more from you than a compare and contrast paper. Remember that this paper is about your claim, your analysis, your ideas about what your readings are arguing, doing, critiquing, saying, or showing. Also remember that you are not just summarizing or repeating what your writers have written, but that you understand what they offer. You will be expected to critically analyze your texts and persuasively articulate how they reveal something significant about the virtual world that exists on the Internet. Keep in mind the exigency for your paper.

Also keep in mind the course outcomes as you work and write. Your claim should be supported with valid evidence from the readings, directly quoting and citing the texts when necessary. You are required to include other outside sources (at least two, not to exceed five) including other texts read for this sequence, scholarly journals, and credible websites, newspapers, and magazines. To summarize, you should be prepared to make a solid and relevant claim using a coherent, complete, and clearly organized analysis of your readings by situating it within a particular and meaningful context, with clear evidence to support your argument.

Audience

At base, you are writing for an audience that includes a general academic community, which includes your instructor, your classmates, and the authors of the essays we have read. You should imagine a larger, more inclusive audience. Keep in mind that your audience is varied in many ways, including academic experience and familiarity with our readings, so you'll need to consider what information each type of reader will need to make sense of your essay. Another good way to think about your audience is to imagine the publication in which your essay could appear such as the reading contexts anthology or a website or scholarly journal.

Format

This assignment is a formal, academic paper and should follow the manuscript guidelines outlined in the course policies:

- ◆ Formal title page, appropriate title for your paper
- ◆ One-paragraph audience analysis
- ◆ Five to seven pages, typed, double-spaced, with MLA citations, stapled
- ◆ Bibliography, correct and current MLA format

Appendix 10B

Guidelines for Developing Effective Assignments

(THUS AVOIDING HELLISH ASSIGNMENTS THAT
UTTERLY CONFUSE, FRUSTRATE, AND LEAD
STUDENTS TO THE DEPTHS OF DESPAIR)

Muriel Harris, 2010

Writing an effective assignment is a very challenging rhetorical task, but the questions to ask ourselves can lead to assignments that truly engage our students and help them produce strong writing. Listed here are some questions to ask yourself about each assignment.

1. **What are the goal(s) and purpose(s) of the assignment?** Articulating your goal(s) to yourself beforehand will guide you as you structure the assignment.

- Do you want your students to learn how to describe concretely?

- Do you want them to learn to write for different audiences?

- Do you want to assess their knowledge of content presented in class?

- Do you want them to practice critical reading and responding to texts they've read?

- Do you want them to learn the art of writing persuasive documents?

- Do you want them to sharpen research skills and practice citing sources correctly?

2. **What will your students need to know to complete the assignment effectively?** Students write better papers if they have the skills necessary to write the papers.

- Have you checked the vocabulary used in the assignment? Are all the terms clear to all the students? Are there any vague generalities such as "have a tight organizational pattern"? Is the level of generality or specificity explained?

- Are you sure you haven't assumed a common background, view of the world, or knowledge of our culture that some students lack?

- Is the wording on the assignment sheet scary for the uninitiated? Does it contain intimidating phrases such as "carefully summarize and articulate in a clear and precise manner" or "synthesize in a mature way what you have learned from your class work, lectures, and readings"?

- Do your students have the necessary skills (library research? critical reading of complex texts? computer skills? practice in interviewing people?) to complete this assignment successfully?

- Have you indicated stages of drafting and possibilities for revision? Will you be reading any drafts-in-progress and offering feedback?

- Would your students benefit from seeing models for the genre of writing expected?

3. **What will your students be graded on?** Students focus more of their energy on what they think you will be grading for.

◆ Does the assignment clearly indicate a hierarchy that lists what the criteria are? Be specific about length of the paper, deadline, formatting concerns, and other requirements, but don't make these instructions dominate the assignment sheet. State any hierarchy you may have for grading by listing which writing skills are more important and which are less important.

◆ Does the assignment sheet spend too much time emphasizing the less important criteria?

◆ Have you spent time discussing your students' perceptions regarding what really constitutes an A paper?

◆ Have you considered having a class discussion about what students think the assignment is asking for? You can ask what they think the goal is, what they think the standards should be for good papers, what previous teachers have stated as qualities of a good paper, what additional assumptions they have (the longer, the better? having "new" ideas? being grammatically correct? playing to what the teacher thinks?).

4. **Does the assignment offer clear choices for the student?** Students who have to write about topics for which they have no interest are not likely to care very much about what they write.

  ◆ If you offer questions to think about, is it clear that students don't have to answer all the questions?

  ◆ Have you either offered a topic that will interest all of the students or offered choices of topics so that all the students can find one that engages their interest?

5. **Is the assignment sheet a visually clear document?** Students may lack the ability to read and comprehend long blocks of closely spaced print with no spacing or subheads to indicate various aspects of the assignment and may miss some of the information you are including.

  ◆ Is the assignment reasonably short—but not so short that relevant information is missing?

  ◆ Is the assignment sheet written so that students do not have to wade through a page or two of dense prose to figure out what the assignment is?

  ◆ Does the assignment sheet use headings and subheadings that make the assignment more readable?

Works Cited

Ballard, Kim. "Re: Problems with Writing Prompts?" Online posting. *WPA-L listserv*. Arizona State University, 6 Jan. 2008. Web. 6 Jan. 2008.

Childers, Pamela. "Re: A Bad Assignment?" Message to the author. 22 Jan. 2008. Email.

Clark, Irene. "A Genre Approach to Writing Assignments." *Composition Forum* 14.2 (2005): n. pag. Web.

Mohrbacher, Carol. "Writing Assignments?" Online posting. *WCenter listserv*. 11 Nov. 2007. Web. 11 Nov. 2008.

Nielsen-Dube, Kathryn. "Writing Assignments?" Online posting. *WCenter listserv*. 11 Nov. 2007. Web. 11 Nov. 2008.

Owens, Derek. "Two Centers, Not One." *Marginal Words, Marginal Work? Tutoring the Academy in the Work of Writing Centers*. Ed. William J. Macauley Jr. and Nicholas Mauriello. Cresskill, NJ: Hampton, 2007. 151–67. Print.

Simpson, Jeanne. "Re: Care to Share?" Message to the author. 11 Nov. 2007. Email.

Skinnell, Ryan. "Re: Problems with Writing Prompts?" Online posting. *WPA-L listserv*. Arizona State University, 5 Jan. 2008. Web. 5 Jan. 2008.

Smith, Trixie G. "Writing Assignments?" Online posting. *WCenter listserv*. 12 Nov. 2007. Web. 12 Nov. 2008.

III

College-Level Writing and the Basic Writing Classroom

"Botched Performances": Rising to the Challenge of Teaching Our Underprepared Students

CHERYL HOGUE SMITH
Kingsborough Community College,
City University of New York

In spring 1997, Barry Munitz of the California State University (CSU) chancellor's office issued to all CSU presidents Executive Order 665 (EO 665), which, in part, detailed the prerequisites for entry-level math and English classes. One clause in EO 665 (II.B.5) led to the CSU trustees' decision that, by fall 2007, each university in the system must reduce remedial course offerings to just 10 percent of regularly admitted students. The universities could still, however, offer remedial classes for all students who qualified as "special admit" students—students who do not academically meet the conventional university admissions guidelines but who are conditionally admitted to the university because they have special needs or because they are from underrepresented or underprivileged backgrounds. In preparation for the reduction of remedial courses, between fall 1998 and fall 2007, students who entered a CSU needing remediation were to complete that remediation by the end of their first academic year or they would be dismissed from the university and readmitted only when they reached junior status at another academic institution. Because the demographics (and therefore special-admit populations) are different at each university in the system, EO 665 affected each of the twenty-three state universities differently. And, as a basic writing instructor for ten years at CSU Bakersfield (I'm now at Kingsborough Community College, CUNY), I can attest only to how this order affected CSU Bakersfield (CSUB).

Bakersfield is situated at the base of the San Joaquin Valley, where farming plays a large role in the community. Hence, CSUB has a large number of students from the migrant-farm population attending the university. It's not surprising, then, that many of the students are from first-generation, low-income, minority families, a large number of whom test into basic writing classes, which are officially regarded as "remedial" courses. Athletes, former gang members from Los Angeles, and students from middle-class homes in the area also are among those who tested into basic writing classes. Regardless of their backgrounds, most of my basic writing students entered CSU Bakersfield because they qualified as special-admit students—not because they met the standard university requirement in academics. The special-admit population at CSUB hovers around 36 percent, so EO 665 does not greatly affect the course offerings; they are, for the most part, able to offer basic writing classes to the numerous students who need them. They still lose some students to the one-year-success rule, but CSUB is at least able to place those who cross their threshold into the appropriate classes.

With the very act of setting the mandates restricting remedial writing, the CSU trustees answered the question of what they feel constitutes college-level writing—a question so complex and multifaceted that NCTE is publishing this second volume of *What Is "College-Level" Writing?* to explore its nuances and implications. For, if EO 665 leads to the mandate that remedial writing must be reduced at all the California State Universities, the CSU trustees established that basic writing classes do not belong at the university and, consequently, that students who need such classes do not write at the "college-level." My first response to these trustees was admittedly flippant: "If students are in my college classes, then the writing that goes on in my classes must, by definition, be at the college level." But my second response was more considered: In spite of such an official declaration by the CSU trustees of what college writing is or isn't, I wanted to demonstrate that these basic writing students *are* characteristically writing at what must be considered the "college-level"—not because they occupy a seat in my class but because they produce the kind of writing that is evidence of the kind of thinking most college instructors would identify as college-level thinking.

CSUB offers sequence courses for first-year students: The students who enroll in a sequence-course section move with their class and instructor from one quarter to the next. The first class of the sequence is, obviously, the lowest level of the first-year composition series, and students do not receive baccalaureate credit for taking this credit/no credit class, but they do receive units toward financial aid. Because this class does not receive baccalaureate credit, the State of California defines it as a "precollege" course, which, again, might make the argument that such basic writing classes do not belong in college because the students who take these courses are not writing at the "college level": If the universities are unwilling to give students credit for taking these courses, then why should the writing that students do in them classify as college level? The answer is thus: Those who say that students in basic writing classes aren't performing at the college level have probably never taught a basic writing course and consequently have no notion of the levels of thinking basic writing students must do. Basic writing classes— and, by extension, the writing done in these classes—should not be deemed "precollege," but, instead, the students who take these classes—some of the hardest-working students on any college campus—should get credit for doing so. Let me tell you why.

I was fortunate that, because of the sequence courses at CSUB, I was able to keep my students for an entire academic year (three quarters). My students may have been a little rough in their first composition course, but they usually met the demands of each writing course in the sequence. To demonstrate why I believed my students were writing at the college level, I provide excerpts from two students who were in my classes for three consecutive quarters. These students were two of my least effective writers when they entered college, but their stories, shown through excerpts of their writing over the span of one academic year, might give readers of this chapter a glimpse into the levels at which my students are capable of thinking.

Firme

"Firme" was a quiet student during group discussions but quite vocal in small groups. By the end of the first quarter, he began to open up to the whole group, and, by the end of the second quarter, he was an active member of the class. Here is an excerpt of Firme's first attempt at college writing:

> (Written in September. From "Misconceived," in response to Brent Staples's "Just Walk on By")

> Staples is viewed in many different ways. For example people may think staples is a thug. They see that his race is African American and without knowing him they automatically think thug. People get scared and when they see him they do not want to get near him because they are afraid he might do something. The people are so afraid that whenever something bad occurs they automatically think of staples and blame him for something he did not do. Other people believe staples is a bad person because of the way he dresses. They look at his style and think bad person. Appearance is no reason for people to start judging you the wrong way. People view staples as a criminal and it is not fair because they do not know him. They should talk to him first and find out what a good person he is before they start talking all this things about him.
>
> People perceive me as the opposite person that I am, which is a gangster, drug user, and a criminal. . . . I get a lot of people that believe I am a gangster that goes around looking for problems, gets into fights and in shootings.

Aside from the ambiguous statement that makes him sound like the very "gangster, drug user, and a criminal" that he is not, Firme completed the assignment at a satisfactory level. He closely read and evaluated Staples's "Just Walk on By" and was able to effectively discuss how he encountered some of the same problems. He moved beyond mere summary and was able to analyze Staples's essay and make connections from Staples's life to his own, which is evidence of his critical thinking ability.

At this point in my discussion about Firme's progress as a writer, I must step back from Firme and address the general question of how writers who lack a command of sentence mechanics and who exhibit awkwardness with sentence phrasing can possibly be considered college-level writers. The question of what constitutes college-level writing in relation to surface-level errors made by basic writers needs to be addressed, especially since my discussion here about my students' writing will undoubtedly raise that issue.

To begin this conversation, I first consult the work of Mina Shaughnessy, who is often credited with establishing basic writing as a field of academic study. In *Errors and Expectations*, Shaughnessy describes how basic writers tend to make certain characteristic errors, and they make those types of errors often, which can deceive an instructor who equates number of errors with skill level. For example, nine incorrect uses of "there" for "their" wouldn't actually count as nine errors but one—because the student is repeating the same error. So papers filled with numerous correction marks don't necessarily mean students are overwhelmingly grammatically deficient; usually, students just need to learn one or two rules and apply them to their writing.

Shaughnessy does not address issues of style, but her discussions of marking grammar can lead instructors to the conclusion that they need to be wary of marking stylistic preferences as grammatical incorrectness. In the first excerpt, Firme makes relatively few mistakes: He confuses a "this" for "these," fails to capitalize "Staples," uses "you" (a cardinal sin in most college writing), and uses "that" instead of "who" when referring to a person (a rule many sophisticated and published writers break). The other "errors" are stylistic. The excerpt is fluent; it's just stylistically unsophisticated. When we talk about "college-level" writing, we have to remember that there is entry-level college writing and exit-level college writing, the latter of which should be stylistically advanced. Yet we often grade our students on stylistic choices as though they have written something incorrectly. At CSUB, the first-year composition courses focus on content and fluency. Not until the upper-division composition class, where instructors assume sentence-level proficiency, does style become a primary focus of the class. Certainly, composition instructors, including basic writing instructors, tackle style in all levels of their composition classes, but instructors must be careful not to overwhelm students by pointing out "errors" that are not mistakes at all.

Shaughnessy tells us that "so absolute is the importance of error in the minds of many writers that 'good writing' to them means 'correct writing,' nothing more" (*Errors* 8). And, since many basic writers care a great deal about "correct writing," premature editing and the focus on "incorrectness" gets in the way of their ability to use writing as a means of exploring ideas. Basic writers struggle to learn the generative value of writing in large part because their focus on surface errors continually interrupts their ability to think productively about what they want to say. John Dewey believed that "insistence upon avoiding error . . . tends also to [the] interruption of continuous discourse and thought" and stated that privileging error can only lead to self-consciousness based upon a "negative ideal" (186), an "ideal" with which some basic writers are all too familiar. As compositionist Sondra Perl has argued, "Editing [early in the composing process] intrudes so often and to such a degree that it breaks down the rhythms generated by thinking and writing" (333). Both Dewey and Perl recognized the danger of premature editing, which, for those basic writers who focus on error, compounds their difficulty in expressing ideas.

This is not to say that surface-level errors or awkward sentencing is something basic writing teachers should ignore. Instead, we should recognize that sentence fluency cannot be mastered in the single term or year that students spend in our composition classes. They need more time and much more practice to build their sentence-level skills (which is just one reason why writing in other classes and disciplines is so important). Sentence fluency isn't valued any less by a basic writing instructor than an instructor who teaches rhetorically and stylistically advanced students, but experienced and knowledgeable teachers of basic writers know that, for our students to succeed in college, they must learn to use writing to generate thought, explore ideas, and advance their thinking—tasks that at first should take priority over mastering surface-level errors and infelicities.

The irony with teaching writing is that we have historically focused on surface-level correctness with basic writers when what they desperately need to learn is how to generate and access their thoughts through writing. We recognize that high-level students can benefit from critical thinking instruction, while we overlook that basic writers need it even more. It's also ironic that some instructors often "forgive" surface-level errors in papers that demonstrate sophisticated thinking because the errors seem inconsequential to the writing, while the same instructors will denigrate basic writers for similar errors. In fact, many instructors feel basic writers need to master surface-level errors before any thinking instruction can begin. Thus, the students most in need of writing-as-thinking instruction are instead in danger of learning more about fragments and run-ons.

Yes, the first writing sample of Firme's is simple and has errors, but, with sustained effort, readers can see in Firme's writing that he understands the Staples's essay and is able to effectively discuss how events in Staples's life mirror his own. Because Firme is providing some analysis of Staples's text, he is clearly demonstrating his ability to think. And *that* is what makes Firme's excerpt, completed in the third week of classes during the first academic quarter, an example of entry-level college writing. Of course, his writing wouldn't pass an exit exam at any institution of higher learning, but Firme isn't at the end of his academic career; he is at the beginning, and the excerpt qualifies as beginning-level college writing.

Subsequent work done by Firme shows him making significant progress as a writer, as this excerpt suggests:

(Written in November. From "*The Fools Run*/Bravery")

The Fools Run also shows a moral type of bravery. There are two types of morals presented in this story. A positive moral is revealed when Kidd, LuEllen, and Dace take a risk and write to the cops for the child pornography they found in one of the houses they broke into. They were brave enough to come forward and write to the cops no matter what the consequences may have been. "After the operation is running, we'll write to the cops. Tell them the truth. That we broke in, what we found. I got a copy of their whole subscription list, print it out and include that, say we found it with the magazines" (Sanford 172). They called the cops because the lives of innocent children were being destroyed with child pornography and did not care if they ended up in jail; they knew that was the right thing to do. The negative moral of the story is that Kidd, LuEllen, forgot about they morals and values because they did whatever it took to get the money, even breaking into houses and stealing.

Firme demonstrates in this excerpt that he is able to better control his language than in his September essay and is able to write effectively about a full-length text. He again moves beyond summary and incorporates analysis into his essay. Up to this point in class, we had not discussed incorporating quotes or explaining a writer's use of quotes, but Firme does both in this excerpt. The writing still contains some errors, but readers can see Firme is beginning to be comfortable with his own writing.

The following excerpt was written three weeks into Firme's second quarter at CSUB:

(Written in January. From "Bad News")

For the first few weeks after my grandfather past away I would have flashbacks of all the fun things my grandfather and I would do. My grandfather and I would go to the park and play and do all kinds of fun things. My grandfather was the one that thought me how to ride a bike, how to fly a kite, and how to play baseball, and much more. I loved my grandfather. My grandfather was like a second father to me. My grandfather would take care of me when my parents would be working and we would have a lot of fun together. I remember that before my grandfather left to Mexico he promised me that he was going to teach me how to ride a horse and take care of all kinds of farm animals at that time I was very excited and could not wait until that day came. Unfortunately, I did not know that was the last time I was going to talk to him and that what he promised me was never going to happen.

The prompt that I assigned for this essay is odd because I removed all the rules, save one: Students had only to evoke an emotion from their reader. I removed all elements of form and structure and pretty much said "all's fair." I wanted students to shed their typical notions of what a "college essay" looks like (à la David Bartholomae's "Inventing the University"), and, by revoking all the traditional rules, I am able to let students focus on their thinking and avoid what Ken Macrorie calls *Engfish* (11) or Shaughnessy calls *written Anguish* ("Diving In" 235). This is the only assignment in all three quarters for which students are not required to write about something they've read. (Note: While my focus here is entirely on the question of what constitutes college-level writing, I also recognize how reading skills critically affect students' ability to write. I believe that students can never outwrite their reading abilities, but the constraints of this chapter do not allow me to discuss this aspect of college writing. See Patrick Sullivan's discussion of the importance of reading in a college writing classroom in this collection (233–253).

Through this assignment, students are concentrating on their thinking, and they are writing without the fear of doing something "wrong." Most students have great success with this essay (a victory instead of the usual defeat), and that success opens them to greater risk-taking in writing for future essays. The January piece shows Firme's comfort level with a personal narrative, and, while his essay is not as sophisticated as some others I received, it shows that Firme does have a command of the language. His next excerpt is from the end of the same quarter, seven weeks later:

(Written in March. From "Technology")

Even though technology has brought positive things to the lives of humans there are still those people who believe technology has only brought negative things to the world. Some people believe that technology has not been used for peaceful purposes, but for negative purposes. "The development of weapons of ever-increasing destructive power has progressed throughout history, from clubs to nuclear weapons" (Technology par 1). Many people find this to be a major problem with technology, and believe technology is only affecting us. . . .

Technology has also brought a series of negative thoughts to people because technology is very expensive; therefore, with newer technology our nation will be in some kind of debt. "Because technology is very expensive only people with money have more opportunity to acquire technology which enables them to acquire even more wealth" (The Social Impact of Technology par 3). Advancements in technology may be occurring each and every day, but because it is so expensive the majority of people do not have access to it. This becomes a problem because that advancement in technology the people cannot afford may change their lives.

While this example shows a backslide in Firme's command of the language (a phenomenon I will discuss later in this chapter), readers can still see a progression in sophistication of sentence structure: Firme moves beyond the simple sentence structures (e.g., incorporating the conjunctive adverb "therefore" and using more subordinating and coordinating conjunctions) and begins to control his punctuation. His writing is still clumsy and may suffer from some logical gaps in the argument, but attentive readers can still manage to understand his ideas.

Firme's last excerpt was written one full quarter later, at the end of the academic year:

(Written in June. From "Gay Marriage")

The topic of gay marriage has most of the nation's votes against gay marriage, but not all. For decades people have come up with many reasonable arguments that have helped them ban gay marriage in almost all of the United States. One common argument that is used against same-sex marriage is simply the definition of marriage. According to Rauch, a correspondent for the *Atlantic Monthly* and writer for *National Journal*, "Marriage is defined as the formal union of a man and a woman typically recognized by law, by which they become husband and wife" (Rauch, 2004, p. 13). This argument uses the definition of marriage to help them show that marriage is and could only be the union of a man and a woman and not two males or females. One of the most popular arguments against gay marriage is morality and God's will. People opposing same-sex marriage argue that marriage is sacred; and is a violation of biblical beliefs and allowing same-sex marriage would be a sin. Should Gay Marriage be Legal (1996) declares that "marriage is already threatened by divorce, and that if gay couples were allowed to marry would set a bad example for children and could spell the downfall of our society" (Should Gay Marriage be Legal, 1996, p. 2). This argument tries to convince people that allowing same-sex marriage will be a disaster for everyone. Another major argument against same-sex marriage is that marriage benefits cost money; therefore, if gay marriage became legal gay couples will be entitled for tax breaks and federal benefits. In Should Gay Marriage be Legal (1996), "It declares that this will eventually place an additional burden on an already strained federal treasury and taxpayers will end up subsiding a lifestyle that many disapprove" (Should Gay Marriage be Legal, p. 2). . . .

I believe that any person that is in love should have the right to marry who they are in love even if it is from the same gender. Rauch mentions, "marriage is for love and we love each other; therefore, we should marry . . . the commitment to care for another for life is the love which exceeds all others, the love of another even oneself" (Rauch, 2004, p. 13–27). This is explaining that everybody that is in love should have the right to marry even if it's from the same sex. Why are people making this so difficult? All gay people are asking for is for a different and better kind of life. Rauch (2004) "A life with all the goods that marriage brings to a couple all they are asking really for a better kind of love" (Rauch, 2004, p. 59) and not to bring harm to society as everybody believes. Allowing people from the same sex to marry is simply equality, pure and simple. Nobody should be able to deny adults the power to marry who they love.

This excerpt comes from an essay at the end of the academic year in a class that fulfills the general education requirement. It begins with Firme's discussion of what the opposing side believes about his argument. He starts his essay by defining the word *marriage*, demonstrates that he understands the complexities of the term, and provides sources that help him explain these complexities. He also provides three very smart points against gay marriage, which shows he understands this issue well because he couldn't have provided compelling counterarguments had he not understood the overall dispute surrounding the issue of gay marriage. In his second paragraph, he shows evidence that he is thinking critically about the issue when he asks the question "Why are people making this so difficult?" and answers with, "All gay people are asking for is for a different and better kind of life." Regardless of what readers believe about this issue, they can't deny that Firme really does ask the best question of all—"pure and simple." Granted, he does still have difficulty incorporating his sources, and readers have to do some of the work to completely see where Firme is going with his argument, but with a little effort on readers' parts, they can surely see what Firme is trying to say.

David Bartholomae believes that basic writing "is not evidence of arrested cognitive development, arrested language development, or unruly or unpredictable language use" if we give basic writers "credit for the sentence [they] intended to write" ("The Study of Error" 254). In other words, we can often tell what basic writers are *trying* to say, as we can see in the June excerpt. Firme has shown that he can write thoughtfully about a difficult topic, even if he still makes errors, struggles with conveying his thoughts, and lacks sophistication in style. Even so, this excerpt shows Firme has improved vastly from the first quarter, when he was writing mostly simple sentences and was writing only about a familiar issue. Any first-year instructor would be delighted with such progress. Nevertheless, the last excerpt also demonstrates that Firme's writing skills have still not caught up with the sophistication of his thinking skills, which may interfere with his ability to write clearly in more academically rigorous classes. Firme passed this course with the lowest passable grade, which is more a testament to Firme's mental acuity than his ability to write up to the level of his thinking. But pass first-year composition Firme did, and, with consistent practice and by continuing to frequent the writing center, Firme should be able to continue to improve his writing skills as he moves on to more taxing thinking and writing challenges in other classes.

Mari

"Mari" was a quiet student who grew up in a very small migrant-farm community. She was a quick learner and was always willing to take risks in her writing. This first excerpt was written three weeks into her first academic quarter:

> (Written in September. From "Example Essay," in response to Brent Staples's "Just Walk on By")

> "Women are particularly vulnerable to street violence, and young black males are drastically over represented among the perpetrators of that violence." (Staples, para. 6). Here he tries to understand why people specially women are treated him as a mugger. He just tried to ask them a question and they ran or cross the street just so they don't passed him. Women always tried to cross the street when ever they are walking at night and they see a man or men in the street. They don't do it unintencialy they do it to protect them self. I as a woman admit that whenever I am walking alone and I see a man that is coming toward my way I cross the street because I feel unsafe.

When I first read Mari's essay, I was worried about her sentence-level skills, but I could easily see that her thinking was well-reasoned and persuasive. Like Firme, Mari also moves beyond summary and, in fact, demonstrates her critical thinking ability when she takes a position that challenges the author's own argument about the racism of white women. That is, Mari moves beyond a conventional racial-profiling reading of this text and instead tackles the problem of the vulnerability of women, arguing that women walking alone on the streets at night should be afraid of *any* man they encounter on the streets. Since this was the first essay of the quarter and since Mari took a challengingly critical stance on Staples's essay, I believed that Mari's writing skills would improve greatly over the next two quarters because her thinking here was so strong.

Below is an excerpt of Mari's last essay of the same quarter, written seven weeks later:

> (Written in November. From "Friendship, in response to *The Fool's Run*")
>
> True friends are the people that can be trusted, and the ones that are always there for each other. LuEllen is considered to be a true friend of Kidd because she was a person that was there, helping him with his job. Kidd saw her as a true friend because he did everything he could to save her life when they were both in danger of getting killed. Dace was also a good friend of Kidd because he was also there helping him on his assignment; however, died at the end. This incident made Kidd feel angry and sad because he lost his close friend. One day Kidd had the doubt that probably either LuEllen or Dace would betrayed him, but then he thought clearly and came to the conclusion that they would never do that. LuEllen might be a thief, but she could never betray him. Kidd stated "I'd never think that LuEllen was the problem. I trust her" (Sanford 115). This quote demonstrates that Kidd did trust LuEllen, and that he knows that she would never betray him. We can see that they were always together; in good and bad moments, just like true friends are.

Even though Mari is still struggling with verb tenses here (something I fear she may always struggle with), her writing ability has clearly improved. Like Firme's, her syntactic structures have become more complicated and varied, and she provides fairly precise cohesive markers in and between sentences. She has more to say about her topic, and, through well-formed, more elaborated sentences, she develops her ideas more fully. Mari has certainly improved over the span of seven weeks since the first paper.

Mari's next paper was written three weeks into the second quarter of her academic career:

> (Written in January. From "American Dream," the creative writing assignment)
>
> When I decided to reach the American dream with my two kids I never thought how hard it would be to survive in a place where you get pointed, laughed at, and some times spit at. Sometimes I have to eat my pride because I do not have a voice and I could be reported back. Working in the hot sun or in the cold weather in poor condition is hard, but I think of my kids and I do not get tired. Sometimes we do not have time to eat because we are told that people depended in that food. I know that people depend on our work, but we also eat these crops as well we buy it too but we are not animals. Why are we treated as animals? I even think that animals are treated better than me.
>
> I love my four-wall house because it's better than where I come from. I have a curtain that separates the side where our mattress is laying. The kitchen is small but has enough food for a two times meal that my kids and I live. The house does not have a lot of decorations, but it has the necessities that we as people have. The bathroom is not inside of the room but it's just outside. The water when taking a shower is cold but every day we are clean.

When I received this essay from Mari, who, like Firme, was among those students who struggled the most at the beginning of the previous quarter, I immediately recognized that she had learned from the styles of two essayists she had analyzed the previous quarter: She took on the same matter-of-fact, nonapologetic tone and process analysis format of coyote Tomás Robles in "Ferrying Dreamers to the Other Side," and she mimicked the repetitive, unforgiving, and highly descriptive style of Jo Goodwin Parker in "What Is Poverty?" She took ownership of others' approaches and created a style all her own. Whereas Firme chose to write about something personal, Mari, who was only nineteen and had no children, chose to combine factual elements of her family's history with imaginative aspects she invented. In this excerpt, readers can see that Mari has an astonishing awareness of her audience, as is shown by her control over the pathos of her essay. She could have written a scathing commentary about the poor conditions immigrants face in the United States, but, instead, through her vivid yet depressing descriptions (e.g., "how hard it would be to survive in a place where you get pointed, laughed at, and some times spit at" or "I even think that animals are treated better than me"), her ultimate appreciation of the opportunities she has in the United States comes through. The descriptions and emotional appeals work, regardless of the incorrect punctuation and syntax. The risks that Mari took in this essay were enormous, yet her willingness to take such risks—whether she had succeeded or not—embodies how we want our students to perform in college. Incidentally, I asked Mari to revise her entire "American Dream" essay and submit it to the William Saroyan Essay Contest sponsored by the Fresno Public Library. She won third place in the college division.

The next excerpt is from a paper written at the end of the same quarter, seven weeks later:

(Written in March. From "Do You Feel Replace by Technology?")

Toffler also argues that "No one—not even the most brilliant scientist alive today really knows where science is taking us" (Toffler 382). This makes sense with this because every day the new technologies grow, and we never know what to expect next. People do not just say that we need the technology, but every day we also ask for more. Everyday devices do work that normally humans can do themselves, as well as resolving some of the problems that we humans have.

People, when using technology, do not think of the harm it causes to humanity and the environment. This is because technology is all over the place from earth to space. The technology is getting better, but the problem is that we are affecting the place that we are living in. Toffler explains the problem that earth faces with all of the technology when he says "This psychic pollution is matched by the industrial vomit that fills our skies and seas" (Toffler 380). New technologies involving gas, oil, food, etc. are affecting the air and the place that we need.

As with Firme, Mari's language becomes strained when she is discussing topics she knows little about. Her arguments are sound, and she uses her research effectively, but the voice is stilted. She understands what Toffler is saying in his essay, and she tries to take his point further by showing that although we have technology, we always ask for more, even if we don't know what we are asking for. She tries to make the distinction between technology that is created for the sake of convenience and technology that is created to help solve problems. She gets all of this from Toffler, but she has difficulty developing her ideas and showing her readers that she really did understand Toffler.

In the second paragraph, if readers take out the word *psychic* from Toffler's quote, Mari's paragraph makes more sense. She wanted to discuss the dangers of technology to "humanity and the environment," and she wanted to use the Toffler quote as evidence. She clearly did not understand how *psychic* fit into the quote, so she ignored the word completely. The paragraph does show that she is considering the dangers of technology compared to the conveniences of technology, but she has trouble making her point. But her point, if readers look at what she is trying to say, shows evidence that she is able, nevertheless, to argue her position and substantiate her thesis.

Finally, the passage below is from Mari's last essay of her first year at CSUB:

(Written in June. From "Death Penalty: Execution Is Needed for the Worst of the Worst):

Innocent people sometimes are in the row of executions, this is why the punishment needs to end. Even though that the punishment is killing many innocent people it is also a cruel and unusual punishment. Henry J. Reske article talks about the punishment been cruel an unusual for Robert Alton Harris "he was executed for kidnapping and murdering two 16-year-old boys so that he and his brother could use their car for a robbery" (Reske, 1992, p. 26). When he was notify that his sentence was to died in a gas chamber, his lawyer argued that the execution was one of the cruelest punishment.

In the other hand Bennett Capers in his article argues that the electric chair is a cruel punishment as "Warhol's use of this particular execution as a referent in his Electric Chair paintings thus asks the viewer to contemplate who is sentenced to death in this country" (Capers, 2006, p. 249). Here the author want to point the chair that gave death to Julius Rosenberg and Ethel Rosenberg were his painting of Andy express the torture of the sentence people to the chair.

In addition the Australian Nursing journal comments the lethal injection that takes place in the city of California, according to The Lancet, which argued the cruelly of the punishment and how it violates the eight amendment because the action is cruel and unusual. Like in the case of Harris that was killed in a gas chamber the Fierro v. Gomez, which argued that the punishment is cruel and unusual. In the American Journal of Law and Medicine mentions the case of Fierro v. Gomez which argues that the eight amendment is been violated when this punishment is apply to a prisoner. Now the court decision says, "this decision clearly states that California may no longer use the gas chamber to execute inmates sentenced to death" (1994, p. 344). This is because doctors proved that the process took long and the pain was severed. In the same way that Harris died and suffer the two boys when they were kidnap and murder suffer.

I chose these paragraphs because they were among of the most troubled in Mari's essay. She struggles with the language in her essay, and this excerpt certainly exemplifies that. Some who read her prose will undoubtedly say that the paragraphs are a jumbled mess and clearly can't be the work of a student who is ready for college. Yet Mari is the same student who, ten weeks before, won third place in a countywide, college-level essay contest. The ideas in the paragraph make sense, if we give Mari "credit for what [she] intended to write." She is identifying three methods of execution that some critics have described as "cruel and unusual": the gas chamber, the electric chair, and lethal injection. She is trying to say that the manner in which we kill people fits the definition of cruel and unusual. She uses sources to help support her claims that these three methods are cruel and unusual, but she does so ineffectively. The excerpt is unified in its objective, but it falls apart when she tries to incorporate so many sources into one argument.

I do think that I should point out that the class in which this essay was written was a class designed around one large research paper at the end of the quarter. Therefore, much of the class focused exclusively on research and incorporating that research into an argument, including how not to plagiarize. This paper is 35 percent of the students' final grade, and only 10 percent of the paper could use direct quotations; the remainder of the sources had to be paraphrased. Part of the problem that both Mari and Firme had with their final papers seems to stem from not wanting to plagiarize. Students have difficulty paraphrasing others, and this is especially so when they have to incorporate those paraphrases into their own argument. So not only is this the first essay Mari has written in which she had to use multiple sources in order to provide evidence supporting her argument, but it's also the first essay in which she had to do so mostly in her own words, *and*, like Firme's excerpt, this writing represents the opposing side's arguments. The complexity of this assignment increased significantly, probably too much so in one quarter for Mari. She clearly struggles here as the academic demands become more rigorous and as she confronts new and difficult rhetorical situations. This struggle becomes visible in the incoherence of her prose. Ultimately, she may not quite understand some of the direct quotations she used and therefore cannot write about them effectively (see Patrick Sullivan's chapter in this book for a discussion of students writing about readings they don't wholly understand), but there is a clear attempt to explain three modes of killing a prisoner and to establish them as cruel and unusual. So, whereas the writing seems to show a backward slide instead of progress, the thinking still comes through. She is grappling, but she is still thinking.

The writing in both Mari's and Firme's final essays clearly appears to undergo a syntactical setback, but, when discussing this very phenomenon of students' writing getting "worse," Mike Rose explains that

> as writers move further away from familiar ways of expressing themselves, the strains on their cognitive and linguistic resources increase, and the number of mechanical and grammatical errors they make shoots up. Before we shake our heads at these errors, we should also consider the possibility that many such linguistic bungles are signs of growth, a stretching beyond what college freshman can comfortably do with written language. In fact, we should *welcome* certain kinds of errors, make allowance for them in the curricula

we develop, analyze rather than simply criticize them. Error marks the place where education begins. (188–89)

Basic writers enter classes deficient in grammar and mechanics, and, of course, we must address these surface-level weaknesses. But if we want our students to progress beyond "correct" but simplistic writing, we must help students understand (and remind ourselves) that sometimes writing that appears "worse" is actually a sign of growth. Ultimately, students must be willing to take risks and accept some syntactical setbacks as they struggle to convey increasingly difficult ideas.

The last paragraph in Mari's essay on the death penalty is difficult to understand, and many who read it will say that Mari does not write at the college level. I would argue, however, that Mari's first attempt at an extended research paper that incorporated several sources and that had to include paraphrasing did, in fact, show that she was thinking critically about the cruel and unusual aspect of the death penalty, and her thinking is an indication of progress. The next time she writes a research paper, she will undoubtedly improve her ability to effectively communicate her ideas as she develops her skills with paraphrasing and incorporating texts into her own arguments. Surface correctness and fluency will develop as she gets more practice and experience. There is no reason to prevent a writer like this from tackling more rigorous college-level work because of a lack of surface fluency.

Conclusion

Clearly, then, it's unfair to punish students with lower grades when they turn in writing that looks inferior to prior work when that inferiority derives from their attempt to meet the demands of a more challenging task than they've ever tried to meet before. This is especially true if we give assignments—as we should—that tax the thinking of our students to the point that their writing becomes muddled. The answer isn't to "dumb down" the tasks but to set and keep the bar high and allow students to struggle along the way. Lynn Quitman Troyka believes that "what basic writers need more than anything . . . is experience with intellectual endeavors of the mind" (196), which suggests that we have to provide challenging writing assignments for our students, and we have to let their sentence fluency develop at a different rate. As Ann Berthoff has argued, "What is good for the best and the brightest is essential for students who have difficulties. Those we used to call slow learners need the freedom and the opportunities we trouble to offer our prize students" (73). Our basic writers need the freedom to explore their ideas, and we must be patient enough to let their sentence-level skills improve along the way.

Just as it's unfair to judge student writing on sentence-level fluency, it's equally unfair to judge whether students write at a college level based on their entry-level writing. Over the span of one ten-week quarter, these students have proven that they can rapidly learn what is required of them in college and can successfully rise to meet the intellectual challenges of writing in college, even if in some moments the progress with their writing at the surface level seems to move backward. Almost all students will struggle with writing when they are challenged with new and complex ideas, yet that struggle does not automatically indicate a deficiency that should disqualify them from more advanced college courses. The point is that writing in college is about the thinking, and, as such, writing at the college level is precisely what my students are doing, even if they are doing it crudely and in a style that marks them as "underprepared."

In terms of reading, many elementary teachers have told me that students begin to dislike reading in fourth grade. When I ask why, every single teacher says it is because in fourth grade students stop learning to read and instead begin to read to learn. Students begin to find inadequacies in themselves (whether perceived or real), and many young students begin to dislike reading (and learn to minimally engage in the reading process). I tell this story because it mirrors a shift in how students engage with writing. In K–12, students are often taught to write—research papers, comparison and contrast papers, process analysis papers, problem/solution papers, literary papers, and so forth. They are constantly presented with new genres to tackle, often in preparation for college. However, once they enter college, a second paradigm shift of their academic careers takes place: The focus shifts from learning to write to writing to learn.

In a longitudinal study that focused on how writing in the first year in college can have an impact on students, Nancy Sommers and Laura Saltz conclude that "the story of the freshman year is not one of dramatic changes on paper; it is the story of changes within the writers themselves" (124). Sommers and Saltz discuss how many students were able to take the focus off the product—the writing task or grade—and put the focus on the process. In doing so, students "began to see a larger purpose for their writing" (139). They add that "students who continue to see writing as a matter of mechanics or as a series of isolated exercises tend never to see the ways writing can serve them as a medium in which to explore their own interests. They continue to rely on their high school idea that academic success is reflected in good grades" (140). In other words, what separates high school writing from college writing isn't what the product *is* or *looks like*, but what the process *does* for the writer: The process helps students discover ideas and make sense of thinking that becomes increasingly more complex as they move deeper into their major fields of study. And it's this generative and explorative type of writing that happens in college that can be classified as "college level." College-level writing is writing that shows students are thinking. The evidence of that thinking—the product—reflects a process that will probably be different for each student and with each situation.

This is not to suggest that no writing-to-learn happens in high school (just look at any National Writing Project teacher's class, for example) or that composition classes aren't geared toward teaching students how to write correctly. But a fundamental change happens in college, and at its core are students who are able to "discover themselves as subjects of inquiry" and who are therefore "free to set their own intellectual agendas" (Sommers and Saltz 140–41). Professors first and foremost want students to master the complexities of the discipline through their writing—not just master the writing itself—and, to do this, college professors assign "real intellectual tasks that allow students to bring their interests into a course" (141). First-year composition classes are often the first step in the academic process that helps college students make this paradigm shift.

For those of us who teach the underprepared, it is especially important that we help students make the transition from learning-to-write to writing-to-learn—a difficult task for us because our students are still learning to write. As long as students "continue to rely on their high school methods and see writing as a mere assignment" (Sommers and Saltz 140), they will be unable to effectively write for college. Therefore, basic writers must simultaneously develop their sentence-level skills while they learn to use writing as a thinking tool, and we have to acknowledge that sometimes students struggle to understand that we are trying to teach them both. As Mike Rose explains,

> Appropriating a style and making it your own is difficult, and you'll miss the mark a thousand times along the way. The botched performances, though, are part of it all, and developing writers will grow through them if they are able to write for people who care about language, people who are willing to sit with them and help them as they struggle to write about difficult things. (54)

While both learning-to-write for college and embracing writing-to-learn, basic writers can learn to accept "botched performances" as paths toward greater understanding. Of course, having supportive instructors "who are willing to sit with them and help them as they struggle" is vital for basic writers to grow, and we must make sure we create assignments that intellectually challenge our students and grade these assignments most heavily on the thinking. Quite simply, it is our job to help this population succeed; we must balance all that we must teach them while at the same time not overwhelm them.

For me, the important question isn't whether our students are ready to be college-level writers, but whether we are ready, as teachers, for those labeled "underprepared." We must also remember that error is easy to recognize and grade, but teaching thinking is much more difficult and takes much more concentration, patience, and attention to detail. It is my belief that teaching thinking is precisely what we need to do. So the issue isn't whether "underprepared students" have the tenacity or desire to learn necessary skills to survive in college—but whether we have the tenacity and desire to teach them.

Works Cited

Bartholomae, David. "Inventing the University." *When a Writer Can't Write: Studies in Writer's Block and Other Composing-Process Problems.* Ed. Mike Rose. New York: Guilford, 1985. 134–65. Print.

———. "The Study of Error." *College Composition and Communication* 31.3 (1980): 253–69. Print.

Berthoff, Ann E. *The Making of Meaning: Metaphors, Models, and Maxims for Writing Teachers.* Montclair, NJ: Boynton/Cook, 1981. Print.

Dewey, John. *How We Think.* 1910. Buffalo, NY: Prometheus, 1991. Print.

Macrorie, Ken. *Telling Writing.* 4th ed. Upper Montclair, NJ: Boynton/Cook, 1985. Print.

Munitz, Barry. *Determination of Competence in English and Mathematics.* Executive Order No. 665. Long Beach: California State Univ., Office of the Chancellor, 28 Feb. 1997. Print.

Parker, Jo Goodwin. "What Is Poverty?" *America's Other Children: Public Schools Outside Suburbia.* Ed. George Henderson. Norman: U of Oklahoma P, 1971. Print.

Perl, Sondra. "The Composing Processes of Unskilled Writers." *Research in the Teaching of English* 13.4 (1979): 317–36. Print.

Robles, Tomás. "Ferrying Dreamers to the Other Side." *Harper's* Oct. 1998: 22–24. Print.

Rose, Mike. *Lives on the Boundary: The Struggles and Achievements of America's Underprepared.* New York: Free Press, 1989. Print.

Shaughnessy, Mina P. "Diving In: An Introduction to Basic Writing." *College Composition and Communication* 27.3 (1976): 234–39. Print.

———. *Errors and Expectations. A Guide for the Teacher of Basic Writing.* New York: Oxford UP, 1977. Print.

Sommers, Nancy, and Laura Saltz. "The Novice as Expert: Writing the Freshman Year." *College Composition and Communication* 56.1 (2004): 124–49. Print.

Staples, Brent. "Just Walk on By: A Black Man Ponders His Power to Alter Public Space." *Ms. Magazine* Sept. 1986: 54+. Print.

Sullivan, Patrick. "What Can We Learn About College-Level Writing from Basic Writing Students?: The Importance of Reading." *What Is "College-Level" Writing? Volume 2: Assignments, Readings, and Student Writing Samples.* Ed. Patrick Sullivan, Howard Tinberg, and Sheridan Blau. Urbana, IL: NCTE. 2010. 233–253. Print.

Troyka, Lynn Quitman. "Classical Rhetoric and the Basic Writer." *Essays on Classical Rhetoric and Modern Discourse.* Ed. Robert J. Connors, Lisa S. Ede, and Andrea A. Lunsford. Carbondale: Southern Illinois UP, 1984. 193–202. Print.

What Can We Learn about "College-Level" Writing from Basic Writing Students? The Importance of Reading

PATRICK SULLIVAN
Manchester Community College

There is no activity more paradigmatic to liberal arts education than reading. At college, that's simply what students do: They read texts, often examining them with great care and attention; they discuss readings with their professors and classmates; and they write about them in journals, essays, reports, and online forums. Students come to college most fundamentally and essentially to read—to encounter new ideas and perspectives; to engage in conversation with important thinkers, artists, and researchers; and to think, speculate, wonder, and explore. Few skills are more essential to success in college, therefore, than the ability to understand, engage, and respond thoughtfully to assigned readings. Unfortunately, however, reading skills are routinely overlooked or simply disregarded in discussions of college-level writing skills. It is my argument here that any discussion of college-level *writing* must always be accompanied by a discussion of college-level *reading*. In fact, I would like to argue that strong *reading* skills may be the most important proficiency a student needs in order to be a successful college-level *writer*.

As I explore the issue of student reading and writing skills in this chapter, I will be working with artifacts from a basic writing class that I teach regularly at my community college. It is the final class in a three-course basic writing sequence. Students need to earn a C or better in this class to move on to first-year composition, and, when they move on, they are expected to enter the mainstream college curriculum as "college-level" writers—ready to successfully navigate the many demands of the college-level curriculum in all the various ways these demands manifest themselves. Students either test into this course via our placement test (currently a combined reading and sentence skills score on Accuplacer) or they "come up through the ranks" of our basic writing program. Student work done at a curricular location such as this one—at the threshold of "college readiness"—offers us an especially promising opportunity to discuss what we mean by college-level writing because issues related to "college-level work" and "college readiness" come into sharp focus almost every day in this class.

The Assignment

Students in this class typically bring with them unique sets of strengths, aptitudes, interests, work habits, motivations, and personal histories. Despite many individual differences in aptitude, motivation, and skill level, however, it has been my experience, having taught this course now for twenty-three years, that students in this final precollege class usually have three very pressing and interrelated needs—and all of them are related to reading:

1. Most students in this class need to improve their ability to read assigned texts carefully. This is particularly noticeable once the readings become more challenging and demanding—that is to say, once they become "college-level" readings, the kind of readings that students routinely encounter in college-level courses.

2. Most students in this class need to improve their ability to think attentively and patiently about assigned readings, especially readings that make college-level demands on readers.

3. Most students in this class need to improve their ability to develop a mature, coherent, and thoughtful response to college-level readings and to do so in a way that does not misrepresent, simplify, or unrecognizably transform these readings.

I have found that the point of greatest risk for students in this course is precisely when I begin to assign more challenging, college-level readings. The assignment that I examine in this chapter is where that process begins in my class (about the third or fourth week of the semester), and it is my argument that this transition point is where college-level writing can be said to begin. I believe, furthermore, that college-level writing must be judged primarily by how well students read (see Bartholomae and Petrosky; Hassel and Giordano; McCormick; Morrow; Salvatori).

In terms of how this assignment is designed and conceptualized, this is the first time in the semester when students are asked to respond to an obvious and traditional kind of college-level reading (*For Better or for Worse*), and most students find this quite challenging, as we will see. This assignment focuses on family, and I have chosen this subject carefully because it is one that students typically find very interesting.

Essay #2: Family Matters

Reading Sequence

1. Alice Hoffman, "Provider"
2. David Sedaris, "Us and Them" from *Dress Your Family in Corduroy and Denim*
3. E. Mavis Hetherington and John Kelly, from *For Better or for Worse: Divorce Reconsidered* (Chapter 1: A New Story about Divorce and Chapter 13: Lessons Learned in Forty-Five Years of Studying Families)

Essay Assignment
Once we have discussed each of these readings in class, I would like you to return to Hoffman's essay and *reread* it.

I would like your essay to focus primarily on your rereading of Hoffman's essay, and this question in particular:

> Have the other readings in this unit in any way affected the way you now read Hoffman?

Please quote at least once from each of the three assigned readings. Essays should be approximately 1,200 words long.

At this point in the semester, students have already written one essay, about James Baldwin's short story, "Sonny's Blues," so this is the first time they are encountering an assignment with multiple perspectives. It is also the first time they are encountering what most of them regard as a "hard" or "confusing" or "challenging" reading—the selection from Hetherington and Kelly. This is by design, as I have assigned shorter, easier, or more accessible readings (Baldwin, Hoffman, and Sedaris) to help them get situated in the course, to help them begin to see the pleasure they can get from reading, and to help ensure that they have some success and build some confidence early in the semester. I am also seeking to prepare them for more challenging readings to come. They generally find these earlier readings engaging or enjoyable in some way—"deep" and "powerful" in the case of Baldwin; "interesting" and also, they say, thankfully "short" for Hoffman; and "funny" in the case of Sedaris.

I would argue that, although the selection from Hetherington and Kelly is almost all of these things (deep, powerful, and interesting) and relevant as well, my students typically do not see it that way. They find this reading, in fact, very difficult to understand and engage. The two chapters I ask them to read are about twenty-two pages in combined length, and that in itself poses problems for many students in this class. It also is clearly college-level reading material and, as I tell them, is the kind of reading they can expect to encounter in mainstream college courses. An important part of my job as a teacher of this class is to help students learn how to effectively engage college-level reading material like this. It is my argument here that students who are ready to be successful "college-level" writers should be able to read such material and then write about it with a fair degree of thoughtfulness.

Artifacts: Student Writing Samples

I would like to consider four samples of student writing in response to this assignment. I focus on what each student has to say about *For Better or for Worse*. Although the writing samples don't tell us everything we need to know about these student writers, they nonetheless give us a general sense of each student's strengths and weaknesses as readers, writers, and thinkers, as well as their potential to be successful in a first-year composition class and in mainstream college courses.

Please note that although this assignment asks students to discuss ways in which the second and third readings in this unit (Sedaris; Hetherington and Kelly) affect the way they read Hoffman's essay, students often have trouble responding to this element of the assignment. (Many, in fact, simply ignore it.) That challenge is reflected in the student writing samples I include here.

Just one more note before I proceed: I would like to thank the students whose work is included here for the privilege of allowing me to use their writing in this essay.

Danielle's Essay

I begin with a writing sample from Danielle, who wrote a strong essay in response to this assignment. Here is what she had to say about the Hetherington and Kelly reading:

> *For Better or for Worse* really got into the struggle of divorce and the effects it has not only on the child but also on the adult. I believe the main point that the author was trying to get across is that, though divorce is in no way an easy thing to overcome, the outcome does not always have to be a bad thing. It is devastating to a family to lose someone they love. Many people carry cherished memories with them for years which make it very hard to let go. "Only the people who shared those moments know what it means to lose them forever." It can be very hard to see the light at the end of the tunnel when everything around you seems so chaotic. I myself struggled with the messy divorce of my parents.
>
> At the very young age of 2 years old, I can honestly say I remember the day as though it was yesterday. I can say that without a doubt their divorce played a huge role in how I turned out today. It took a very long time for me to figure out how I was going to move on. I found it very interesting that many of the effects of divorce occur within the first 2 years. Again, I only being 2 years old when it happened, after 2 years I would have only been 4. I would have thought that I would have moved on a bit easier than I did. With that said,

I found it interesting that the 1960's study they did, showed that fathers play the more important role in both the boys' and girls' lives. I lived with my father for 10 years after their divorce. Not until I was about 11 years old had I went to live with my mother. I find it interesting that even with all those years of living with him I still got attached very quickly to others. This was not a good thing either. Because, I would get so easily attached it took a very long time to be able to let go.

In the article it said that the negative effects of divorce were exaggerated. I don't know that I find this to be 100 percent accurate however; I do believe that in some cases there are those who dwell, making it harder for them to move forward. A very good friend of mine that went through this has a very negative outlook on life. Not that I am a mean person, but it's almost pathetic. Listening to how they justify themselves for doing what they do. Or listening to them complain over and over about their hardships but never doing anything to change. I would have to say that they are unfortunately one of those who would be considered "the defeated." [Hetherington and Kelly identify six common ways people respond to divorce: "enhanced," "competent loners," "good enoughs," "seekers," "libertarians," "the defeated."]

Going through the experience myself, it does take a very long time to reassure yourself that everything is going to be okay. You really must look deep inside and figure out what positive learning experiences you can take out of it and leave the negative behind. Those involved must remember that it takes time. In the authors' studies, the first and second year after seemed to be the hardest. "About 75 to 80 percent of adults and children show few serious long-term problems in adjustment following divorce and are functioning within the normal range."

Luckily, through the years I have turned out to be a very strong individual. I would have to say that I consider myself "enhanced." Most people who know me often say to me, "With all that you've been through, I'm surprised you turned out the way you did." Most of the time, I have to sit back and think about it. Sometimes even I wonder how I ended up having such a positive outlook on things. I really would have to say that I just try to keep a positive outlook on what happened and not let the negative stuff affect me. If I sit and dwell on the past I would never move on. I just have to give myself a constant reminder of what I want my life to be. I am not my parents, and I do not have to live my life correcting their mistakes.

As most readers of this excerpt will probably note, this writer has a number of strengths. Although there may perhaps be an over-emphasis on personal experience for some readers, Danielle none-theless shows that she has at least a basic grasp of Hetherington and Kelly's major argument. In terms of her attitude as a writer, Danielle appears to be curious and interested in the enterprise of encountering new ideas and talking about them—a very impor-tant college-level disposition, it seems to me. She also maintains a strong sense of her own self and voice as she interacts with Hetherington and Kelly in this conversation. In addition, she has a solid sense of the rhetorical conventions of the academic essay, and she uses paragraphs effectively to help present her ideas. She also seems comfortable in the world of abstract ideas and aca-demic discourse. Overall, and to put it most simply, this student appears to be ready to do college-level work.

The single most important element of this essay, for me, is Danielle's engagement with the assigned reading. She has read Hetherington and Kelly carefully, and she has a solid and accu-rate understanding of the main outlines of their argument. As a teacher of this "gateway"/transition class, I can look at writing like this and say, "This writer is ready to be a successful college writer. With a little more polish, during the next nine weeks or so, she should be ready."

Michael's Essay

For purposes of comparison, I would like to share with you a few selections of work from other students in this class whose work (when considered in comparison to Danielle's) clearly shows for me the difference between basic writing and college-level writing. Here is the first sample, written by Michael:

> The boy found that the Tomkey family would never watch TV; instead Mr. Tomkey stated that he didn't believe in televi-sion. Once finding out that the Tomkey's didn't watch TV the boy began to monitor the family to find out what they really do. He found that the Tomkey family would talk to each other about their day during dinner. Because the Tomkey's didn't watch television, the boy believed that "They didn't know

what attractive was or what dinner was supposed to look like or even what time people were supposed to eat." This quote had made me understand a similar quote written by Alice Hoffman, "having once believed that her life would sort itself out to be like those television shows." In both readings the television is shown to give off an image of what the ideal family was supposed to look and act like. To those who follow this image, that person would sometimes feel as if they have the power to judge others differently because they don't act like everyone else.

Probably one of the most hurtful things which happened in Alice's life would be the divorce of her parents. A divorce of a child's parents has a large impact on their emotional and physical status. Authors E. Mavis Hetherington and John Kelly constructed a study over the years on the after affects of a divorced family. The authors were able to conclude three major topics, most important being that divorce is usually brutally painful. After reading the "better or for worse" study, Alice and her mother's struggle become more serious to me. Every day these two women feel the power of others judging them because of every move they make from taking out the garbage to how Alice's mother simply goes to work just to feed her child's mouth.

Michael is only able to devote a few sentences in his essay to Hetherington and Kelly, and, unfortunately, his comments here (unlike Danielle's) simplify and, in so doing, misrepresent the conclusions Hetherington and Kelly report about divorce. He has missed some important nuances of their argument. So a lot is at stake here—how a student understands or does not understand this landmark study on divorce. Although Hetherington and Kelly do, indeed, say that divorce is "usually brutally painful to a child" (7), they do this in a section devoted to a "myth" about divorce:

Myth Two: Children Always Lose Out After a Divorce

This is another article of faith in popular wisdom and it contains an undeniable truth. In the short run, divorce usually is brutally painful to a child. But its negative long-term effects have been exaggerated to the point where we now have created a self-fulfilling prophecy. At the end of my study, a fair number of my adult children of divorce described themselves as permanently "scarred." But objective assessments of these "victims" told a different story. Twenty-five percent of youths from divorced families in comparison to 10 percent from non-divorced families did have serious social, emotional, or psychological problems. But most of the young men and women from my divorced families looked a lot like their contemporaries from non-divorced homes. Although they looked back on their parents' breakup as a painful experience, most were successfully going about the chief tasks of young adulthood: establishing careers, creating intimate relationships, building meaningful lives for themselves. (7)

Hetherington and Kelly also spend a great deal of time discussing the many different ways that adults and children respond to divorce. They attempt to replace "myths" about divorce with research data:

> On one level, *For Better or for Worse* is a portrait of the new ways that Americans have learned to live and love and parent in a divorce-prone society. On another level, the book serves as a primer on what might be called the postnuclear family experience. . . .
>
> At the center of this primer is a new and, I think, more balanced view of divorce and its consequences. After forty years of research, I harbor no doubts about the ability of divorce to devastate. It can and does ruin lives. I've seen it happen more times than I like to think about. But that said, I also think much current writing on divorce—both popular and academic—has exaggerated its negative effects and ignored its sometimes considerable positive effects. Divorce has undoubtedly rescued many adults and children from the horror of domestic abuse, but it is not just a preventative measure. I have seen divorce provide many women and girls, in particular, with a remarkable opportunity for life-transforming personal growth, as we shall see later.
>
> The reason our current view of marital failure is so unremittingly negative is that it is based on studies that have only examined people for a year or two after their divorce, and a year or two is not enough time to distinguish between short- and long-term effects. Additionally, many divorce studies do not employ a comparison group of married couples, and thus are unable to distinguish between problems common to all families and problems unique to divorced families. (4–5)

Furthermore, in their final chapter, Hetherington and Kelly summarize their key findings. The first one they list is related to "diversity":

> What are the lessons my research colleagues and I have learned in over forty-five years of studying families over time? What have we learned about what sustains families and nurtures family members' well-being or leads to conflict, distress, and marital breakup? What helps or hurts adults and children as they deal with the changes and stresses in their lives associated with divorce, life in a single-parent household, and remarriage?

> ### Lesson One: The Diversity Lesson

> Be suspicious of averages and focus on diversity. Averages conceal the great variability in how individual men and women, boys and girls, function in intimate relationships, and how they cope when these relationships alter or break down and they have to build a new life. It is the diversity rather than the predictability or inevitability of pathways in intimate relationships over the course of life that is striking. (275)

So Michael has simplified and misread this reading in some important ways. That Michael struggles with this reading suggests that he is not yet a college-level writer.

This writing sample also suggests why "college-level writing" is so difficult to define—because when we talk about writing, it seems to me that we must also talk about reading and thinking (Sullivan). The material Michael has been asked to address here is a finely nuanced argument, and this is something that many students do not appear to encounter very often. We devoted more than two hours to this reading during class discussion, and during one of our conferences about his essay for this assignment, Michael indicated that he still really "struggled" with it. To help a student like Michael become a college-level writer, a teacher will need to sit down and attempt to help him discover not only what he's missed in this reading but also try to help him understand why what he's missed is important. A teacher will also need to help Michael see the importance of making a long-term commitment to improving his reading skills. In other words, to make

Michael a better *writer*, Michael's teacher is first going to have to help him become a better *reader*.

Josiah's Essay

Here is an excerpt from Josiah's essay. This essay appeared to me at first glance to be a skillfully crafted model of organization, paragraphing, and sentence mechanics, but as I read further into the essay, the content turned out to be quite weak, as I think this excerpt suggests:

> *For Better or for Worse* was a very interesting writing by E. Mavis Hetherington and John Kelly about divorce and the effect it has on the father, mother, and children in both the short and long run. Divorce has a huge effect on the relationship between a father and children. "And I know none of them ever thought that talking to their children would become almost as difficult as talking to a stranger," says Kelly. In this quote he's talking about in the result of a divorce, the mother is gone which is almost like the missing link in the family chain. The father, without his wife being there to help out with the kids, is having a hard time communicating and spending quality time with his children. Although the mother isn't there in the bonding between father and child, she still plays a part in it.
>
> What I think he is saying in this quote is that having the two parents there together is all the world easier for them to talk to their kids. With the mother being there, just the feeling of having the whole family together makes everything better, thus chatting with the kids is easy. But when there is a divorce it's like the family ties are all broken, and knowing that as a father is heartbreaking, and having a normal chat with your kids is one of the hardest things in the world to do. Also, if the kids are living with their mother, living under her roof and her rules possibly remarried, being a father and knowing this has to make him feel as if he isn't the true father anymore, and that he isn't even a big part of the kids' lives anymore. That would make me feel like I don't know them anymore, and that I am talking to a complete stranger.

Josiah has a very strong sense of how an essay is structured and what a paragraph should "look" like. In terms of his content, however, these paragraphs don't convey much information and they certainly don't engage Hetherington and Kelly in any significant way. These are, alas, "empty calorie" paragraphs—they fill out space and look like paragraphs, but they don't engage ideas or communicate anything very substantial. As a writer, Josiah seems almost entirely concerned with form rather than content (perhaps because of exposure to certain kinds of teaching strategies that focus on the five-paragraph essay; see Edward White's and Alfredo Luján's essays in this collection). Obviously, and like Michael, Josiah has missed almost all of the important content in the Hetherington and Kelly selection. Unfortunately, work like this—which displays an obvious command of essay form and conventions, features an authoritative "voice" and "self," and is "tidy" in some obvious ways (Bartholomae)—is often valued and rewarded in high school and college English classes and in many other places as well. For all the wrong reasons, Josiah may well be prepared to be a successful college-level writer.

Amel's Essay

Finally, I would like to conclude with an excerpt from Amel's essay:

> Because of the narrators isolation issues [in "Us and Them"] and lack of family communication is something that was considered to be common among children in divorced families. However in the research by E. Mavis Hetherington and John Kelly, in the excerpt "A New Story about divorce" from the book *For Better or for Worse*, they discovered that these traits were not common in all divorced families, and the divorce was something that was affected different families in many ways and not the ways one may believe. For example, they brought up the point that most children of divorced families, unlike their parents, were successful in "creating intimate relationships" and "building meaningful lives for themselves." They also discovered that their research, which began in the 1960s, had to be modified and not based on life and marriage pre 1960, because as time change society changed dramatically and after the '60s.
>
> There are many interesting things in Hetherington's and Kelly's research that makes one think twice about preconceived notions on how divorce affects each spouse. For example in the section titled "Men Are the Big Winners in Divorce,"

shows us that women are actually the "big winners," because they tend to do ". . . better emotionally after divorce than men. . . ." Though men may do better financially after a divorce, since most added a significant amount of income into the home prior to the divorce. However, as women are now beginning to depend less on the man's income after he's left the home, due to "better education of women" today, that gap of men has the financial advantage over women is vastly closing.

Another interesting thing about their research on divorce is that they discovered they had to add a new element to their research. This is the "post nuclear" or the conjoined family that emerged soon after the "divorce revolution of the 1960s." They Hetherington and Kelly found the many of these marriages worked better than the first marriage of their subjects. They believed or hoped that these families would not get remarried or get another divorce, at least for the sake of science, in order to prove their research right that that conjoined families cannot work. However, because the change that many of these people had within them to make in the second marriage as well as the shift in society in accepting these types of families, the "post nuclear" families worked. Although there were many that did not work as they predicted, the fact that more than some did work the second time around showed that there was an importance of family community that needed to be. Therefore, since it did not work in the first marriage they were determined to make it work in the second marriage.

I like Amel's work here a great deal, even though it has some obvious weaknesses. Amel may not have the "fluidity" or sureness we expect of a college-level writer, and he struggles in a few places to find the language to express his ideas, but he has read Hetherington and Kelly patiently, and he is working in good faith to engage this reading thoughtfully. Even though Amel may still be in the process of finding his voice and acclimating to the demands of academic writing and the academy, I think this excerpt shows him to be working patiently and in good faith toward becoming a skilled and resourceful reader and thinker. In my judgment, this is perhaps the most important hallmark of a college-level writer—an eagerness to engage readings patiently and thoughtfully. This is the kind of cognitive engagement that Cheryl Hogue Smith discusses in her chapter in this collection (209–232). I believe we are essentially in agreement about the importance of this kind of thinking as a measure of college readiness.

Reading Skills in Decline

On those dark days when discussions don't go particularly well in my basic writing classes—or when my students seem to miss the most important parts of assigned readings when they discuss them in their essays—I sometimes wonder if it's just not a matter of *effort*. "Why can't they try harder?" I think. "Why don't they reread? Why don't they get help at the writing center with reading material they don't understand? Why don't they visit me during my office hours?" At times like this, I turn for solace to my favorite section of Angela Duckworth and Martin Seligman's essay, "Self-Discipline Outdoes IQ in Predicting Academic Performance of Adolescents":

> Underachievement among American youth is often blamed on inadequate teachers, boring textbooks, and large class sizes. We suggest another reason for students falling short of their intellectual potential: their failure to exercise self-discipline. As McClure (1986) has speculated, "Our society's emphasis on instant gratification may mean that young students are unable to delay gratification long enough to achieve academic competence" (p. 20). We believe that many of America's children have trouble making choices that require them to sacrifice short-term pleasure for long-term gain, and that programs that build self-discipline may be the royal road to building academic achievement. (944)

I think there is a great deal to be said for Duckworth and Seligman's argument.

But this may also be a matter of *skill development* as well. Reading skills have been eroding nationwide in the United States for some time now, and this is an often invisible and overlooked variable in many discussions of college-level writing skills and overall college readiness. As I have been suggesting in this chapter, I believe that reading skills are probably the single most essential skill for both predicting and achieving success in college. Unfortunately, a recent report by the American College Testing Program (ACT) titled *Reading between the Lines: What the ACT Reveals about College Readiness in Reading* indicates that many high school graduates lack the reading skills they need to be successful at college. This study is based on approximately 1.2 million high school students who took the ACT and indicated that they would graduate from high school in 2005 (1), and, unfortunately, as the editors of the report note, only 51 percent of these students appear ready to be successful college-level readers:

> Just over half of our students are able to meet the demands of college-level reading, based on ACT's national readiness indicator. Only 51 percent of ACT-tested high school graduates met ACT's College Readiness Benchmark for Reading, demonstrating their readiness to handle the reading requirements for typical credit-bearing first-year college coursework, based on the 2004-2005 results of the ACT. (1)
>
> ACT's College Readiness Benchmark for Reading represents the level of achievement required for students to have a high probability of success (a 75 percent chance of earning a course grade of C or better, a 50 percent chance of earning a B or better) in such credit-bearing college courses as Psychology and US History—first-year courses generally considered to be typically reading dependent. The benchmark corresponds to a score of 21 on the ACT Reading Test. (1)

I would argue that unpreparedness in terms of reading (and what this suggests about student ability to think carefully, critically, and maturely) is at the heart of most writing problems we encounter in our composition classrooms (see Hassel and Giordano; Jolliffe and Harl; National; Rothstein).

The Accuplacer reading comprehension placement scores of the student writers that I have included in this study are intriguing in this regard. Danielle had a 78. Josiah had a score of 38. Both Amel and Michael had strong reading scores: 87 and 91, respectively. Our college defines scores above an 86 as "college level" in terms of reading proficiency. We are following Accuplacer's own guidelines for cut scores here (College Board), along with statewide data collected and shared systemwide and our own local data and institutional research. Most of the twelve community colleges in our system have historically defined "college level" in roughly the same way (plus or minus 5 points). But Michael's scores, it seems to me, are misleading. Although Michael earned a 91 on his reading placement test, for example, it is difficult to say precisely what such a score might mean in terms of college-level proficiency, both theoretically and operationally. We know, for example, thanks to the work Achieve has done examining college placement and admissions tests, that placement instruments like Accuplacer and Compass *test certain kinds of reading and thinking skills—and not others.* Unfortunately, these are mostly lower-level reading skills such as "literal recall," "low inference," and "high inference" (13–18). As the editors note, "Very few items on either test [Accuplacer or Compass] require analysis, which is regarded as the most demanding performance and is cited as an important skill by college professors" (16). In terms of "cognitive demand" or "cognitive challenge," only 1 percent of the questions on the Accuplacer test, for example, require "analysis" (16).

So Michael's score of 91 confirms his ability to handle what Accuplacer calls "informational texts" effectively, but his ability to engage more abstract or complicated reading texts—and his ability to analyze ideas or think abstractly—has apparently been left untested. If it is true, as the editors of this report claim, that "most of what students read in college is informational in nature, such as textbooks" (14), then such a score does, indeed, indicate "college readiness." If not—or if more advanced kinds of reading and thinking are either practically or ideally the primary focus of the college curriculum—then we have no way of knowing from this test whether Michael is ready to read at a college level. I would argue, however, that being able to understand and analyze abstract ideas in readings may well be the single most important college-readiness skill. Without it, as we have seen, students like Michael will struggle, regardless of how well they may read informational texts.

Assignments Can Tell Us a Lot—Or Not Much at All—about What Students Can Do as Writers

Finally, I would like to comment briefly here on student responses to another assigned project in this class, an interview project. I mention this assignment in order to show how important reading is to our definition of college-level writing. For this project, I ask students to conduct an interview with a person they admire and then write a profile of the person they've selected. I include this assignment to give students variety in terms of the written work

I assign during the semester and to encourage them to have some fun with a writing assignment. This assignment almost always is a favorite for many students. Many report that they welcomed the chance to acknowledge the person they chose to interview and write about. Most students also have little trouble putting together a solid essay—organized, focused, and generally free from punctuation and spelling errors. Why is this the case? Well, for starters, it appears that students *care more* about the writing they do for this assignment. They generally want to present the people they admire in the best possible light, and this level of engagement usually leads to more effort with organization, focus, and detail, more careful proofreading and editing, and more care and attention to the finished product overall.

The other main reason that students do well on this assignment is because, well . . . it's very easy. They simply have to interview someone, take notes, and arrange their material in some way (usually chronologically). This usually does not pose major cognitive challenges for most students in this class (see Willingham). There is also, of course, no reading involved, and I think this assignment shows how crucial reading is when trying to assess college-level writing skills. I am often amazed at how well some of my weakest writers do on this assignment (when judged by their performance on other assignments that require them to deal with college-level reading material and abstract thought). In fact, sometimes they seem like completely different people and completely different writers.

At its most basic, then, my point in this essay is simply this: *We can't tell if students are college-level writers until they are asked to write about college-level readings.*

Conclusion

It is my argument that we can't assess a student's readiness to be a college-level writer until we have assessed her or his ability to be a successful college-level reader. Furthermore, I don't believe that students can demonstrate college-level writing skills until they are responding to college-level readings. Unfortunately, as the editors of ACT's *Reading between the Lines* note, "What appears, according to our data, to make the biggest difference in students' being ready to read at the college level is something that, for the most part, is neither addressed in state standards nor reflected in the high school curriculum" (i). As the editors suggest, "Not enough high school teachers are teaching reading skills or strategies and many students are victims of teachers' low expectations":

> Another likely reason that high school students are losing momentum in readiness for college-level reading is that reading is simply not taught much, if at all, during the high school years, not even in English courses. As one educator explains: High school English teachers . . . are traditionally viewed—and view themselves—as outside the teaching of reading, because the assumption has been that students come to them knowing how to read. . . . High school English teachers rarely have the backgrounds to assist the least able readers in their classes, and additionally are often uncertain about what reading instruction actually involves. (9)

The problem appears to be the cognitive demand made by texts assigned in high school:

> The type of text to which students are exposed in high school has a significant impact on their readiness for college-level reading. Specifically, students need to be able to read complex texts if they are to be ready for college. All courses in high school, not just English and social studies but mathematics and science as well, must challenge students to read and understand complex texts. (23)

I believe high school students and basic writing students in college need to regularly encounter true college-level readings, even if this means they must ultimately struggle with or only imperfectly understand such texts. Here I would recommend that we be guided by David Bartholomae and Anthony Petrosky's advice in *Facts, Artifacts, and Counterfacts*:

> There [is] no reason to prohibit students from doing serious work because they [can]not do it correctly. In a sense, all courses in the curriculum ask students to do what they cannot yet do well. [Therefore,] there [is] no good reason to take students who were not fluent readers and writers and consign them to trivial or mechanical work in the belief that it would

somehow prepare them for a college education. It would make more sense, rather, to . . . provide the additional time and support they needed to work on reading and writing while they were, in fact, doing the kinds of reading and writing that characterize college study. (Preface)

I also believe that the high school English curriculum needs to be less exclusively focused on literature and should include a mix of historical, sociological, scientific, theoretical, personal, and literary readings. A curriculum designed this way would more effectively help prepare students for the types of reading they will encounter (and have to write about) in college. Such a curriculum would also help students begin to understand the role academic discipline plays in framing questions about knowledge, value, and meaning.

Finally, as we continue to discuss and clarify what we mean by "college-level" writing, it is my hope that we will continue to regard reading as an important variable in this discussion. It seems to me that when we talk about college-level writing, we must also talk about college-level reading.

Works Cited

Achieve. *Aligned Expectations? A Closer Look at College Admissions and Placement Tests.* Washington, DC: Achieve, 2007. Print.

ACT. *Reading between the Lines: What the ACT Reveals about College Readiness in Reading.* Iowa City, IA: ACT, 2006. Web. 17 June 2010.

Baldwin, James. "Sonny's Blues." *Going to Meet the Man.* New York: Vintage, 1993. 101–41. Print.

Bartholomae, David. "Inventing the University." *Writing on the Margins: Essays on Composition and Teaching.* Boston: Bedford/St. Martin's, 2005. 60–85. Print.

Bartholomae, David, and Anthony Petrosky, eds. *Facts, Artifacts, and Counterfacts: Theory and Method for a Reading and Writing Course.* Upper Montclair, NJ: Boynton/Cook, 1986. Print.

College Board. *Accuplacer Online Technical Manual.* Jan. 2003. Web. 17 June 2010.

Duckworth, Angela L., and Martin E. P. Seligman. "Self-Discipline Outdoes IQ in Predicting Academic Performance of Adolescents." *Psychological Science* 16.12 (2005): 939–44. Print.

Hassel, Holly, and Joanne Baird Giordano. "Transfer Institutions, Transfer of Knowledge: The Development of Rhetorical Adaptability and Underprepared Writers." *Teaching English in the Two-Year College* 37.1 (2009): 24–40. Print.

Hetherington, E. Mavis, and John Kelly. *For Better or for Worse: Divorce Reconsidered*. New York: Norton, 2002. Print.

Hoffman, Alice. "Provider." *New York Times Magazine* 1 Nov. 1992: 22–23. Print.

Jolliffe, David A., and Allison Harl. "Texts of Our Institutional Lives: Studying the 'Reading Transition' from High School to College: What Are Our Students Reading and Why?" *College English* 70.6 (2008): 599–617. Print.

Luján, Alfredo Celedón, "The Thirty-Eight-or-So Five-Paragraph Essay (The Dagwood)." *What Is "College-Level" Writing? Volume 2: Assignments, Readings, and Student Writing Samples*. Ed. Patrick Sullivan, Howard Tinberg, and Sheridan Blau. Urbana, IL: NCTE. 2010. 142–169. Print.

McCormick, Kathleen. *The Culture of Reading and the Teaching of English*. Manchester, UK: Manchester UP, 1994. Print.

Morrow, Nancy. "The Role of Reading in the Composition Classroom." *JAC* 17.3 (1997): n. pag. Web. June 2009.

National Endowment for the Arts. *To Read or Not to Read: A Question of National Consequence*. Washington, DC: National Endowment for the Arts, 2007. Print.

Rothstein, Richard. *Class and Schools: Using Social, Economic, and Educational Reform to Close the Black-White Achievement Gap*. Washington, DC: Economic Policy Institute, 2004. Print.

Salvatori, Mariolina. "Conversations with Texts: Reading in the Teaching of Composition." *College English* 58.4 (1996): 440–54. Print.

Sedaris, David. "Us and Them." *Dress Your Family in Corduroy and Denim*. New York: Little, Brown, 2004. 3–12. Print.

Smith, Cheryl Hogue. "'Botched Performances': Rising to the Challenge of Teaching Our Underprepared Students." *What Is "College-Level" Writing? Volume 2: Assignments, Readings, and Student Writing Samples*. Ed. Patrick Sullivan, Howard Tinberg, and Sheridan Blau. Urbana, IL: NCTE. 2010. 209–232. Print.

Sullivan, Patrick. "An Essential Question: What Is 'College-Level' Writing?" *What Is "College-Level" Writing?* Ed. Patrick Sullivan and Howard Tinberg. Urbana, IL: NCTE, 2006. 1–28. Print.

White, Edward M. "My Five-Paragraph-Theme Theme." *What Is "College-Level" Writing? Volume 2: Assignments, Readings, and Student Writing Samples*. Ed. Patrick Sullivan, Howard Tinberg, and Sheridan Blau. Urbana, IL: NCTE. 2010. 137–141. Print.

Willingham, Daniel T. *Why Don't Students Like School? A Cognitive Scientist Answers Questions About How the Mind Works and What It Means for the Classroom*. San Francisco: Jossey-Bass, 2009. Print.

IV

Student Perspectives: Transitioning from High School to College

Home Schooled

CASEY MALISZEWSKI
Raritan Valley Community College,
Class of 2007

It is incredible to think that all of us have a very unique educational path. Before I was even born, my parents had decided my educational path would be a home-schooled one, just like my three sisters before me. Through trial and error, my parents believed that the best approach to education was as little structure as possible, crossing superstrict, ultrastructured home-schooling with "unschooling," a method that holds children accountable for deciding what they want to study. After they taught me to read and do basic math, my parents gave me a stack of curriculum-based books and left me to my own learning devices. Fortunately, I was always the type that took the initiative, so I adapted well to this method of taking charge of my education. I fell in love with the books on literature and history, but I loathed the books on science and math.

My parents' creative approach to English was no formal writing—none. My writing assignments consisted of fiction, poems, fables, and journals—just enough to get a handle on basic grammar. I remember marveling when my friends told me of their latest book report due. When I asked my mother why I never had to do any book reports, she responded with a shriveled face, as if she had just tasted bad milk: "Book reports made me hate reading when I was kid. I don't want to do the same thing to you." I suppose my parents' approach worked because I always was and still am an obsessive reader.

One story assignment comes to mind during my earlier years of high school work. My assignment was to write a fable about why robins are red breasted. First, I had to do research on the computer about what a fable was and what components it consisted of (a brief story that features animals, inanimate objects, and forces of nature to illustrate a moral lesson). Then, I had to find a fable already written to get an example. I had to let my imagination do the rest. Such an assignment might seem odd, but, by this time, I was used to these creative assignments from my parents.

The Red Breasted Robin

Do you ever wonder why a robin is red breasted? There is a specific reason, along with a specific story to go with it. It begins with the Goddess Mother Nature.

She was within the wind. She was within each of us. She was the protector of animals and the controller of storms. She could make the rain come as easily as the sunshine, and the snow come just as effortlessly. She loved all of nature, and all of nature loved her. She respected life, and likewise, life respected her. She was supreme. She was Mother Nature.

Now there are exceptions to every rule, as well as every story. This particular exception was a man named Alfred.

Alfred was a horrid man. He was ugly, stupid, and mean. All three of these things were by his own choosing. He had black, piggish eyes, a crooked nose, and long scraggly hair, which was full of lice and fleas on account he never took a bath. He was tall and had gangly limbs that seemed to never end. He had brown, crooked teeth, and long fingernails, dirt underneath them, of course. He walked with a limp and had a snort to make one cringe.

As ugly as his appearances and mannerisms were, even uglier was his mind. It was filled with selfish, egotistical thoughts. He thought only of himself and was delighted to do so. He never challenged himself, and was never challenged by anyone else. He was quick to temper, and even quicker to act upon it. He spoke only of gossip, with bad feelings toward others. He did speak of good sometimes, but they were usually only compliments to himself. His brain was the size of peanut. All it contained was rubbish.

As ugly as he was, and as stupid as he was, worst of all was his heart. Most people would agree that he didn't have one, but there are those who say everyone has one. Little though it may be, whatever heart he did have was filled with greed, selfishness, and cruelty. He was abusive toward others, abusive toward nature, and abusive, though unknowingly so, toward himself. He was consumed by hate. He hated others, nature, and sometimes even himself.

The Goddess Mother Nature took a look at this man. She saw that Alfred had taken everything in life for granted. He was filled with greed, stupidity, and cruelty toward every form of life. He questioned everything that life was about. He had forsaken the love within his heart and all that the God of Love had given him. Mother Nature saw all of this and decided something had to be done.

Mother Nature was very powerful. She had a great deal of love in her. She was not one to trifle with, and certainly not one to anger.

She decided to use her power of rain. She brought down heavy rains. The rains lasted long and soon became floods. The floods lasted three days.

You may be asking why Mother Nature brought down these rains, and why she did it to teach Alfred a lesson. The reasoning behind it was that Alfred had a house with plentiful fields. He had bountiful crops that stretched several acres. As the rain continued, they flooded over his fields.

After the floods went down, Alfred stepped out of his soggy house. He saw that all of his precious crops were ruined. He was devastated. His devastation, however, lasted only for a while. After the devastation came the outrage.

Alfred felt outrage like he had never felt before. Anger-filled words poured out of his mouth. His blood boiled, and his face turned red. He hastily grabbed his bow and arrow and decided he would kill Mother Nature. He would have his revenge!

He ran out of the house and down the steps. He ran through the forest, on and on, for what seemed like an eternity. Then, he came to a glade, and there she was.

She was radiant and beautiful. She had sparkling, crystal eyes, and long flowing silver hair. She was glowing in a mixture of colors. The colors were vibrant shades of blue, lavender, and pink. The goodness and love seeped out of her soul. Within a glade full of beautiful flowers and animals, big to small, she was a sight to be seen.

Alfred, not forgetting his anger, took a breath and reached for his arrow. He pulled the arrow back into his bow and aimed right for Mother Nature's heart.

At that moment, a robin saw what was about to be done. The robin was black and brown with a breast of bright white. With all of the robin's love for Mother Nature, she flew straight for her.

Alfred took a deeper breath and let go of the arrow. Mother Nature heard the whistle of the arrow and the flutter of wings behind her. She turned around. The arrow hit the robin straight through the heart.

Mother Nature bent down and picked up the little bird in her delicate hands. The robin's beautiful white breast was now covered in red. Mother Nature began to cry. "Why have you done this?" she asked him.

Alfred fell to his knees and began to cry as well. He cried, but he could not answer Mother Nature's question.

Mother Nature looked into Alfred's eyes and saw that he had learned his lesson. She also realized that she, too, had learned a lesson. She could not judge Alfred's evil ways because he had known no other way.

She helped Alfred up to his feet and said to him, "I think you should go home now. Before you go, please remember this: every time you see a robin with a red breast, I want you to remember that white-breasted robin that showed compassion and love. With that, you will learn to have love for nature, others, and yourself, as I do, and as that robin did."

In remembrance of that compassionate robin, Mother Nature gave all robins a red breast. And that's why all robins are red breasted.

Though these assignments through my high school years gave me a great interest in writing, I still had no formal writing instruction and had no idea how to structure a basic essay. It was not until the year came to take my General Equivalency Degree (GED) tests that I had to sit down and learn the format of a basic essay. I will always remember that first day with my GED instructor, when she sat down next to me to help me work through an essay. She patiently explained to me a basic five-paragraph essay format. My topic for that day was fruit. I learned the first paragraph was called an introduction and was used not only to introduce the fruit but was also used to introduce which one I thought was best. Each of the following three paragraphs was used to describe a fruit and why they are or are not a good fruit. The fifth paragraph, called a conclusion, was used to summarize my points. It seems like such a simplistic approach, but it made sense to me. Breaking down the essay into digestible parts made writing seem simple. The approach worked because I passed my GED with flying colors, and, in fact, it is still a method I use in my own work and in tutoring.

Moving into college, the work became a little more challenging. As I sat in my very first college class, I was nervous not only about being in a classroom for the first time but was also apprehensive about my writing abilities. On the first day of class, my professor told us about the various assignments throughout the semester, including a ten-page research paper. Her assignment was met with a wave of groans from the students. She shrugged her shoulders and said, "Oh, by the end of your college career, you'll be writing ten-page papers like it was nothing." I was skeptical.

It was this professor who introduced me to college-level writing. She taught that the introduction should include something called a thesis statement, which was more than just your own opinion but instead a point around which you surround the essay, a central focus. This was also my first experience with comparing and contrasting two essays or articles to come up with a thesis and using the material to support it. She taught how to incorporate research and quotes to help prove your point. My first essay of the class focused on the writings of Lucy Grealy and Nancy Mairs. Here readers will see a more structured essay, with a more defined thesis, and the use of quotes to support the central focus.

Images

We often hear the popular phrase, "Sometimes it's best to learn a lesson the hard way." While sometimes it is truly best to learn the hard way, there are other times we may learn by listening to another person's story. Such is the case with two authors' stories, Lucy Grealy's "Mirrors" and Nancy Mairs's "Carnal Acts." They share with us how they learned the hard way life's lessons involving society's harsh demands of beauty and how they fell short of it, what it meant for their self-image, how they coped with it, and how they overcame their feelings.

Grealy and Mairs tell us about the hardships they endured while struggling with physical abnormalities. Grealy suffered cancer as a child, giving her a misshapen face. Mairs, though she lives normally into the beginnings of adulthood, is stricken with MS in her early adulthood and has to deal with her body being destructed day by day. Both of these authors make a valid point of how society sets a high standard for beauty. Mairs says, "I was never a beautiful woman, and for that reason I've spent most of my life (together with probably at least 95 percent of the female population of the United States) suffering from the shame of falling short of an unattainable standard" (Page 370). Grealy suggests that society feeds us images that make us want to be someone else. "Society is no help; the images it gives us again and again want us to believe that we can most be ourselves by looking like someone else" (Page 60). It is clear that society standards are not helpful to us.

Given these standards, both of these authors suffer from very low self-esteem. Mairs says, "Afflicted by the general shame of having a body at all, and the specific shame of having one weakened and misshapen by disease, I ought not to be able to hold my head in public" (Page 372). Grealy experiences such shame when teased by other people, "I was a dog, a monster, the ugliest girl they had ever seen. . . . I was too ashamed to lift my eyes off the ground" (Page 54).

How could one cope with such inner turmoil? Grealy valued her intellect, which gave her a sense of self worth, "I decided to become a deep person. I wasn't exactly sure what this would entail, but I believed if I could find just the right philosophy, think just the right thoughts, my suffering would end" (Page 54). Mairs realized that despite her disability, she still had her voice, which she took comfort in. "Here is where my 'voice' comes in. Because, in spite of my demurral beginnings, I do in fact cope with my disability at least some of the time. And I do so, I think by writing about it" (Page 372). Both of these authors use their internal voices to cope with their negative feelings.

Grealy and Mairs did suffer a lot in learning how to cope with their images. However, they did come out of their dark, hopeless cave, but in very different ways. Grealy came out of the darkness by shedding her image. She writes, "But where as a child I expected it to come as a result of gaining something, a new face, it came as a result of shedding my image" (Page 60). Mairs, on the other hand, comes out by accepting her image. She says, "Paradoxically, losing one sort of nerve has given me another. No one is going to take my breath away. . . . I've found my voice, then, just where it ought to be. . . . No body, no voice; no voice, no body. That's what I know in my bones" (Page 375).

In reading both of these stories, we learn we should not live by society's standards. If we do, they will destroy us. When people read these two stories, it should not only teach us this lesson, but also give us the strength and inspiration to accept ourselves for who we are.

This essay was a large stepping stone in my development as a writer for several reasons. First, I learned to formulate a more complex thesis, my central focus. This is a pivotal step in college-level writing, something that distinguishes college writers. Second, I learned that when writing supporting paragraphs, every single paragraph must relate to and support the thesis. This is important to keep the essay on track and not confuse writers by adding more than is necessary. Third, I learned to incorporate quotes to support my thesis. This is also incredibly important in college-level writing. It is not enough to create a thesis: You must support it with facts. In this case, the facts came from the writings of Grealy and Mairs. Lastly, I learned the proper way to document such quotes and sources. As the first semester progressed, I improved upon all of these things. Later in the semester, I felt I was beginning to understand the components of a thesis and how to support it.

Yet if I had to choose one class that pushed my writing ability farther than anything, it would have to be my English II Honors course. The course only had three papers, but, to the professor, it was not about quantity, it was about quality.

Instead of a writer's anthology, she used books from various time periods. The works included Shakespeare, Jane Austen, Virginia Woolf, Zora Neale Hurston, and Anzia Yezierska. In preparation for each class, we had to read a section of each book and write responses to some of the professor's questions. This was probably the biggest shock of all because these questions seemed to me at the time incredibly hard! To answer the questions, you had not only to read the selection several times but you had to think about what was beneath the text. Our professor introduced each book with a brief history of the author, an explanation about what the author's life was like, and an overview of what was going on in the world that could have influenced the author's writing. This helped give us insight into what we might be looking for in answering her questions and helped us look for patterns, such as social patterns, gender issues, or economic stratification levels. These responses were compiled in a journal we kept, which, at the end, totaled fifty pages of writing.

This professor taught me how to distinguish a weak thesis from a strong thesis, which depended upon how creative your thesis was and how well you could support it. I learned this from trial and error as I submitted thesis after thesis only to have them turned down, one right after the other. "Most people would agree with your statement. Choose something that is more difficult to argue," she said for one. "Now your argument may be too difficult. You may not have enough material to support your argument," she said for another. "Your argument is too broad. You would have difficulty covering all of the points in this particular length of a paper." Or she would say, "Your topic isn't broad enough. You would run out of things to say." But throughout this entire process, she always said, "You're getting closer. Don't give up!"

My first essay in the class felt like a major breakthrough in developing a strong thesis. Here readers will see two things that helped me mature more as a writer. The first is a more balanced thesis (i.e., not too narrow, not too broad), which arose from going through each of those points my professor made to me. The second is a more complex argument that came from reading beneath the text to determine broader patterns within the work. This essay excerpt discusses a common theme between two works of William Shakespeare and Jane Austen:

Big Boys Don't Cry

> In William Shakespeare's *As You Like It* and Jane Austen's *Pride and Prejudice*, it is easy to see the competition and struggles in life that women encounter. It is much less easy to see the struggles and competition that men experience, yet in their own way, these can be more intense and oppressive than the struggles and competition between women. While women compete with each other to obtain the most profitable marriage they need in order to survive, men compete with other men not only for a profitable marriage but also for wealth, power, and status. This competition affects all aspects of men's lives much more so than women's, including their relationships with men, women, and their families, and ultimately affects their own emotional well-being.

By the time this class ended, I felt my writing had improved greatly. I was now able to distinguish strong thesis statements from weak ones. Newly inspired by the end of the semester, I decided to declare myself an English major. The major required me to complete four elective courses to further my growth in connecting ideas with research. The professors in these courses taught me to push my ideas just a bit farther and how to concisely express my ideas. I also learned to broaden my research base by using different sources such as journal articles, newsletters, and literary magazines.

As I look back on my interactions with other college writers transitioning from high school to college from my work as a college writing tutor, I have noticed two unfortunate things in many students fresh from high school. One, many high school students come to college without understanding basic grammar and sentence structure. Without this foundation, these students seem doomed to a miserable and incredibly challenging college experience. Two, most students did not enjoy, and many even hated, reading and writing in college. These students often came to the tutoring center saying, "I hate writing" or "I'm terrible at writing." Thankfully, I was fortunate enough to avoid these problems. I came to college needing help with essay formats and understanding a thesis, but I could construct clear sentences with proper grammar. Plus, I loved reading and writing! Other students were not so lucky.

In thinking through my own educational path, there are certain aspects I would keep and other things I would change. I would never get rid of the early creative writing I did because it helped me learn basic grammar while developing my passion for writing. However, I wish I had been given some more formal writing assignments with specific sets of questions to help me learn to think critically. I am grateful that I never had a list of specific books to read but instead was given a choice in what I read. While I know that not all students will learn to love to read and write, I can't help but think that maybe more of them would be passionate about those pursuits if they had more of a choice in what to read and write.

Many experts are calling for higher standards in schools, while others may claim that a freer, creative approach is the way to achieve better student outcomes. I do not see why we cannot have a little of both. If students were assigned creative or free-choice assignments, they would have a fun way to learn better grammatical structure. Creative writing assignments might also help students learn to enjoy the basics of writing, such as grammar and punctuation. Once they have a firm grasp on these things, they can then move onto learning the more advanced concepts of essay and paper writing. I do think it is imperative that students have some say in what they read and write. While some students need a teacher to give them a topic for writing assignments, other students feel stifled by such a process. Perhaps a choice should be given to them in the process: Either the teacher can give them a specific topic to write about, or they can create their own topic.

In reference to higher standards, there are two additional things high school students can learn before coming to college, yet these are things that come with maturity. One is more critical thinking through understanding articles, essays, and books. The other is a greater understanding of a true thesis.

In learning critical thinking, it is important that students be given specific questions that challenge them to critically analyze a reading. Even though it was frustrating at first, I am glad my English II professor gave the class those tough questions. She would ask questions such as "What does the author want the reader to get from this work?" "If the author says this, . . . what does that *really* mean?" "Is the author implying something about society in general?" "Is the author giving a recommendation to society?" and "Is the author influenced by his or her surroundings and background?" She would assign a specific passage and ask us to give our opinions about its deeper meaning. She was always asking us to delve deeper into the text, or, in other words asking us, "What does that *really* mean?"

In teaching students to write a thesis, it is important that they understand it is an argument. A thesis should strive to achieve a perfect balance: not too broad, not too narrow, with enough material and points to support it. Students may need much practice to get this balance right, but it also may take some one-on-one coaching in order to understand it correctly.

My journey from high school to college-level writing has been challenging. The transition to college-level writing was shocking at first, but practice and persistence provided a great reward. I know that I will take my writing skills with me not only throughout my education but throughout my working career as well. My English I professor was right. Though I sat with skepticism in that first class, I can now write longer papers with greater ease. I am grateful to my professors for their dedication to my education. And, to all of you, I wish you a happy writing or teaching journey of your own.

Moving the Tassel from the Right to the Left

Steven Schmidt
Trinity College, Class of 2008

I recently completed my undergraduate studies in the field of psychology, and when I moved that tassel from the right to the left on that joyous day in May 2008, I was one year shy of 40. My journey to that point was not one of a traditional college student. It took well over a decade to get my degree, and, along the way, I got married, was diagnosed with cancer, underwent a life-threatening bone marrow transplant, got divorced, started an annual 5K fundraiser for pediatric cancer, bought my first home, and received three prestigious national scholarships. While I did not take the traditional route to obtain my bachelor of science degree in psychology, my story is certainly an interesting one, which I hope will highlight some important issues regarding the transition into college for traditional and nontraditional students alike.

The Early Years

I don't remember much from my K–12 years; however, what I do remember is that I had a very creative mind in elementary school. On more than one occasion, my teachers would comment on my creative writing ability to my parents, naturally bringing smiles to their faces. I loved writing assignments at an early age because they were a way for me to tell my fantastic stories. I was eight years old when the original *Star Wars* movie came out, which energized my love for science fiction. Indeed, there was a time when I dreamed of being a science fiction writer when I grew up.

Unfortunately, it was not long before I began to view writing as a chore—something forced upon me at a young age. During my junior high years, I attended a Catholic school, and my creative writing was not enthusiastically accepted. The humor I injected into my writing was regarded as mere fluff, and the feedback I received turned off the joy I took in writing. My dislike for writing and reading was evident in high school: My grades in English classes were C's and D's. However, in my junior year I began writing poetry on the side. Along with a dear friend from my French class, I would spend much of my free time crafting wonderful poetic masterpieces (at least that is how they existed in my mind). Away from the pressures of the classroom, writing poetry was something I enjoyed. Being able to write freely and under my own direction was exciting and liberating. I even had one poem published, but, alas, once I entered the workforce the free time I once had to devote to this hobby disappeared. There just wasn't the time to allow any hidden talents I might have had to flourish.

Another factor that drastically changed my interests away from writing was the introduction of the personal computer in the mid-1980s. I was fascinated by what could be done with computers, and programming provided me with a new outlet for my creativity. Following my graduation from high school, I completed a five-month program at a local computer school and graduated at the top of my class. I quickly got a job with a large manufacturing company as a night-shift computer operator. Early in my career in information technology, I had little opportunity for writing, but the programming I did on the side was a much-needed creative release. Nonetheless, I loved my job, worked extremely hard, and, as a result, moved into a supervisory position within five years. In that role, writing became more critical and salient. Memos and documentation had to be focused, comprehensive, and clear. Because of my strong work ethic and the diversity of the work staff, I developed certain routines to ensure that my memos and documentation were clear and concise. This included careful proofreading, often at least a day after the initial draft was written, time permitting.

Additionally, for a few months, one of my employees was being monitored closely after several negative performance issues were identified. Proper documentation of poor performance in a corporate environment is critical if the employee is terminated, and, since I was new in the position, I forced myself to be critical of my own documentation. Legal issues that could arise fostered the need for unambiguous and lucid writing, which further forced me to be even more analytical and conscious of my writing.

The Community College Years

Seven years after my graduation from high school, I decided to attend college. Since I knew I would need a college degree to continue climbing the ladder at work, I enrolled part time at a local community college in the computer information systems program. My first seven classes were computer or math courses with few writing requirements. After relocating to a new town, I transferred to a different community college and took an economics course before the unthinkable happened. At the blissful age of 28, just four months after my wedding day, I was diagnosed with cancer.

My cancer treatment (bone marrow transplant) and recovery kept me out of classes for four years. However, during the five months of my actual treatment, I was three thousand miles from home and maintained a daily log of my progress on the Internet for my family and friends. This certainly kept my mind fresh as the chemicals and emotions I was dealing with took their toll. I knew it was not easy on my family and friends to be so physically removed from me during such a critical time. I had to keep my log truthful, but I also peppered it with humor and optimism. This activity, along with my experiences as a supervisor, taught me the skills of writing for an audience. It also compelled me to reflect on my own thoughts and priorities. Deep inside my battered self, it was also the time I decided to change my career goals. I no longer found the corporate life rewarding. I felt the need to do something more meaningful with my life. This was the beginning of a new chapter for me.

After my diagnosis of cancer, I renewed two of my passions— reading and programming. I read almost constantly. Memoirs were my literature of choice, but I also immersed myself in resource books, technical books, and coping books. If it had to do with cancer, I would read it. I enjoyed learning about other people's

struggles and triumphs. During my recovery, when I wasn't reading, I would be at my computer creating code for a card game that
was not available commercially. Writing a computer program was
challenging and enjoyable. It was a long and tedious project that
culminated in a copyright. Reading and programming were the
fuel that fed my empty days of recovery, but I would realize much
later that they were also the tools helping build both my creative
and analytic writing skills.

Because of my weakened immune system, I took online
courses when I returned to college, one of which was a course in
college reading and writing. It had been years since I had written
creatively, and I was eager for this course to start. I remembered
the times when writing had been an exhilarating release for me,
and I was hoping to rekindle that feeling through this class. I was
not disappointed.

In that class, I received A's on my assignments. It was an
ecstatic feeling to use those creative (albeit rusty) skills. Patrick
Sullivan in his chapter in this collection suggests that reading
skills are critical to being a successful writer at the college level,
and I strongly believe that my love for reading (along with my
strong work ethic) helped me develop the skills to do well in this
course, despite not having taken a writing class in more than
a decade. Indeed, while I didn't have free choice in my reading
assignments in college, I did spend my free time while recovering
from cancer treatment reading narratives of my choosing. I agree
with what Casey Maliszewski suggests in her chapter in this collection: that greater choice in reading can foster the development
of a passion for writing. I thrived at college-level writing.

However, looking back I see that while my analytic ability
was fine, my grammar and style were not where they are today.
Over the years, I have honed my skills in paragraph development,
transitions, and grammar and usage. Much of this development
came from feedback from professors and peer reviews, which I
will discuss in more detail.

While reading has become more of a chore for me over the
years, it has clearly been instrumental in the development of my
writing skills. However, another medium that has been helpful to
this development is public speaking, something I have done on
numerous occasions, including during a public speaking course

at the community college. During my time as a part-time community college student, I was invited to join Phi Theta Kappa, the honor society for two-year colleges, and I took on several leadership roles, including presidency of the New England region. Additionally, I was involved in volunteer work for the American Cancer Society, National Marrow Donor Program, Leukemia and Lymphoma Society, and Nikki's Run, a local fundraising event I helped start in 2003 for pediatric cancer research and support programs. All of these activities included public speaking engagements, which further helped in the development of my writing style. Knowing what I wanted to say to an audience was a great motivator for focusing on my writing.

Scholarship essay writing was yet another aspect that fostered the development of my writing abilities. I took this endeavor so seriously that I took time off from work to focus on the writing portion of my scholarship applications. My concentrated focus and feedback from those willing to provide it allowed me to pen my essays well enough to receive three national scholarships, which paid for my educational expenses at the private four-year college to which I transferred.

Although several external and internal factors contributed to the development of my writing and reading skills to this point, it was the encouragement and praise from my professors at the community college that instilled in me the confidence to apply these skills in the academic environment.

My success at the community college level is certainly something I am proud of, but it didn't come easy. Dealing with cancer and my eventual divorce added a significant amount of stress to the pressures of trying to succeed in college. Fortunately, I started off as a part-time student, never taking more than two classes per semester. This schedule eased me into a comfort level with my academic work and allowed me to better meet the requirements of college-level work. Despite the stress, anxiety, and self-imposed pressures, I graduated salutatorian, with a 4.0 grade point average.

That being said, I am unsure that my experiences at the community college prepared me as well as they could have for the challenges at the small liberal arts college to which I transferred. The writing assignments were less demanding, and there were few opportunities to improve following feedback. The transition to a four-year college turned out to be more challenging than the transition from working to attending community college. The demands at the four-year institution as a full-time student were far greater than what I had experienced previously. In fact, the time and effort required at the four-year college to complete assignments were significantly greater than what was required previously during my time at the community college. The community college offered an optional honors program, which would have been beneficial during my transition to the four-year institution. Unfortunately, I was unaware of this option until I was in my last semester, and the offerings were limited. Certainly, for a large number of students looking for no more than a two-year degree, the honors program would not be so beneficial. However, for students wishing to continue their studies at a four-year institution and beyond, I would strongly recommend such a program as one means to prepare for the transition. Furthermore, I believe that two-year colleges need to do more to promote their honors programs and increase their availability to cover all courses. It would be a tremendous value to have the benefits of an honors program communicated to students by professors at the start of each semester.

Aside from the need for more honors programs at two-year colleges, writing needs to be a primary focus for courses, whenever practical. I recommend both formal and informal writing assignments. Although grades for informal writing should count less, these assignments are critical to a student's development. Exploratory writing assignments such as journals, reflection papers, and one-minute papers give students the means to discover and reflect on their thoughts about particular topics and develop analytical thinking styles, which will aid them in the development of their writing skills. However, formal writing assignments are ultimately the best measure of a student's skill and progress. Providing students with sample papers of good writing and poor writing can benefit students and clarify expectations. It is important that a short, formal paper be assigned early in the course to provide a baseline assessment. This assessment is critical to the professor and the student alike, and prompt feedback is crucial. More substantive formal assignments throughout the course need to include a process for reflection and revision. This can be accomplished through draft submissions, peer reviews, individual conferences, or other processes that allow for critical feedback (see Merrill Davies's essay in this collection for examples and ideas).

Furthermore, self-reflection from students throughout the course can be a vital tool for professors to gauge comprehension and progress, and it can be advantageous in guiding the professor's feedback early on. Opportunities for self-reflection can be provided through weekly one-minute papers on the content of the material covered in class. It is equally important to implement paired or small group breakout sessions throughout the semester to facilitate group interaction and shared learning. With this approach, professors can implement a scaffolded scheme for learning, providing more individual support early on and stepping back as students develop.

My time at the community college certainly did a fine job adjusting me to college life after being out of the classroom for so many years. The student population at the community college level is diverse, and the expectations at four-year institutions cannot be broadly applied to the community college setting, which is populated with every demographic from fresh high school grads to single mothers to retired individuals. Nonetheless, the two-year college curriculum needs the added demands of a writing-intensive focus, which would be of tremendous benefit to all students, whether they plan to enter the workforce after graduation or transfer to a four-year institution.

The Liberal Arts College Years

In the end, I appreciate greatly what the community college environment did for me academically. However, my professors at the four-year college pushed me much harder and also invested time in me outside the classroom. The workload was immensely greater, and my professors demanded excellence and perfection of me, just as I did of myself. But they also provided the critical one-on-one feedback, encouragement, and resources to achieve excellence. My first semester there, I earned a 3.51 grade point average, which disappointed me. In my second semester, I was more comfortable and understood the demands of the environment; by the time I completed my studies, I had raised my GPA to 3.86.

During my academic career at the four-year college, two factors were particularly critical to my continued growth as a scholar: feedback and note-taking. I cannot emphasize the importance of the former enough. Critical feedback for me was the primary source of learning and being able to retain and implement what I learned. Class lectures and textbooks are great sources of learning, but the best way for students to learn and retain is through practical experience with critical feedback and advice. Nevertheless, providing critical feedback can be difficult for students who review each other's papers, and it can be challenging as well to some professors in fields outside the language and literature domain who give writing assignments. Certainly, when I give feedback to peers, I almost always feel bad pointing out mistakes and areas in need of improvement, but I know this is an important aspect of the process, not only for the student whose paper I was reviewing but also for me.

The other factor that contributed much to my academic growth was note-taking. As a cancer survivor, I was forced by issues such as osteoarthritis, memory problems, and limited concentration to record class lectures on tape. Yet having to do so was a highly beneficial side effect of my cancer treatment. Transcribing notes is a tedious and time-consuming activity most students would rather not take on. But the benefit of hearing the class material outside the classroom and writing down the key points is immeasurable. This benefit has become evident in recent years as professors from around the world use modern technology to make their lectures available via podcasts. Moreover, taking notes while reading can be advantageous. Since my cancer treatment, I have discovered that I read at a considerably slower pace and often have to go back a few paragraphs, if not pages, because my concentration has waned to the point where I sometimes have no idea what I just read. Of course, interrupting reading to jot notes is not productive. To this end, I employed the strategy of highlighting while reading, followed by going back to take notes on key points. This process was extremely beneficial to me, especially in conducting research for essays.

Fortunately, writing was a primary focus in virtually all of my courses at the four-year college, and my professors would critique every aspect of my writing carefully, which I learned to welcome. It was also common to integrate peer reviews, which helped the student whose paper was being reviewed, as well as the reviewer. To exemplify the impact of peer reviews and draft feedback, I offer two examples of opening paragraphs from papers I wrote without feedback early in my community college days:

Sample #1

This essay will cover a topic that has been argued for centuries. I will discuss the various differences between the genders and offer explanations about where these differences arise from. Men and women are different, and as a result, our society has created stereotypes that are unjustly placed on all members of each gender. Not all women have the stereotypical traits that people assume and the same could be said for men. While men and women are different, so too are men different from other men and women are different from other women. After all, we are all unique individuals. My focal point will be that, yes, men and women are very different and these differences start with inherited genes. However, culture and society play a huge role in defining these differences.

Sample #2

Animals play a large part in the human race. From our pets, to the foods we eat, to the clothes we wear, to the products we use, to the entertainment we enjoy, animals are in our lives every day. There are many issues related to animal rights but the one that I will focus on is the moral and ethical issue of toxicity testing of consumer products on animals. Do we as humans have the right to cause pain and suffering while testing ingredients and products on other living creatures for the purpose of marketing items such as makeup, laundry detergent, perfume, crayons, air freshener, and oven cleaner? Or is it our moral responsibility as a species with the ability to comprehend the consequences of our actions to research and create new methods of testing products or even to refrain from making these products (most of which serve no purpose to the survival of mankind) in an effort to stop the torment that animals go through to insure such products are safe for human consumption?

While I consider these samples to be good opening paragraphs, they could have been improved through the addition of brief yet striking examples of stereotypical traits in the first sample and tests performed on animals in the second. Moreover, the flow of each is a bit choppy, and they don't grab the reader as well as they could. Comparatively, the following is a sample of an opening paragraph before and after peer review, written for a class at my four-year college:

Before Peer Review

Sex is the oldest and most important dichotomy in human culture. The human race would not exist without either men or women. Despite the mutual contributions each gives to evolution, cultural evolution has divided the two by defining behaviors, roles, and identities for each sex. This process has contributed to the stereotypes and stigmas assigned to each gender and in turn have fostered prejudice, discrimination, and oppression. It is my contention in this paper that the study of sex differences is important in order to address these harmful issues. Differences between men and women do exist, but it is only by studying these differences ethically and without bias that we can control, if not overcome prejudice, discrimination, and oppression based on sex.

After Peer Review

Sex is the oldest and most important dichotomy in human culture. The human race would not exist without men or women. Despite the mutual contributions each gives to evolution, the two are divided by culturally defined behaviors, roles, and identities for each sex. This process of division has contributed to the stereotypes and stigmas assigned to each sex and in turn has fostered prejudice, discrimination, and oppression. My contention in this paper is that the study of sex differences is important in order to address these harmful issues. Over the last thirty years, women have made progress in achieving higher education, employment, and income. The *Convention on the Elimination of Discrimination against Women* was published. Laws to protect women from domestic violence have been enacted. Without the analysis of the differences between men and women, these changes may never have happened. Differences between men and women do exist but only by studying these differences ethically and without bias can we control, if not overcome prejudice, discrimination, and oppression based on sex.

At the four-year college, I was also put in a position to think more holistically. I was no longer writing only short reflection papers on single topics, as was common at the community college level. I was now expected to routinely integrate ideas from multiple sources and theories into cohesive and analytical essays. This expectation was highlighted by the culmination of my yearlong undergraduate senior thesis. The research, readings, and writing assignments from my classes early on at the four-year college prepared me well for my thesis. My skills at note-taking and the critical feedback I received throughout the semesters helped me to develop the skills to work on such a massive project. My thesis included fifty-nine references, which I had pulled together to compose one cohesive, sixty-three-page manuscript. The following is the opening of my thesis:

In capitalistic societies, certain traits are highly valued for corporate managers, and these traits are usually considered masculine by cultural definitions. Men are socially groomed to see paid employment as being of primary importance in their lives (Aaltio-Marjosola & Lehtinen, 1998; Lee & Owens, 2002), and toughness, stoicism, and competition are valued (O'Connell, 2005). For managers, masculinity persists as the socially preferred role and has been considered key to career progression (Kirchmeyer, 1998; Powell & Butterfield, 1989). Indeed, the success of men's careers often is critical to their self-identities and sense of self-worth (Lee & Owens).

Although masculine traits are highly valued in corporate managers, they have a more contradictory role in romantic relationships. Research has shown that women are more likely to be initially attracted to men with masculine traits, specifically the ability to provide resources and income (Bogg & Ray, 2006; Ickes, 1993); yet this same category of traits is often reported as a primary source of relationship dissatisfaction (Bradbury, Campbell, & Fincham, 1995; Langis, Sabourin, Lussier, & Mathieu, 1994). So if masculine traits are reinforced in corporate climates and rewarded in dating situations, yet are also deemed detrimental to long-term relationships, it would seem that men in these positions are in a predicament requiring a delicate but deliberate balance of masculinity across these social contexts.

Surviving versus Thriving

My initial transition entering the community college system was relatively easy, as I attended part time and mostly took computer courses, which were already my expertise. However, my transition following cancer treatment was more difficult. I took courses outside my field of expertise and was also dealing with the lingering effects of cancer and divorce; however, making the transition a gradual one with online courses helped. Taking on more courses over the years, along with my extracurricular duties, helped build my tolerance for the time demands of college.

While the community college gave me the confidence and basic skills to survive at the four-year college, I feel that more could have been done regarding the development of my writing skills outside my language and literature courses to prepare me adequately for the demands of the four-year college. My transition to the four-year college was difficult, and my first semester was incredibly challenging. However, through the processes of feedback, reflection, and review, along with my own work ethic, I became comfortable with the new demands I faced in the four-year setting by my second semester. Certainly my experiences with reading and note-taking were important during my thesis work, but the development of my writing skills was most significantly influenced through informal writing, peer and faculty feedback on formal writing assignments, class presentations, and exercises to integrate material from multiple sources. Undoubtedly, a more writing-intensive focus using these strategies at the two-year college would have aided my transition greatly. Survival is one thing. Thriving is another.

Works Cited

Davies, Merrill. "Making the Leap from High School to College Writing." *What Is "College-Level" Writing? Volume 2: Assignments, Readings, and Student Writing Samples*. Ed. Patrick Sullivan, Howard Tinberg, and Sheridan Blau. Urbana, IL: NCTE. 2010. 119–133. Print.

Maliszewski, Casey. "Home Schooled." *What Is "College-Level" Writing? Volume 2: Assignments, Readings, and Student Writing Samples*. Ed. Patrick Sullivan, Howard Tinberg, and Sheridan Blau. Urbana, IL: NCTE. 2010. 257–266. Print.

Sullivan, Patrick. "What Can We Learn about College-Level Writing from Basic Writing Students?: The Importance of Reading." *What Is "College-Level" Writing? Volume 2: Assignments, Readings, and Student Writing Samples*. Ed. Patrick Sullivan, Howard Tinberg, and Sheridan Blau. Urbana, IL: NCTE. 2010. 233–253. Print.

Disappearing into the World of Books

LINDSAY LARSEN
University of Connecticut
Class of 2009

L anguage and writing have always fascinated me. I was a voracious reader starting at a young age, and my love of words hasn't ceased. Words could comfort me when I was upset, and I enjoyed disappearing into the different worlds of books. The power of words and the infinite possibilities of words compelled me to become interested in writing. I have always enjoyed my English classes the most throughout my school career, and, even though I recently graduated from the University of Connecticut with a degree in English, my love and enjoyment for reading and writing continue.

The transition from high school and college is sometimes a difficult and intimidating experience for students. Students are expected to produce college-level work, and, if their high school career does not prepare them well, they may have difficulty. Students also need to be prepared to be conscientious in college. My high school teachers had high expectations, so I learned the importance of self-motivation and diligence. In college, no one is hovering over your shoulder, telling you what to do. This newfound independence is often thrilling and frightening at the same time. You must learn to depend on yourself, which can be a difficult lesson for some. I feel my work in high school prepared me for college, but no one can teach the importance of meeting deadlines or being organized; I had to learn that for myself.

I took AP English classes at RHAM High School in Hebron, Connecticut, and the amount of writing that was required and the literature that I read helped me prepare for college. For my AP English classes, we read a new work every few weeks, and we were expected to read several chapters each night. We read vastly different works, from the early English novel *Tom Jones* to modern works such as *Beloved,* but they were all challenging and required a great deal of thinking. Some of the books we read were a bit dry, but the reading did help me become a good English student. In one of my AP English classes, we had to read a modern novel and give a book talk on it. I chose *The Lovely Bones,* by Alice Sebold, and it became one of my favorite books. I enjoy it when instructors select a book from outside the literary canon, such as a modern novel or one that is not considered a classic.

I believe that English teachers should teach a variety of novels and even include nonfiction books such as biographies. The readings should be from different time periods and of different experiences. There is more diversity in this world than that represented by English white males from 1850. Teachers should also consider mediums not usually considered "literature," such as graphic novels. I recently read *Persepolis* by Marjane Satrapi for a modern English literature course, and I loved it. It told a story of a place I was not familiar with—Iran—and was fascinating. I bought the sequel on my own because I was so intrigued by the novel and wanted to know what happened next.

By the time I completed high school, I had read *Romeo and Juliet, King Lear, The Odyssey, The Iliad,* and more recent works such as *The Crucible* and *Beloved.* The advanced reading and high expectations of my high school prepared me for college-level work. If students read easier books and write simple essays, they will never gain experience and will remain at a lower level of learning. Adult-level works can be difficult and frustrating, but they open students to new ideas and help them as writers, introducing them to a variety of writing styles and a larger vocabulary. I consider the "classics" of literature, by authors such as Ernest Hemingway, Jane Austen, and Nathaniel Hawthorne, to be more adult-level works. However, there is a fine line between adult and young adult literature; it all melds together, with books such as the Harry Potter series aimed at children but loved by readers of all ages. Books with more challenging or provocative themes should be taught, not ones that are too simplistic or easy.

I will admit that some of the books were not my favorites, but one can learn from different styles of literature. Although exposure to a variety of ideas and stories can be tedious at times, it can also be beneficial. I learned to analyze and understand literature through research-based and creative assignments. Writing was required in all of my classes, and we often had writing portfolio assignments in which we explained how we worked on a math problem or translated a passage of Latin, depending on what subject we were writing in. If writing is considered essential across all disciplines, it will become more important and, most of all, come more naturally to a student. One must practice writing in order to become skilled at it. College consists of much independent essay writing. There isn't much hand-holding. Students often have to come up with their own topics based on what they have studied. In high school, students should be required to become more independent and think of their own topics.

Teachers should prepare students from the very beginning of high school for college-level writing. If students are taught how to edit their work early on, they will become better writers. Teachers should require drafts in the early grades of high school for some assignments, so students can learn how to edit their essays and perfect them. However, they should also let students write some essays without several drafts or meetings with the teacher. In college, multiple drafts are not normally required, so students should be taught how to edit on their own without support from an instructor. By the end of high school, students should be able to write strong essays on their own. If they create their own topics and research them, students will usually be more interested, and this simulates college conditions. If the students fail at essay writing, they should meet with the teacher to go over what was wrong, and they should be given a chance to fix it. Short writing exercises should also be done, such as composing a brief paragraph on a topic or even a poem or short story. Writing a persuasive essay is an important type of assignment as well and sets the stage for more advanced writing.

Teachers should also keep in mind that there is nothing worse than stifling a student's creativity. One of the best assignments I had in high school was to create a newspaper about *Romeo and Juliet*. My friend and I wrote articles about the tragic events in the play, including police reports about the deaths of Romeo, Juliet, Mercutio, and other characters, and we developed an investigative article on apothecaries. In middle school, a teacher had us produce creative works about every book or poem we read. We created a poem version of Poe's "The Pit and the Pendulum" and wrote a creative piece on the Holocaust after reading about Anne Frank. Creative assignments helped open my imagination and helped me grow as a thinker. With creative writing assignments, students are not restricted to a certain form and their ideas are not stifled. The world is filled with different problems and issues, and dealing with them in creative ways can help immensely in real life. Creative assignments provide more freedom and less boredom for students. It is important to master all forms of writing; it will, in turn, improve a student's essays.

I strongly believe teachers should instill a love of words into their students. Not everyone is going to enjoy the process or value a mastery of words, but it is worth a try. Teachers do have to follow a curriculum and state standards, but when the passion goes out of teaching, the passion goes out of learning as well. I would tell high school teachers that they should challenge their students to achieve to the best of their ability and try to teach in ways that capture student interest. I always enjoyed creative projects or learning something new and fascinating; it helped my writing a lot. The best teachers open up their students' minds to new possibilities and new ways of thinking, and this includes writing as well. Teaching a new book or a new writing style may help students improve their own writing.

In the remainder of this chapter, I present and discuss selections from the writing I did in high school and college.

Writing Sample 1

My writing has improved immensely since the beginning of high school. I understood the basic structure of an essay, but the analytical skills and depth of a more mature writer didn't exist yet. My writing was not bad for someone who was fourteen, but I definitely grew as a writer and learned to expand my ideas, as well as express original ideas and interpretations of the works I wrote about. The first sample was written at the beginning of my first year in high school. It is simplistic and illustrates how much I have grown since then. My sentences are short and choppy, and I often repeat myself. The essay is rather short as well, and my ideas could have been fleshed out much more. I used quotes to support my ideas, but I used too many of them in places where my ideas should have stood alone. An excessive use of quotes does not let your ideas shine through, and it can also mean you do not really understand what you are writing about. My ideas on the oppression of women in Greek myths were good, and I was going in the right direction, but the essay is mainly a plot summary:

> In ancient Greece, women were not equal to men. This belief is echoed in their mythology. All the main heroes, like Odysseus, Perseus, and Jason, were men. Most women played minor roles in the myths; the male characters overshadowed them. Even the only woman hero, Atalanta, is forced to marry a man in the end.
>
> In all the myths, women are judged by their beauty; the more beautiful they are, the more men like them. For instance, in the myth of Pygmalion and Galatea, Pygmalion, a woman-hating sculptor, makes the statue of a "perfect" woman. Pygmalion then becomes obsessed with Galatea because of her immense beauty. In the myth of the Trojan War, Paris, who is told to judge who is the most attractive of the goddesses, accepts Aphrodite's bribe of the most beautiful woman in the world, Helen of Troy. A whole war is fought over Helen. Paris claims his prize by running away with Helen, even though she is married to Menelaus. Thus, Menelaus declares war on Paris' home, the city of Troy. Even before that, Helen had so many marriage proposals, she didn't know what to do. "Such was the report of her beauty that not a young prince in Greece wanted but to marry her" (pg. 187–188). Women were prized for their looks and nothing else. No one cared if she was intelligent or had a personality. In ancient Greek times, appearance mattered greatly. What was on the outside counted more than what was on the inside.
>
> Greek women were treated as property; they had no say in their fate. In the story of the Trojan War, Agamemnon sacrifices his daughter just because the hunter goddess, Artemis, is angry the Greeks have killed her favorite hare. So Iphigenia, Agamemnon's daughter, was told that she was to be married. Instead, her father led her to an altar and murdered her. "And

all her prayers—cries of Father, Father/Her maiden life/These they held as nothing/The savage warriors, battle-mad" (pg. 190). Other women were also tricked like Iphigenia was. The great heroine Atalanta refused to marry a man, but one suitor tricked her. Atalanta said that she would only marry a man who could beat her in a race, but she could beat anyone in a race, so she would never marry. The man, Melanion, rolled some golden apples into her path as she was racing. These apples distracted her, so he won the race. "But then the third golden sphere flashed across her path and rolled far into the grass beside the court. She saw the gleam through the green, she could not resist it . . . She was his" (pg. 184).

Some Greeks believed that women were cursed. Pandora was made by the gods to be sent down to earth as revenge to the mortals. Since she was the first woman on earth, she was a temptation to men. Her story says, "From her, the first woman, comes the race of all women, who are an evil to men, with a nature to do evil." However, a kinder story about Pandora says she wasn't evil, but merely curious about the world. She was sent down with a box, but told never to open it. Unfortunately, Pandora's curiosity got the better of her, and she opened it. Out flew all the horrible things in the world—plagues, sorrow, mischief, and crime. Luckily for Pandora, Hope also flew out, to calm people in times of trouble. Epimetheus, who married Pandora, was warned by his brother Prometheus never to take Pandora as a gift from Zeus. "He took her, and afterward when that dangerous thing, a woman, was his, he understood how good his brother's advice had been" (pg. 74). Women were often viewed as dangerous if they thought too much, or were curious about something, as the myth of Pandora and the box illustrates.

Atalanta was the only woman hero the Greeks had in their myths. When she was born, her father was angry she wasn't a boy and decided that she was worthless. He left her in the mountains to die, but she was found by bears and then raised by kind hunters. Atalanta grew up, and became a wild and fierce huntress. When it came time to kill the Calydonian boar, she entered the hunt. However, some of the men were angry. "Some of the heroes resented her presence and felt it beneath them to go hunting with a woman . . ." (pg. 181). The men felt that a woman should not be part of a man's world. Later on, after Atalanta killed the boar, some hunters "felt themselves insulted and were furiously angry at having the prize go to a girl" (pg. 182). After this, she was tricked into marrying Melanion. The story of Atalanta is bittersweet; she is an exception to the sexism in Greek myth, but she herself cannot avoid the prejudice. The men don't want her in the hunt, and later a huge tragedy ensues. They are very angry since Atalanta killed the Calydonian boar and end up getting killed. Even the end of Atalanta's story isn't happy. After she is forced to marry Melanion, "her free days alone in the forest and her athletic victories were over" (pg. 184).

Women are portrayed in Greek mythology as weak and unintelligent people. Their only saving grace is their beauty. Greek mythology seems very sexist to us, but is an accurate reflection of the thinking of the times. Luckily, nowadays, women are being portrayed in literature as they truly are: strong, smart, and outspoken.

Writing Sample 2

High school helped me grow as a writer, and, by my senior year of high school, I was able to write longer essays comparing different works of literature and containing a lot of analysis. For our final paper in AP English, I read *Jane Eyre,* by Charlotte Brontë, and *Wide Sargasso Sea*, by Jean Rhys, and compared the two works while discussing social issues in both novels. I have always enjoyed *Jane Eyre*, and it was fascinating to read the story behind Bertha, Rochester's mentally ill wife who is locked in the attic, in *Wide Sargasso Sea*. Since the books are related, it was easier to find connections between them, but the paper was the longest I had ever written. The minimum requirement was twenty pages, and it was difficult at first to find that much to say, but once I started writing the paper, the ideas started to flow. The paper represents my growth as a writer and illustrates how I improved throughout high school. I learned to elaborate on my ideas, as well as support my ideas soundly. I was more confident in my writing ability, and I included more description and well-thought-out ideas. I consider this essay to be college-level writing because of the amount of analysis and the deeper understanding shown about the novels. My first sample essay was shorter, but it also lacked content. This second essay shows a better understanding of the material. I was able to comprehend the novels fully and connect them to real social issues and the theme of oppression.

The ability to find connections between works is important, and I was able to compare and contrast the books easily.

Here is an excerpt from the beginning of that essay:

Novels often deal with serious issues within society. *Jane Eyre* and *Wide Sargasso Sea* are both concerned with the volatile issues of class and race and gender in their respective societies, Victorian England and Jamaica in the 1800s. Both were very different societies, but the issues reappear again and again. Victorian England was filled with whites who strived to be high society, and poor people were looked down upon. Women had no voice and men were their masters. The Caribbean contained mostly blacks, and Caucasian people were the minority. The white people could even be considered lower than the blacks, as Antoinette and her family are in *Wide Sargasso Sea*. Jean Rhys and Charlotte Brontë were both influenced by the societies they lived in, and issues of class and race that they dealt with are pervasive in their novels *Wide Sargasso Sea* and *Jane Eyre*. *Wide Sargasso Sea* is a prequel to *Jane Eyre*, and its societal conflicts are very different than *Jane Eyre's*. However, the novels mirror each other in many ways. Both contain a similar thread—Rochester's mad wife, Bertha—and a woman's struggle in an oppressive society.

Wide Sargasso Sea is a prequel to *Jane Eyre*. It tells the story of Antoinette Cosway Mason, who will later marry Rochester and become Bertha Rochester. Antoinette grows up in Jamaica, the daughter of a beautiful yet troubled mother and a father who dies when she is a child. Antoinette is similar to Jane in that they are both abandoned as children. Antoinette's mother pays her little attention, and Antoinette is scorned by the black people of the island because she is poor and fatherless. "I got used to a solitary life . . . ," says Antoinette of her childhood (Rhys 18). Antoinette leads a loveless life full of rejection (Angher 534–535). Her mother doesn't love her, and although her stepfather Mr. Mason and nurse Christophine are fond of her, Antoinette never knows love. She may be tricked into love, like her marriage with Rochester, but it is never real (Angher 535). It is no wonder she becomes disillusioned with the world and turns into the mad monster that is Bertha Rochester.

Antoinette's experiences shape her and cause her to become mad. The first problems she faces are race-related. The society was mainly black people, and white people were the minority by far. Black people respected the rich, white English people. However, Antoinette's family is Creole and poor. The white Creole people were disliked because "there is often the well-grounded supposition that the Creole may have mixed blood" (O'Connor 21). They, like Jane Eyre, had an odd place in society—they were not native Jamaicans, but they thought of it as their home (O'Connor 21). In the Jamaicans' eyes, the Cosways are little better than white trash. Her mother is a ruined, crazy beauty; the father is dead; Pierre, Antoinette's brother, is mentally challenged; the family is poor, a broken shell of what it once was. To the black people of the island, it was reason enough to hate the Cosways. The family was slaveowners, and there were rumors of Antoinette's father sleeping with black women, which was not uncommon practice, but it was still looked down upon. Antoinette says:

> I never looked at any strange negro. They hated us. They called us white cockroaches. Let sleeping dogs lie. One day a little girl followed me singing, 'Go away white cockroach, go away, go away. Nobody want you. Go away.' (Rhys 23)

Antoinette starts to believe that nobody wants her, and for the most part, it's true. Soon, her mother remarries to Mr. Mason, a wealthy Englishman. There are rumors about that marriage, too. Antoinette hears someone say, "Then why should he marry a widow without a penny to her name and Coulibri a wreck of a place?" (Rhys 28).

Everyone in Jamaica is constantly judging the family. Even in the Caribbean, which would appear to be more carefree and less restrictive than stuffy England, appearances matter. The family has problems, such as drunkenness and poverty and madness, but no one ever pities them. All of Jamaica seems to scorn the Cosways, and even when Antoinette's mother marries Mr. Mason, there isn't much of an improvement. Everyone gossips about why he married a woman like her. Then there is a riot at the estate where the family lives, Coulibri. Blacks come to the house and throw rocks and burn the house down. Pierre dies in the ensuing turmoil. Antoinette describes the violent scene:

> "Some yelled, 'But look at the black Englishman! Look at the white niggers!' and then they were all yelling 'Look at the niggers! Look at the damn white niggers!' . . . But we could not move for they pressed too close 'round us. Some of them were laughing and waving sticks, some of the ones at the back were carrying flambeaux and it was light as day." (Rhys 42)

Antoinette's mother is forever scarred from the death of Pierre, and she goes insane. Antoinette is sent away to a school at a convent, but the incident haunts her. She is even more rejected by her mother, and she barely ever sees her.

Society has strict rules that one must follow. Both Jane and Antoinette have troubles being accepted in society, and Antoinette's difficulties never improve. She is always perceived as white trash, even after her marriage to Mr. Rochester. He is a rich, proper Englishman—the kind of man her reputation needs for salvation. But the blacks never truly accept her—one rude servant girls sings about Antoinette being a cockroach. Antoinette is downtrodden all her life because of her family; the world never sees who she truly is, a beautiful, emotionally fragile girl who just needs someone to care for her, and accept her for all her faults and her dark past. She is not strong-willed and self-sufficient like Jane Eyre; Antoinette is childlike and breakable. However, Mr. Rochester cannot accept her for who she is. In Wide Sargasso Sea, he is concerned with social status and appearances. He is a cold, unfeeling man whose marriage is one of convenience. Rochester puts on a show of loving her, but that's not how he truly feels. "When at last I met her I bowed, smiled, kissed her hand, danced with her. I played the part I was expected to play. . . . Every movement I made was an effort of will and sometimes I wondered that no one noticed this," admits Rochester (Rhys 77). He is playing the role of a dutiful son; his father wants him to marry, since he is the youngest son and will not receive a huge inheritance. He receives a large dowry for marrying Antoinette; she is now rich because of her stepfather, Mason.

Class plays a large role in Mr. Rochester's motives—he needs to remain wealthy, and she has the money. It is a marriage of convenience, although both Antoinette and Rochester pretend there is passion. They want to believe there is love, or at least give the appearance of it, but this attempt does not succeed. Then Mr. Rochester discovers the secrets of Antoinette's family, and this revolts him. Daniel Cosway, who claims he is the son of Antoinette's father and a black slave, writes him a letter describing the family's faults. "The young Mrs. Cosway [Antoinette's mother] is worthless and spoilt, she can't lift a hand for herself and soon the madness that is in her, and in all these white Creoles, come out," writes Daniel (Rhys 96). Rochester is horrified and feels like no one tells him the truth. He starts calling Antoinette Bertha, since it is a plain English name, and almost an insult to a beautiful, exotic island girl. Antoinette hates the name, but he calls her it anyway, and it degrades her. Rochester never again pretends to love her, and soon their relationship crumbles. Rochester hates her, and she slowly starts to go mad at his treatment.

Writing Sample 3

The following is an excerpt from an essay I wrote on William Butler Yeats for a modern English literature course in college. I discussed Irish nationalism in Yeats's poetry, and what his view on events such as the Easter Rising were. Yeats's poems are not always straightforward, and for this paper, I had to find the meaning and connect it to political issues of the time, as well as his own views.

I feel like this piece really exemplifies my growth as a writer. By this point, I was able to take historical background and themes in his poetry and analyze them, and then draw conclusions about what his personal beliefs may have been. I became a much more confident writer, and I was not afraid that my ideas might be wrong. I could interpret the literature and express my ideas in detail. This essay demonstrates my belief that I have come a long way from my first essays in high school:

> In "Easter 1916," Yeats describes the participants in the nationalist movement, and how they were executed for their involvement in the Easter Rising. The opening of the poem is a list of the people involved, and how their involvement changed their lives, and Irish history, forever. The tone is solemn and full of remembrance for the executed; they have been "transformed utterly" by the Easter Rising and it is not a positive change (Yeats 39). Yeats obviously considers the deaths and the rise of Irish nationalism to be a serious matter but he refers to the participants as taking part in a "casual comedy"; he is mocking because the situation is neither casual or amusing (Yeats 37).
>
> The end of the first stanza introduces the refrain "A terrible beauty is born." Yeats has created a paradox, because something that is beautiful is usually not considered terrible; to most people, they are two opposing ideas. Beauty is associated with good and happiness, while terror is associated with

evil and darkness. A terrible beauty has arisen out of the ashes of Easter Rising, and one that will be unstoppable. The devotion to one's country and the fight for independence can be considered a beautiful and positive thing; for example, the American Revolution is often seen as good, since it created an independent nation. Freedom usually has positive connotations. The refrain is simple but strikes the reader; it is powerful in shaping what the reader thinks of the Easter Rising, and creates an effect that lasts throughout the whole poem.

The line is repeated several times for more emphasis; we as readers are supposed to realize the horrible costs of attaining freedom. Critic Peter Koch writes that the refrain has been associated in readers' minds with the Easter Rebellion, and the present tense of the sentence emphasizes its importance and influences the reader (200). Yeats seems to think that a certain amount of nationalism is good, but the good can quickly be erased and become dark. Yeats writes, "Hearts with one purpose alone/Through summer and winter seem/ Enchanted to a stone/To trouble the living stream" (Yeats 41–44). If the nationalists narrow their focus too much, and become obsessed and violent, it will change the world. This ultimately does happen and Ireland suffers from nationalistic violence for many years after it was divided into two separate nations. Their desire for independence will harden their hearts, and ruin their lives. They cannot forget what else life has to offer, and that change will come; it is inevitable. As critic Neville F. Newman writes, "This recognition exposes the political and moral paradox with which the poem wrestles. The fundamental political changes represented by the Easter rebellion contain the potential for a political and moral petrification. The very act of change can result in entrenchment, establishing a position resistant to the idea of improvement. Out of such situations, hearts of stone are created. And so Yeats argues vehemently for a change of sorts, while warning that if change is to be justified, it must be viewed as the precondition for yet further change."

The nationalism of the Irish people could be making the situation worse, and the country could become stuck in a political limbo, instead of improving. The fighters' hearts have turned to stone, and the rebellion has created a tense political situation that could make Ireland much worse than when it started. Political unrest and violence are on the horizon, and Yeats is cautioning the nationalists. However, he is not saying they are completely wrong; he just does not agree with their means of gaining independence. Yeats sees the beauty in freedom, but also sees the terrible, and very real, possibilities of the future.

Recommendations

Writing is an ongoing process; students are always improving and learning, and teachers should always be ready to teach their students new things. High school teachers should be prepared to teach their students the fundamentals of writing, including the editing process and how to critically analyze literature to write better essays. High school students should be taught to argue their point thoroughly, and they should also learn to be creative with their essays. They should be encouraged to think of their own essay topics, to further help them as writers and thinkers.

College-level writing is not as scary as some students think it is. It can be challenging, but if students write essays in high school on a regular basis, critically analyze readings, and provide convincing support for their arguments, they should be prepared for college. Students have to understand that the biggest challenge they face in college is their own independence; their instructors will not support them along the way as they do in high school. Students must be prepared to write essays on their own and to be confident in their abilities. That is the most important aspect high school teachers need to prepare them for.

---V---

Ideas, Observations, and Suggestions from Our Respondents

College-Level Writing and the Liberal Arts Tradition

EDWARD M. WHITE
University of Arizona

It is clear that the concept of "college-level writing" is not solely a matter of location. College-level writing goes on in many secondary schools, while much writing that takes place in a first-year college course would be unlikely to be called college level. Indeed, as the essays written by the student contributors to this collection make clear, many students remember fondly their work preparing them for college and often consider it more significant and challenging than some of their college-level writing. No, the overall impact of this volume, with its variety of voices, suggests that college-level writing, wherever it occurs, makes certain kinds of demands on student abilities that depend on cognitive growth, emotional maturity, and intellectual flexibility that some students gain early and that others, well, might gain later in their lives.

Further, it is clear that US colleges and universities differ strongly in their demands on student writers, not only from one to another but also from one kind of curriculum within a college to another. The standardization implied by a single term *college level* is not only foreign to the diversity of US universities and colleges but actually runs counter to the great strength offered by this diversity. Yet though the term resists simple definition, it is also clear that it is much in use as a way of speaking of a refined ability to express oneself.

And it is the great strength of this volume (as well as the first one), that it circles around its topic, looking at it from a wide variety of perspectives. We sense that there is something inside this circle, what psychologists would call a *construct*, that exists, despite our inability to pin it down and determine all of its characteristics. In order for readers to respond to this book, we need to seek for certain essences: What characteristics clearly must be present in writing for us to call it *college level*?

A good place to start is with the opening essay in the volume, where Tom Thompson and Andrea Gallagher present high school and college readings of the same papers. High school and college teachers, they point out, inhabit different worlds, and Thompson and Gallagher go on to explain some of the key differences. The high school world is more constricted, particularly by the ever-present competency tests that inevitably emphasize form. The college world is less structured, even more chaotic, and teachers there are able to value thoughtfulness and originality in ways that high school teachers cannot. The source paper, for example, at the high school level, tends to stress research skills, bibliography compilation, and footnote form as well as organization and correctness. In addition, since so much high school writing is attuned to test preparation, teachers necessarily insist that the writing focus on responding to the assignment.

While these matters remain important in college-level work, they are not necessarily at the top of a professor's criteria. There is a slight but very significant shift in the use of sources: In college, the writer needs to put sources in context, say why the source is being cited, and relate what the source says to what the writer has to say. Those teaching college-level writing work hard to help students distinguish between using a source to *substitute* for their ideas and using a source to *support* their ideas. This is a very difficult matter for students to understand and put into practice, since it assumes that writing is a discovery process during which the writer's ideas come into focus. It also assumes that the writer has an intellectual identity distinct from the sources cited. Notice that a certain amount of maturity is necessary for this scenario to occur.

Too many college students fail to write college-level papers because they feel they have nothing to say, particularly when they stand in the shadows of their sources. So they list sources, or summarize them, or even plagiarize them, relying on the knowledge of forms they may have gained in high school. But the key element in a college-level source paper is the writer's use of sources to support or discuss positions and assertions that the writer has come to defend and develop. The goal of the high school source paper is to help students learn how to locate and document sources, an important and necessary ability; the goal of the college-level source paper—which may, I repeat, occur in high school—is to help students learn how to use sources as evidence for the discovery and development of ideas and arguments.

Perhaps the best example of this difference is the five-paragraph theme, a format frequently taught in the schools but generally mocked and deplored in college. My satire of the format included in this volume is at heart an attack on the dominance of form over content, arguing, satirically, against the limitations on discovery and thought imposed by the form. Returning from an Advanced Placement essay scoring session recently, I imagined myself at age seventeen and set out to write a defense of the five-paragraph theme. I was a good high school writer and I think my seventeen-year-old self wrote a pretty good paper. College professors laugh heartily at the satire, while high school teachers are not nearly as amused. They point out that when students are learning to write essays, they need to learn about organization of ideas; at that stage, a primitive format is extremely useful. Notice that the student contributors to this volume appreciated the limits of the five-paragraph theme, though—in order to have writing mature enough to be published here—they have moved well beyond those limits. And several of the authors in this volume, most notably Alfredo Celedón Luján, have written about the constructive ways they adapt the formula for teaching college-level writing. Nonetheless, one of the hard lessons that students must learn is that formula writing is at most a starting point for college-level work, which requires genuine thought and development of ideas.

Another hard lesson for students has to do with writing assignments. High school teachers often give clearer and more effective writing assignments than do college professors. And the incessant pressure to do well on tests in school leads to clear grading rubrics in many cases. Yet college-level assignments, despite their less structured nature, have a curricular focus that requires considerable reading related to the college course. Only in rare cases will students have free choice to write about what they want to write about or to experience what Steven Schmidt calls "being able to write freely and under my own direction, [which] was exciting and liberating" (268). College papers exist because writing is a student's chief means of learning, and college-level writing is usually designed to move students out of their comfort zone into new ways of thinking about complex matters. That is a different kind of liberation than Schmidt is praising.

If we step back and think about this volume and its predecessor, we can see an important and original contribution to the way we as a culture have come to value college-level study. Despite, or perhaps because of, its diversity and range of studies and standards, college-level work in the United States at its best offers all its students opportunity for moving beyond the formulas and conventions of earlier education. Or, at least, that is the tradition and the reason writing is generally regarded as the most paradigmatic aspect of college-level work. That ideal needs constant defense, since it is perennially under attack by proponents of vocationalism, corporate conventionalism, and pragmatism. This volume, with all its variations in perspectives, offers, by example and by definition, an excellent defense of that liberal arts tradition.

Works Cited

Larsen, Lindsay. "Disappearing into the World of Books." *What Is "College-Level" Writing? Volume 2: Assignments, Readings, and Student Writing Samples*. Ed. Patrick Sullivan, Howard Tinberg, and Sheridan Blau. Urbana, IL: NCTE. 2010. 280–292. Print.

Luján, Alfredo Celedón. "The Thirty-Eight-or-So Five-Paragraph Essay (The Dagwood)." *What Is "College-Level" Writing? Volume 2: Assignments, Readings, and Student Writing Samples*. Ed. Patrick Sullivan, Howard Tinberg, and Sheridan Blau. Urbana, IL: NCTE. 2010. 142–169. Print.

Maliszewski, Casey. "Home Schooled." *What Is "College-Level" Writing? Volume 2: Assignments, Readings, and Student Writing Samples*. Ed. Patrick Sullivan, Howard Tinberg, and Sheridan Blau. Urbana, IL: NCTE. 2010. 257–266. Print.

Schmidt, Steven. "Moving the Tassel from the Right to the Left." *What Is "College-Level" Writing? Volume 2: Assignments, Readings, and Student Writing Samples*. Ed. Patrick Sullivan, Howard Tinberg, and Sheridan Blau. Urbana, IL: NCTE. 2010. 267–279. Print.

Thompson, Tom, and Andrew Gallagher. "When a College Professor and High School Teacher Read the Same Papers." *What Is "College-Level" Writing? Volume 2: Assignments, Readings, and Student Writing Samples*. Ed. Patrick Sullivan, Howard Tinberg, and Sheridan Blau. Urbana, IL: NCTE. 2010. 3–28. Print.

Responding Forward

KATHLEEN BLAKE YANCEY
Florida State University

When the editors of this collection invited me to respond to the good thinking here, I was glad to say yes. The connections between high school writing and college writing are ones I've been interested in for a long time, based largely on three experiences: my own teaching (in addition to teaching college writing classes for longer than I care to admit, I taught high school and middle school English classes for several years); my work with high school teachers in Virginia Beach City Schools, a decade-long labor of love that continues today; and my recent research on what we call the transfer question. Put simply, what is it that students learn in our classes about how to write that they carry forward with them into other sites of writing? This volume, of course, implicitly makes a response to that question, at the least because transfer of some kind is what we *all* hope for: We want our students' learning to have both immediate effect and enduring value. At the same time, we know—and as this volume makes clear—we have very different cultures of writing in high school and in college. I hasten to point out, however, that even a *single* high school or college has within it *multiple* cultures of writing, and, given that writing is rhetorical—designed for a given purpose and audience—that's a good thing, in my view. The "problem," if there is one, isn't the diversity of cultures, but rather *how those cultures connect,* or put somewhat differently, *how we might better connect them.*

To think about this—about how our writing cultures might connect—I'm going to do exactly what our editors asked Ed White and me to do in our responses: " . . . to identify important points of agreement among contributors and to offer us pragmatic advice for moving forward." To help us move forward, then, I'll think in three movements: first, identifying points of agreement within the chapters of this collection; second, connecting those points of agreement to selected research findings; and third, proposing a very specific approach that could both connect and enhance our cultures of writing.

Points of Agreement

How do we find points of agreement? Inside a book, we often read chapters individually and then read across them to discern patterns, a practice nicely evidenced in Ed White's response. I did that, too, and so I also have some impressions of what I read. But in the age of digital technologies, I decided to try two other quick but useful strategies. First, I used a visualization technique provided by Wordle[1] (www.wordle.net) that shows themes according to word counts: The more often the word is used, the larger it is. To create this visualization, I simply copied and pasted the contents of this volume, except this chapter, into the program, and it created a "wordle" depicting the themes of the volume. Indeed, as Figure 17.1 shows, *What Is "College-Level" Writing?* focuses on

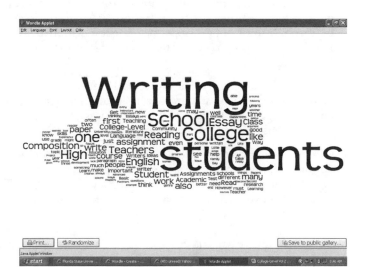

FIGURE 17.1. *The themes of this volume as visualized by Wordle.*

writing for students in high school and college! This, then, would seem to be the major point of agreement.

Are there others? Second, and to answer that question, I identified some key terms and used the search function in Microsoft Word to see what I'd find. My first search term was *writing process*, used because there's a common assumption that English teachers on both sides of the high school–college divide teach writing as process, and, in my reading of this volume, that assumption seemed accurate. According to the search results, however, *writing process* is used only four times in this book. I then tried the word *process*, which occurred more than a hundred times. But when I took a closer look at *how* the term *process* was employed, it defied any central meaning. Here is an almost-random sample:

- But throughout *this entire process*, she always said, "You're getting closer. Don't give up!" (264)

- While some students need a teacher to give them a topic for writing assignments, other students feel stifled by such a process. Perhaps a choice should be given to them *in the process*: Either the teacher can give them a specific topic to write about, or they can create their own topic (265–266).

- More substantive formal assignments throughout the course need to include *a process for reflection and revision*. This can be through draft submissions, peer reviews, individual conferences, or other processes that allow for critical feedback (272–273).

- Certainly, when I give feedback to peers, I almost always feel bad pointing out mistakes and areas in need of improvement, but I know this is *an important aspect of the process*, not only for the student whose paper I was reviewing but also for me (274).

- Of course, interrupting reading to jot notes is not productive. To this end, I employed the strategy of highlighting while reading, followed by going back to take notes on key points. *This process* was extremely beneficial to me, especially in conducting research for essays (274).

So is *process* a central term here? My answer: yes and no. Certainly, it's used often, as shown in these quick examples, to describe the learning process, the process of assigning writing, the process of reflection and revision, the process of responding to writing, and the process of reading and researching. At the same time, the usage we see is sufficiently varied that it doesn't point to a common reference. Put simply, *process* is a key term, but, in its differentiation, it doesn't provide for the critical mass or coherence we expect of a key term. Without that, it's difficult to see how it could serve as a connection between high school and college, or even between us and our students.

I tried a second term, *genre*, and, again, found more than a hundred instances of it. But in this case, there was a different kind of pattern: *Genre* wasn't used throughout the volume, as *process* was, but rather appeared predominantly in two chapters. In other words, *genre* as a term was used nearly as often as *process*, but it figured primarily in only two chapters. Based on this analysis, it's not a central term in the book, either. I tried other terms as well—terms that many in the high school community might value. One key term, *literature*, came up eighty times. Other terms those in the college community would likely find important were *digital* (used only once); *visual* (eight); and *rhetorical situation*, perhaps the most salient expression in college composition,[2] was used only once. By itself, however, *rhetoric* occurred twenty-two times, and more than another fifty if we count uses stemming from the root—*rhetorical*, for example.

What does all this mean? My assumption is that shared key terms could provide a connection, and that those key terms need to be more than the terms we saw in the Wordle image—students, high school, college, and writing—as useful as those terms are. If that's so, what might those key terms be?

Recent Research

Within the last ten years, many studies in higher education have focused on the transfer question, and, of these, I'd like to highlight three research findings because of their relevance to what we mean by "college-level writing" in the context of high school and college writing cultures.

The first of these, a longitudinal study conducted by educational assessment researchers reported in the University of Washington's Study of Undergraduate Learning (UW SOUL), located a writing gap between high school and college and identified its causes. In design, this study tracked 304 undergraduates through their undergraduate writing experience in order to gather information that would help us improve teaching and learning. The study was designed to discover what undergraduates learned, how they learned it, what obstacles or challenges they faced along the way, and how they assessed their own learning in six areas:

- writing
- problem solving/critical thinking
- quantitative reasoning
- understanding and appreciating diversity
- information literacy
- general growth as learners (n.p.)

Of these areas, the two that were most difficult, the ones that constituted serious gaps between high school and college, were math and writing. The problems in writing were twofold: (1) as we see in this volume, students bring with them to college a conception of writing misshaped by testing; and (2) students don't understand writing as disciplinary. What we see in this large study, then, aligns nicely with what we see in this volume.

A second finding, from a joint study conducted at the University of Washington and the University of Tennessee (Bawarshi and Reiff), also aligns nicely. Interested in how the key concept of genre might transfer from high school into college, faculty at both institutions interviewed numerous college students to learn about their understanding of genre and how they use the concept in composing. What they found was that the students brought limited genre knowledge into college with them and didn't use that knowledge when writing. Rather, when asked about genre, the students began to describe rhetorical strategies or approaches.

> During our coding and analysis of the interviews, two inter-
> esting patterns emerged: the relationship between genres
> and strategies, and the move from genres to what we termed
> "not" genres. When we asked students what genres they were
> reminded of or drew on, they would often name genres such
> a five-paragraph essay, book review, literary analysis. But they
> would also name what we began identifying and coding as
> "strategies." (n.p.)

In other words, in spite of all the time these students had spent
learning a set of genres in literature, they didn't have the category
of genre as one that informed their writing. Put differently, perhaps it was too much to ask these students to make the connection between reading genres and their own writing in genres.[3]

The last finding concerns the connection between assuming
the rhetorical stance of a novice as one moves from one large
context, that of high school, to another, that of college. In 2004,
Nancy Sommers and Laura Saltz reported on the Harvard Study
of Writing, and one of their findings focused on what we might
call the role of noviceship. Basically, they found that the most successful writers were those who understood that, as new writers—
that is, new writers in college—students needed to begin anew
and write from a position of noviceship:

> A major conclusion of our study is that students who ini-
> tially accept their status as novices and allow their passions
> to guide them make the greatest gains in writing develop-
> ment. As novices who care deeply about their subjects,
> these students have a reason to learn the methodologies of
> their chosen disciplines, encouraged to believe that follow-
> ing their own interests is important to their success as stu-
> dents. (145)

Interestingly, this finding corresponds to what Kristine Hansen
and her colleagues at Brigham Young found in examining the
success of Advanced Placement students. That study showed that
students who attempt to *replace* college composition with high
school AP scores, particularly those with scores in the 3 range,
find themselves at a distinct disadvantage:

> Our results show that students who score a 3 on the AP exam
> and do not take a first year writing course are likely to suffer
> real consequences in sophomore courses that require writing
> assignments. . . . At BYU, as is likely true of most institutions,
> FYC provides an introduction to the discourse of the univer-
> sity, to a university library, and to genres of writing students
> have likely not encountered before. (41)

In other words, as a site of writing, college is different than high
school: It's sufficiently new that entering students are novices.
Moreover, when they embrace the rhetorical stance of novice,
they develop more fully as writers. Perhaps not surprisingly, this
is precisely the point made by one of the students in this volume,
Steven Schmidt:

> My transition to the four-year college was difficult, and my
> first semester was incredibly challenging. However, through
> the processes of feedback, reflection, and review, along with
> my own work ethic, I became comfortable with the new
> demands I faced in the four-year setting by my second semes-
> ter. (278)

How can these findings—about the writing gap between high
school and college, about *genre* as a potentially useful term that
hasn't thus far helped students bridge the high school-college gap,
and about the rhetorical stance of noviceship—help us create
connections between the writing cultures in high school and those
in college?

A Modest Proposal

A quick glance at what high school teachers are expected to
teach, regardless of whether the classrooms are in Alaska or Alabama, demonstrates that it's a good deal more than writing: It's
listening, speaking, media, reading, and, perhaps most important, literature. At the college level, we teach literature, too, but
in literature classes not, any longer at least, in writing classes.
It wasn't always so: Seventy years ago, college writing classes
were English classes, too, where introductions to literature were

taught alongside of writing (Yancey 2006). Today, however, with the advent of writing process research and pedagogy, introductory collegiate English classes have become *writing* classes in their own right, expected to introduce students to the world of college writing, where they, in David Bartholomae's famous expression, "invent the university"—in a trend that matches the growth of and is fueled by the field of rhetoric and composition.[4] In fact, college writing classes are increasingly housed *not* in English departments at all but rather in a "room of their own": inside their own independent writing programs or writing studies departments. Indeed, one of the more interesting current trends in the teaching of writing at the college level is using writing itself—an approach that's called writing about writing—as the material of such classes (Downs and Wardle; Slomp and Sargent). The point: that the high school *English* class and the college *writing* class inhabit very different cultures and help students meet very different outcomes.

But I wonder if there aren't key terms or expressions that we share, or could share, that would provide a stronger connection between these two larger cultures. To test this small theory, I'd like to begin with three expressions, phrases, or terms, where in each case a foundation is available, one we see inside the pages of this volume, but a foundation we would need to define, agree upon, and build into curriculum documents, assignments, and reflections. I believe such a set of key terms, in valuing our differences yet at the same time emphasizing what we share, would help students precisely because it would provide a new shared *vocabulary of practice*.

A first expression is *writing processes*, but it likely needs to be a different *writing process* than has been employed in the past. Too often that process is a one-size-fits-all mechanistic approach, or one keyed to a teacher's own practices rather than to the needs of a genre (writers of fiction ordinarily do use a different process than composers of a biology lab report), or one keyed to a testing situation, or one innocent of technology—and all this is before we talk about the composing students *already* do outside of school, a point I've made elsewhere and often (see, for example, "The Impulse to Compose and the Age of Composition"). If we—high school and college teachers together—agreed on *writing processes* as one of our three expressions, we might then work together to define it fully, to connect it to out-of-school literacies, and to enact it differentially in our classrooms.

A second expression is *genre*, a term that also seems to bring the high school and college writing cultures together in a "natural" way. Genre is at the heart of literary study: in fact, we read a sonnet differently than we do a novel, even when a novel is poetic (as most good novels are; see *Teaching Literature as Reflective Practice*). Genre is likewise at the heart of many, if not all, first-year college composition classes, as the WPA Outcomes Statement, a widely adopted statement about what students should know and be able to do by the end of first-year composition, suggests:

> By the end of first year composition, students should
>
> ◆ focus on a purpose
>
> ◆ respond to the needs of different audiences
>
> ◆ respond appropriately to different kinds of rhetorical situations
>
> ◆ use conventions of format and structure appropriate to the rhetorical situation
>
> ◆ adopt appropriate voice, tone, and level of formality
>
> ◆ understand how genres shape reading and writing
>
> ◆ write in several genres

In other words, genre is already embedded in the high school culture, although we know from the research reported here that it would need to be highlighted in different ways in order to provide a link to college composition. For their part, college programs would then need to build in a link to this prior knowledge their students bring in with them. In sum, although we might need to adjust its usage, *genre* is available as a term to connect our writing cultures; we'd simply need to make it count.

And last, but perhaps most important, is *rhetorical situation*, an expression created by Lloyd Bitzer more than forty years ago, with three characteristics: an exigence, or occasion for writing; a purpose for writing; and an audience to whom a composer writes. All writers, according to Bitzer, write within a rhetorical situation—be it Charles Dickens, Toni Morrison, or the students in our classrooms.

I'll note that this past summer, I used this expression with a group of high school teachers in a literacy institute I led. The expression was completely new to them, but of all the terms we used (and we had ten), they found this one the most useful, in part because it can be used both as a tool of analysis—what is the rhetorical situation in which Shakespeare is writing?—as well as a heuristic for the design of writing that emphasizes its rhetorical nature—its purpose, its audience, its occasion. So I think it has much promise to align both high school and college writing cultures. Put differently, while the expression *rhetorical situation* is likely new to most high school contexts, I think it could well serve as a welcome addition.

In Sum

Our writing cultures in high school and college are different, as the volume here shows us, although we share an abiding faith in processes of all kinds and a commitment to help students develop those processes. As this volume shows, however, the high school and college writing cultures are different, and in making those differences visible and articulated, this collection has also made them available for discussion—and for change. In sum, this volume implicitly asks us how we might move forward *together*.

The good news is we have much to build upon—our students, our pedagogies, our writing cultures. Building together doesn't mean, in my view, collapsing difference or making it invisible; it does mean identifying shared vocabulary and practices. And my hope is that with a central set of fundamental terms—writing processes, genre, and rhetorical situation—we can begin building a new writing future for all our students.

Notes

1. Wordle is a wonderful tool for classroom practice. For example, before peer review, students can "wordle" a draft to see if their sense of focus is matched.

2. See, for example, the comments of well-known compositionists in the *Take 20* DVD.

3. As I make clear later, I think this term is available for connection making, but we'd have to decide upon that as a common outcome. I'll note that *genre* is a relatively recent addition to the vocabulary of college composition (and, indeed, many of the early efforts of writing process treated all genres as alike); the WPA Outcomes Statement, for example, includes in the introduction to the outcomes an expression of anxiety about including it as a term, which is pretty interesting given that it's a familiar term in high school.

4. An unexplored speculation on my part here has to do with the different education we teachers bring to the classroom. Anecdotally, the claim is that many high school teachers have had very little, if any, formal education in writing theory, research, or practice. In my own experience, I had a single methods course that addressed literature, writing, media, etc., which was the same single course required of preservice teachers twenty years later at UNC Charlotte, a course I consistently taught during my decade-long tenure there. It was a good course, but it was only a single course with too many demands on it. In contrast, more and more often, teachers in college classrooms bring at least one dedicated course in writing into the class with them, and others, like our students at Florida State completing a master of arts degree in rhetoric and composition, bring with them *at least* three courses—composition theory; rhetorical theory; and research methods in rhetoric and composition—and often more. If this observation is correct, we'd expect our understandings of writing to vary.

Works Cited

Bartholomae, David. "Inventing the University." *When a Writer Can't Write: Studies in Writer's Block and Other Composing-Process Problems.* Ed. Mike Rose. New York: Guilford, 1985. 134–65. Print.

Bawarshi, Anis, and Mary Jo Reiff. "Researching Transfer of Writing across Situation, Time, Medium, and Genre." Writing Research across Borders Conference. Santa Barbara. 22 Feb. 2008. Address.

Beyer, Catharine Hoffman, Gerald M. Gillmore, and Andrew T. Fisher. "UW Study of Undergraduate Learning (UW SOUL)." *http://www.washington.edu/oea/soul/index.html.* University of Washington Office of Educational Assessment. Web. 1 July 2010.

Bitzer, Lloyd. "The Rhetorical Situation." *Philosophy and Rhetoric* 1.1 (1968): 1–14. Print.

Council of Writing Program Administrators. "WPA Outcomes Statement for First-Year Composition." *http://www.wpacouncil.org/ positions/outcomes.html.* WPA, Apr. 2000. Web. 21 June 2010.

Downs, Douglas, and Elizabeth Wardle. "Teaching about Writing, Righting Misconceptions: (Re)Envisioning 'First-Year Composition' as 'Introduction to Writing Studies.'" *College Composition and Communication* 58.4 (2007): 552–84. Print.

Hansen, Kristine, Suzanne Reeve, Richard Sudweeks, Gary L. Hatch, Jennifer Gonzalez, Patricia Esplin, and William S. Bradshaw. "An Argument for Changing Institutional Policy on Granting AP Credit in English: An Empirical Study of College Sophomores' Writing." *WPA: Writing Program Administration* 28.1–2 (2004): 29–54.

Maliszewski, Casey. "Home Schooled." *What Is "College-Level" Writing? Volume 2: Assignments, Readings, and Student Writing Samples.* Ed. Patrick Sullivan, Howard Tinberg, and Sheridan Blau. Urbana, IL: NCTE. 2010. 257–266. Print.

Schmidt, Steven. "Moving the Tassel from the Right to the Left." *What Is "College-Level" Writing? Volume 2: Assignments, Readings, and Student Writing Samples.* Ed. Patrick Sullivan, Howard Tinberg, and Sheridan Blau. Urbana, IL: NCTE. 2010. 267–279. Print.

Slomp, David M., and Elizabeth Sargent. "Response: 'Thinking Vertically.'" *College Composition and Communication* 60.3 (2009): W25–34. Web. 8 July 2010.

Sommers, Nancy, and Laura Saltz. "The Novice as Expert: Writing the Freshman Year." *College Composition and Communication* 56.1 (2004): 124–49. Print.

Take 20. Dir. Todd Taylor. Bedford/St. Martin's, 2008. DVD.

Yancey, Kathleen Blake. "Delivering College Composition into the Future." *Delivering College Composition: The Fifth Canon.* Ed. Kathleen Blake Yancey. Portsmouth, NH: Boynton/Cook, 2006. 199–209. Print.

———. "The Impulse to Compose and the Age of Composition." *Research in the Teaching of English* 43.3 (2009): 316–38. Print.

———. *Teaching Literature as Reflective Practice.* Urbana, IL: NCTE, 2004. Print.

ADDITIONAL ESSAYS
AVAILABLE ONLINE

The following essays are available on our companion website (www.ncte.org/books/collegelevel2):

Tony Cimasko: "A Little More Relevance"

Jason Courtmanche, with participants in the Connecticut Writing Project 2007 Summer Institute at the University of Connecticut: "Writing on the Same Page: Teaching Writing from Kindergarten through College and Beyond"

Tom Liam Lynch and Kerry McKibbin: "When Writers Imagine Readers: How Writing for Publication Affects Students' Sense of Responsibility to Readers"

Milka Mustenikova Mosley: "Preparing Students for Georgia's State-Mandated Practice Writing Assessment Test: A Day in the Life of a High School Teacher"

John Pekins: "Mandatory Testing in Florida: The K–12/College Disconnect"

Yufeng Zhang: "The Impact of ESL Writers' Prior Writing Experience on Their Writing in College"

INDEX

EDITORS

Patrick Sullivan teaches English at Manchester Community College in Manchester, Connecticut. He believes deeply in the community college mission, and he has greatly enjoyed his many years teaching at MCC. When not at MCC, he likes spending time with his wife, Susan (who is an artist and ceramics professor), and his two amazing children, Bonnie Rose (who is working on an MFA in illustration at Western Connecticut State University) and Nicholas (who just graduated with a BFA from the University of Massachusetts, Amherst). His scholarly work has appeared in *Teaching English in the Two-Year College, Academe, College English, Journal of Developmental English, Community College Journal of Research and Practice,* and the *Journal of Adolescent & Adult Literacy.* He is also the editor, with Howard Tinberg, of *What Is "College-Level" Writing?* (2006).

Howard Tinberg is professor of English at Bristol Community College in Fall River, Massachusetts, and is the author of three books—*Border Talk: Writing and Knowing at the Two-Year College* (1997), *Writing with Consequence: What Writing Does in the Disciplines* (2003), and *The Community College Writer: Exceeding Expectations* (with Jean-Paul Nadeau, 2010). He is coeditor, with Patrick Sullivan, of a fourth book, *What Is "College-Level" Writing?* (2006). He is past editor of the journal *Teaching English in the Two-Year College.* Tinberg is the 2004 recipient of the Carnegie/CASE Community College Professor of the Year award and served as a Carnegie Scholar in 2005–2006.

Sheridan Blau is the Distinguished Senior Lecturer in English education and coordinator of the English education program at Teachers College, Columbia University. He is also professor emeritus of English and education at the University of California, Santa Barbara. He has been honored with awards from the university and from national professional associations for teaching, research, and contributions to the profession of English. For thirty years, until his retirement from UCSB, he directed UCSB's South Coast Writing Project and Literature Institute for Teachers. He also served for many years as director of the campus composition program and program head of the teacher education program in English. Beyond the university, he has served as a member of the Assessment Development Panel for National Certification in English for the National Board for Professional Teaching Standards, as a senior advisor to the California Test Development Committee for statewide assessments in reading and writing, as a member of the English Academic Advisory Committee to the College Board, and director of the National Literature Project Network. For twenty years, he was a member of the National Writing Project Advisory Board and Task Force. He is also a former president of NCTE. His publications have focused mainly on the teaching of composition and literature, seventeenth-century British literature, professional development for teachers, and the ethics and politics of literacy. He has also written and edited textbooks in composition and literature for students in middle school, high school, and college classrooms. His widely influential book, *The Literature Workshop: Teaching Texts and Their Readers* (2003), was named by the Conference on English Education as the winner of the 2004 Richard Meade Award for outstanding research in English education.

CONTRIBUTORS

Deborah Coxwell-Teague currently serves as director of Florida State University's first-year composition program. In this capacity, she is involved in the training and supervision of almost 150 individuals who teach approximately 450 sections of first-year composition annually. She has also taught writing at both the high school and community college levels, and she has served as director of FSU's reading/writing center for four years. Deborah holds undergraduate degrees in English education and journalism, a master's degree in reading and language arts, and a PhD in composition/rhetoric. Her research interests focus on teacher training and teaching composition. Her publications include *Finding Our Way: A Writing Teacher's Sourcebook*—a book that explores seldom-discussed issues in teacher training—coauthored with the late Wendy Bishop, and *Multiple Literacies*—a composition textbook coauthored with Dan Metzer.

Merrill J. Davies, a retired English teacher in Rome, Georgia, spends much of her time writing, attending writing conferences, and enjoying her six grandchildren. She is also very active in her church and her local Toastmasters club and continues to be active in the Georgia Council of Teachers of English and NCTE. She is in charge of GCTE's annual student writing contest and editing the magazine *Mindscapes*, which publishes the work of the contest winners. Her most recent publication was an article, "Teaching Writing without Becoming Buried in Paperwork," in the spring 2009 issue of *Connections*, a GCTE journal.

Andrea Gallagher is a teacher at Wando High School in Mount Pleasant, South Carolina. Claiming no political affiliation, she actually buys into the premise of No Child Left Behind and strives to help each and every student who crosses her path find academic and personal success. She is grateful that her husband and son support, or at least tolerate, her quixotic ventures.

Muriel ("Mickey") Harris, emerita professor of English, Writing Lab director (retired), and editor of the *Writing Lab Newsletter*, is ready to stand on any soapbox and proclaim the merits of writing center theory, pedagogy, and, most of all, the tutors who inhabit those centers. Should anyone be interested, her awards, honors, keynote speeches, workshops, conference presentations, articles, book chapters, and books are detailed on her curriculum vitae (http://writinglabnewsletter.org/mh.pdf). Her proudest accomplishments are her family: husband Sam; daughter Bekki and her husband, Dan; Bekki and Dan's kids, Hannah and Eitan (whose photos will gladly be shown to anyone who even hints they're interested); and son David and his wife, Megan.

David A. Jolliffe is professor of English and curriculum and instruction at the University of Arkansas at Fayetteville, where he holds the Brown Chair in English Literacy. His most recent book is an updated edition of *Everyday Use: Rhetoric at Work in Reading and Writing* (2008), coauthored with Hephzibah Roskelly. Jolliffe was chief reader for the Advanced Placement English language and composition examination from 2002 through 2007. He now works on community literacy issues throughout Arkansas.

John Kiser's career as an educator spans thirty-four years and includes a wide variety of educational experiences. He spent twenty-seven years in the Charlotte-Mecklenburg Schools in Charlotte, North Carolina, where he taught nearly every grade and academic level. He also taught AP for more than twenty years, including both English literature and composition and English language and composition. As an administrator, he served as English vertical teaming coordinator and English curriculum specialist. In addition, he taught a variety of literature and writing courses at the University of Alabama in Huntsville. John has also served as a reader of the AP English literature and composition examination. He retired from public education in January 2003, and he now spends his time as a consultant for the College Board and conducting workshops in AP, vertical teaming, and writing tactics using SOAPSTone.

Peter Kittle and **Rochelle Ramay** teach English in northern California. Kittle directs the Northern California Writing Project and is professor of English at California State University, Chico. Ramay chairs the English Department at Corning Union High School and teaches English to first-year students and seniors. Their collaboration began with a plea from Tom Fox—"Wanna lead a professional development institute? It's only a two-hour drive from here. Oh, and it's eighty hours—Fridays from 5–9, and Saturdays from 8–4. For a mere three months in the middle of the school year . . . Please?" Nonplussed, they nonetheless took on the challenge, and similarly daunting opportunities have fueled their collaboration since. They work best when the stakes are highest. Visitors at their respective homes are greeted with genetically delightful pets: mustachioed dog Phoebe at the Ramay household, and Emma, a cat formed in the image of a Dachshund, at the Kittles's place. As an antidote for the lassitude of tweedy cerebral endeavors, the pair can be found racing through Chico's Bidwell Park, Kittle pedaling his mountain unicycle, and Ramay training for yet another marathon.

Lindsay Larsen is a graduate of the University of Connecticut with a bachelor of arts degree in English. She plans to pursue a career as a middle school English teacher. Lindsay has always enjoyed literature and writing and hopes to spread that love to her future students. In her spare time, she enjoys reading, traveling, movies, and anything British.

Alfredo Celedón Luján is a graduate of the schools that changed his life: Bread Loaf School of English (1987), New Mexico State University (1972), Pojoaque High School (1967), and Nambe Elementary School (1961). He is also a graduate of several other learning institutions: He has been a carryout boy, stocker, and cashier for Safeway, Piggly Wiggly, and 7-Eleven grocery stores; he has dug *acequias*; he has been a gas station attendant, a state department go-fer, a dump truck driver, a weed chopper, a fence post hole digger, and a teacher; he has coached basketball, volleyball, and track; he's been an NEH Fellow ('85, '89, '90), a bedfellow, and a rock-throwing fellow. He's a northern New Mexican–Chicano Boston Celtics fan. Luján's passions include hiking, walking the family dog Brutus, writing, being husband to Amy and father to Amanda, Mabel, and Peter. He's okay with the cats but resents the guinea pigs.

Ronald F. Lunsford is professor of English and director of the graduate program in English at the University of North Carolina at Charlotte, where he teaches courses in composition theory, rhetoric, and linguistics. His publications include: *Twelve Readers Reading: Responding to College Student Writing, Noam Chomsky, Research in Composition and Rhetoric*, and *Linguistic Perspectives on Literature*.

Casey Maliszewski is a student pursuing a career in educational policy. She graduated from Raritan Valley Community College with an Associate of Arts in 2007 and Mount Holyoke College with a Bachelor of Arts, majoring in sociology. She has been an active campus leader serving in such roles as international president of the Phi Theta Kappa Honor Society, founder and executive director of the Roosevelt Institute at Mount Holyoke College, and education policy senior fellow of Roosevelt Institute Campus Network. When she is not working on policy projects and research, she loves to read, knit, and play with her dog, Ollie.

Steven Schmidt is a cancer survivor and a doctoral student at the University of Connecticut in the field of human development and family studies. He is currently developing his pedagogical skills and conducting research on psychosocial factors that influence and are influenced by cancer survivorship. His career goals include teaching at the college or university level and continuing his research in the field of cancer survivorship. He is actively involved with numerous cancer advocacy causes, and, in 2003, he helped start Nikki's Run, an annual 5K fundraiser for pediatric cancer research and support programs.

Cheryl Hogue Smith is an assistant professor of English at Kingsborough Community College–City University of New York. She is a member of the board of the California Association of Teachers of English, a fellow of the National Writing Project, and an assistant to the director of Camp Shakespeare at the Utah Shakespearean Festival. She earned her PhD in language, literacy, and composition from the University of California, Santa Barbara. Current publications include articles in *California English*, *English Journal*, Utah Shakespearean Festival's *Insights: Scholarly Articles on the Plays*, and the *Journal of Adolescent & Adult Literacy*.

Tom Thompson had a brief career teaching high school before retreating to the ivory towers for a lighter workload. He still visits high school regularly, though—both to teach a research-based paper every semester at Andrea Gallagher's school and to supervise student teachers in surrounding districts. He also directs the Lowcountry Writing Project, the National Writing Project site in Charleston, South Carolina, which allows him to work with great teachers in many grade levels and disciplines. He has published several articles on teaching and assessing composition and edited *Teaching Writing in High School and College: Conversations and Collaborations*, which was published by NCTE.

Edward M. White has written or edited thirteen books and nearly one hundred articles or book chapters on writing, writing instruction, and writing assessment. In 2007, he coedited (with a former student) his fifth textbook for college writing students, *The Promise of America*, and fully revised the fourth edition of his book for teachers, *Assigning, Responding, Evaluating: A Writing Teacher's*

Guide. His best-known books are *Teaching and Assessing Writing*, which won a Shaughnessy Award from the Modern Language Association in 1994, and *Assessment of Writing*, an MLA research volume, in 1996. After taking early retirement in 1997 as professor emeritus of English at the California State University, San Bernardino campus, where he was named outstanding professor in 1994, he joined the University of Arizona's Department of English, where he has taught graduate courses in writing assessment, writing research, and writing program administration, completing his fifty-first year of college teaching in 2009. Now a visiting scholar at the University of Arizona, he lives in Flagstaff.

Kathleen Blake Yancey, the Kellogg W. Hunt Professor of English at Florida State University, directs the graduate program in rhetoric and composition. A past president of the Council of Writing Program Administrators, a past chair of the Conference on College Composition and Composition, and a past president of NCTE, she focuses her research on composition studies generally; on writing assessment, especially print and electronic portfolios; and on the intersections of culture, literacy, and technologies. She has authored, edited, or coedited eleven scholarly books and two textbooks as well as more than sixty-five articles and book chapters. Her edited collection *Delivering College Composition: The Fifth Canon* received the 2006–2007 Best Book Award from the Council of Writing Program Administrators, and she was recognized in 2010 with the Florida State University Teaching Award for her work with graduate students. Currently the editor of *College Composition and Communication*, she is coauthoring a study of the transfer of knowledge and practices in college writing situations called *The Things They Carried: A Study of Transfer of Knowledge and Writing Cultures.*

This book was typeset in Sabon.
Typeface used on the cover is
Brioso Pro.
The book was printed on
50-lb. Opaque Offset paper
by Versa Press, Inc.